Grand
Prix
Culinaire

Grand Prix Culinaire

Gerold Berger

CBI

CBI PUBLISHING COMPANY, INC.
51 Sleeper Street
Boston, Massachusetts 02210

PHOTO CREDITS

Cover photograph is courtesy of The Royal Hawaiian
Hotel, Honolulu, Hawaii.
*The following photographs were produced by Stoeckli Inc., CH
8754 Netstal—Switzerland:*
Emince a la Fridolin, Color Plate 5
Pot au Feu Bonne Menagere, Color Plate 7
Flaming Steak Zermatt, Color Plate 7
Classical Gourmet Punch, Color Plate 8

*The following photographs were furnished courtesy of Kraft
Foodservice:*
Brazilian Lagosta Cocktail, Color Plate 1
Mediterranean Rice Classic, Color Plate 1
Aloha Macadamia Pie, Color Plate 2
India Chicken Classic, Color Plate 2
Sukiyaki Classic, Color Plate 3
Tsugaru Classic, Color Plate 3
Kama Boko Classic, Color Plate 3
Sweet and Sour Pork, Color Plate 4
Ho Salad, Color Plate 4
Lo Mein, Color Plate 4
Kwangtung Shrimp, Color Plate 4
Marco Polo Beef, Color Plate 4
Almond Orange Festival, Color Plate 4
Rice Crunch, Color Plate 4
Apple-Pecan Classic, Color Plate 5
Big Apple Kebob Classic, Color Plate 7
Somerset Salad, Color Plate 7
The World of Cheese, Color Plate 8
Photograph courtesy of Marriott's Essex House:
Rock Cornish Hen Earl of Essex, Color Plate 6
*Photograph courtesy of The Pineapple Growers Association of
Hawaii:*
Hawaiian Plantation Cake, Color Plate 8

Production Editor: Deborah Flynn
Text Designer: Roy Howard Brown
Compositor: Trade Composition, Inc.
Cover Designer: Designed For

Library of Congress Cataloging in Publication Data

Berger, Gerold.
    Grand prix culinaire.

    Includes index.
    1. Cookery, International.   I. Title.
TX725.A1B38   641.59   81-12280
ISBN 0-8436-2196-6   AACR2

Contents

Preface

Cooking is an art which has always been fascinating to human beings. Achieving its highest expression requires years of experience with ingredients and the subtle blending of flavors.

Fire was perhaps the first experiment with food. Primitive ancestors experienced a new taste in meat. As the human population grew, eating habits changed over thousands of years. Farmers cultivated plants and spices. In the time of gladiators, regional cooking with sauces and herbs created a classical world of gourmet eating. Empires exchanged exotic dishes.

During my years of travel, I have collected many awards and prizes. I would like to share some of my knowledge of adventurous cooking with you. These are classic, not complicated, dishes. Think of the ancient Greek or Roman who prepared masterpieces simply by seasoning and colorful presentation. The appearance of various garnishes with a meal can whet your appetite. This is your first consideration. Just imagine lobster meat with an orange colored sauce, an eggplant with its dark purple skin, green grapes and a tomato in the center surrounded by white rice, with sliced peaches and mint leaves, all on a china plate with a gold rim. Now, for the classical gourmet, a touch of seasoning.

I wish to extend my thanks to the many individuals who have helped with the preparation of *Grand Prix Culinaire:*

CBI Publishing Co., Boston
The Pineapple Association of Hawaii
Twinings Tea of London
Kraft Foodservice, Inc., Chicago
Guaranteed Pure, Solid Copper Produced by Stockli, Inc., CH 8754,
    Netstal, Switzerland
Kutchera Wine Export of Austria
Swiss Rose International, Inc., New Jersey
Brotherhood, America's Oldest Winery, New York
Haagen Dasz, New York
Marriott's Essex House, New York
La Touraine
Joan Braun, my secretary

Grand Prix Culinaire will be of valuable interest to all who love simple gourmet food.

This work is dedicated to my wife, Anne, and my son, Gary.

Gerold Berger
The Classical Gourmet

I
Wide World
of
Gastronomy

1. Menus Throughout the World

During my travels by train, ship, and plane, the different cuisines and cultures have always fascinated me. Various culinary customs or styles are represented in this section by selected menus from throughout the world. (Note that recipes may not be supplied for standard items in the menu, such as beverages.)

Austria

During the Hapsburg Empire, Austria stretched from Poland to the blue waters of the Adriatic. Spain, the Netherlands, and Mexico were its provinces, and it boasted the most elegant cuisine ever created. In Vienna, food and waltzes go hand in hand.

> *Speckknodel Suppe—Consomme with Bacon Dumplings*
>
> *Gemischter Salad—Salad Variety*
>
> *Wiener Tafelspitz—Boiled Beef Viennese Style*
>
> *Apfel Kren—Horseradish Sauce*
>
> *Gebackene Champignons—Fried Mushrooms*
>
> *Salzburger Nockerln—Souffle Salzburg Style*
>
> *Espresso*

Speckknodel Suppe
Consomme with Bacon Dumplings

INGREDIENTS   YIELD: 8 to 12 servings

3 onions, finely chopped
1 lb. bacon, diced
3 tbsp. oil
8 small rolls, diced
4 eggs
¼ cup milk
6 tbsp. flour
salt and pepper, to taste
1 tbsp. parsley, chopped
1 gal. beef consomme

Saute onions and bacon in oil for 10 minutes; the bacon should not be crisp. Combine with small diced rolls, or process in chopper for several seconds. Combine with eggs mixed with milk, and soak; add flour, seasonings, and parsley. Form small dumplings and place in boiling salted water. Boil for 12 minutes, remove, and add to consomme.

NOTE   If dumplings are too soft from the absorbed liquid, add a little more flour. Dumplings can be refrigerated, covered with a wet cloth, and cooked at a later time. Never leave dumplings in water more than 30 minutes.

Gemischter Salad
Salad Variety

Dip six Boston lettuce leaves in water mixed with equal amounts of vinegar and oil, and season with salt, pepper, a dash of sugar, and the juice of one lemon. Place on serving plate and arrange with ½ cup of pickled beets, ½ cup of cole

(Cont.)

slaw marinated in oil and vinegar with caraway seeds, ½ cup of German potato salad, 1 cup of cauliflower marinated with green pepper, two tomatoes sliced and marinated with two onions, and 1 cup of cucumber salad. Garnish with watercress and six radish roses. Yields 8–12 servings.

Wiener Tafelspitz
Boiled Beef Viennese Style

INGREDIENTS   YIELD: 8 to 12 servings

4 onions, cut in half

3 lb. Tafelspitz (cut from tip of beef brisket)

2 celeriac, julienne

3 carrots, julienne

2 celery stalks, julienne

2 leeks, julienne

1 tbsp. peppercorns

¼ cup chives, cut

salt, to taste

3 gal. water

Place onion halves on top of stove and burn till black. Put onions and remaining ingredients in soup pot and bring to boil. Skim soup and simmer for 3 to 4 hours. Season. Remove meat, strain soup, and reduce to half. Slice meat and arrange on serving platter with creamed spinach. Sprinkle chives on meat and pour some of the stock over. Garnish with boiled potatoes and horseradish sauce.

Apfel Kren
Horseradish Sauce

INGREDIENTS   YIELD: 8 to 12 servings

3 horseradish, freshly grated

6 apples, peeled and shredded

¼ cup vinegar

2 tbsp. oil

1 tsp. sugar

Combine all ingredients. Serve in side dish with Wiener Tafelspitz.

Gebackene Champignons
Fried Mushrooms

INGREDIENTS   YIELD: 8 to 12 servings

3 lb. mushrooms, quartered and cleaned

flour, to dredge

2 eggs, whipped

salt and pepper, to taste

breadcrumbs, for breading

oil for frying

Dredge mushrooms in flour. Dip in eggs mixed with seasonings, and bread in breadcrumbs individually. Fry in oil at 375° F. till golden brown. Garnish with lemon slices and parsley.

Salzburger Nockerln
Souffle Salzburg Style

INGREDIENTS YIELD: 8 to 12 servings

4 oz. butter
6 tbsp. sugar, 10x
9 eggs, separated
salt to taste
3 oz. flour
¼ cup milk
2 cups vanilla sauce

Whip butter with 3 tbsp. sugar till creamy. Add egg yolks and whip for 3 minutes. In separate bowl, whip egg whites with remaining sugar till firm. (Egg whites must stay on the whip when lifted.) Carefully add salt and flour. In a large pyrex dish heat milk with 1 oz. butter. Form three large dumplings, or 8 to 12 dumplings by using a ladle. Sprinkle with additional 10x sugar, place in 375° F. oven, and bake for 12 minutes. Serve vanilla sauce on the side.

NOTE Souffle must be served immediately, when golden brown. It should be creamy inside, not completely baked.

Africa

Morocco, Algeria, Tunisia, Egypt—from Casablanca to Alexandria—the Arabic tribes have contributed couscous to the culinary art.

Mediterranean Rice Classic

Couscous Pharaoh

Sahara Salad

Arabian Coffee with Cardamon Seeds

Mediterranean Rice Classic

INGREDIENTS	For 4	For 24
chicken breasts	4	24
water or chicken stock	to cover	to cover
white wine	2 oz.	1 cup
onions, finely chopped	1	6
butter	3 oz.	½ lb.
flour	4 oz.	2 cups
ground nutmeg	dash	¼ tsp.
salt and pepper mixture	dash	to taste
long grain rice, cooked	8 oz.	3 lb.
walnuts	12	72
parsley, chopped	for garnish	for garnish

Poach chicken breasts in stock and wine. Remove. Saute onions in butter, add flour and stock, and whisk until cream is smooth. Add seasoning and simmer for 25 minutes. Arrange rice on individual plates, top with sliced breast of chicken, cream sauce, and 3 walnuts, and garnish with parsley. Serve remaining sauce separately. See Color Plate 1.

Couscous Pharaoh

INGREDIENTS   YIELD: 4 to 6 servings

2 cups couscous
¾ cup water
4 tbsp. raisins
5 tbsp. sweet butter, melted
5 tbsp. peanuts
6 tbsp. fresh raspberries
5 tbsp. confectioner's sugar

Moisten couscous with water. Using a double boiler or couscouserie, steam with raisins for 30 minutes. Remove, place in individual serving dishes, and toss with butter and peanuts. Place fresh raspberries in the center and sprinkle with sugar. See Color Plate 1.

Sahara Salad

Two freshly sliced apples, 2 bananas, and 5 orange sections topped with bing cherry slices centered with ½ cup of cottage cheese and topped with several pomegranate seeds. Yields one serving. See Color Plate 1.

Arabian Coffee with Cardamon Seeds

Bring 1 cup of water to a boil, and add 2 tsp. Arabian coffee and 1 tsp. sugar. Return to boil, add 5 cardamon seeds, and let stand several minutes. Yields one serving.

France

Paris, the Arc de Triomphe, the gracious Champs Elysees where Napoleon marched, the many regions including Monaco and Corsica. French cooking is renowned throughout the world. Paris in the spring—it could almost be a culinary song.

Saumon St. Tropez—Salmon with Vegetable

Potage Rossini—Duck Soup

Casserole Rennes—Clams, Scallops, and Langoustine Casserole

Charlottes Napoleon

Cafe Elysees

Saumon St. Tropez
Salmon with Vegetable

INGREDIENTS   YIELD: 8 to 12 servings

2 lb. salmon
¼ cup heavy cream
3 egg whites
salt and pepper, to taste
3 cups white wine
1 bouquet garni
¼ cup carrots, diced
¼ cup shallots, diced
4 oz. butter
dash cayenne pepper
2 tbsp. flour

Finely grind salmon meat, mix with heavy cream and egg whites; season. Make quenelles with spoon. Bring white wine, bouquet garni, and carrots to boil. Strain the sauce and some of the carrots. Drop in quenelles and poach for 10 minutes. Remove from stock. Saute shallots in butter, add flour and some wine stock, and whisk till sauce is smooth. Season to taste. Strain remaining liquid, remove. Add carrots to sauce, pour over quenelles.

Potage Rossini
Duck Soup

INGREDIENTS   YIELD: 8 to 12 servings

1 2½-lb. duckling
1 gal. bouillon
1 cup carrots, diced
1 cup celeriac, diced
1 leek, cut
2 onions, finely chopped
2 oz. butter
2 tbsp. flour
1 cup white wine
1 small bouquet garni
¼ cup heavy cream
salt and pepper, to taste

Remove all skin from duck, and bone meat. Set bones aside. Dice meat, keeping larger parts whole. Boil meat and bones in bouillon for 50 minutes; remove. Saute vegetables in butter. Add flour, wine, bouquet garni, stock, and simmer for 30 minutes; strain. Add diced duck meat. Place larger parts in bowl. Bring soup to a boil, add heavy cream, and season. Pour over large pieces of duck meat.

Casserole Rennes
Clams, Scallops, and Langoustine Casserole

INGREDIENTS   YIELD: 8 to 12 servings

¼ cup shallots
12 mushrooms, sliced
2 carrots, sliced
1 leek, julienne
4 oz. butter
1 cup rice
2½ cups water
salt and pepper, to taste
4 lb. lobster meat, cut in 1-inch cubes
1 lb. scallops
1 lb. clams
dash saffron
2 cups wine
1 fennel

Saute shallots, mushrooms, carrots, and leek in butter. Add rice, water, and seasoning. Bring to a boil and simmer for 20 minutes. Place seafood in a casserole with layers of rice. Add saffron, wine, and fennel. Cover and bake for 30 minutes at 375° F.

Charlottes Napoleon

INGREDIENTS   YIELD: 8 to 12 servings

24 ladyfingers
2 cups whipped cream
2 lb. marron puree
3 oz. kirschwasser
24 glazed marrons
1 pint strawberries

Place waxed paper in a charlotte form. Cover the sides and bottom with ladyfingers. Mix half of the whipped cream with marron puree and kirschwasser; fill mold. Cover with ladyfingers. Refrigerate. Turn upside down to remove from pan. Decorate with whipped cream topped with marrons. Arrange strawberries around the mold.

Cafe Elysees

INGREDIENTS   YIELD: 1 to 2 servings

2 tsp. sugar
1 lemon peel
1 cinnamon stick
2 cloves
1 oz. cognac
1 oz. Grand Marnier
2 cups espresso coffee

Place sugar, lemon peel, cinnamon stick, and cloves in chafing dish over flame. In heated ladle, ignite cognac and pour over ingredients until sugar is dissolved. While flaming, add Grand Marnier and, gradually, espresso coffee.

United Kingdom

Where Caesar and his army once feasted on oysters. The Isle of Man and Ireland, Wales, and Scotland—surrounded by salt water. The British highlights are Sunday brunch, high tea, and dinner parties.

Dundee Mousse

Sauce Cumberland

Lady Van Cursen

Shrimp Grasmere

Glazed Ham Thomas

Plum Pudding

Somerset Salad

English Chiffon Pie Classic

High Tea

Dundee Mousse

INGREDIENTS   YIELD: 8 to 12 servings

2 lb. venison meat
1 cup heavy cream
5 egg whites
salt to taste
cayenne pepper, to taste
2 oz. cognac
4 oz. butter
cumberland sauce
mint leaves, to garnish

Finely grind venison meat. Mix with heavy cream and egg whites. Season and add cognac. In buttered ramequins, divide mixture and poach in water for 45 minutes. Turn upside down and cover with cumberland sauce. Garnish with mint leaves.

Sauce Cumberland

INGREDIENTS   YIELD: 8 to 12 servings

1 lb. lingonberries, in syrup
4 oranges, quartered
2 lemons, quartered
½ cup sugar
4 cloves
1 cinnamon stick
2 cups red wine

Combine all ingredients and simmer for 45 minutes. Strain and chill thoroughly.

Lady Van Cursen

INGREDIENTS   YIELD: 8 to 12 servings

1 qt. turtle consomme
6 oz. sherry
8–12 egg yolks
1 cup whipped cream
2 tbsp. curry powder

Heat turtle consomme with sherry, and divide between serving bowls. Add one egg yolk to each bowl, place whipped cream on each, and top with curry powder. Brown under a salamander for several seconds and serve.

Shrimp Grasmere

INGREDIENTS   YIELD: 8 to 12 servings

10 lb. shrimp, peeled
flour, to dredge
2 onions, diced
4 oz. butter
2 tbsp. chutney
2 tsp. curry
6 oz. whiskey
2 cups heavy cream
salt and pepper, to taste

Season peeled shrimp, and dredge in flour. Saute diced onions in butter, add shrimp and chutney, and simmer for 10 minutes. Add curry and flame with whiskey. Add heavy cream and season.

Glazed Ham Thomas

INGREDIENTS	For 4–6	For 24
Twinings spiced tea	1 tbsp.	4 tbsp.
apricot preserves	1 cup	3 cups
water	¼ cup	1 cup
arrowroot	1 tbsp.	3 tbsp.
ham, smoked	1 5-lb.	2 10-lb.
pineapple juice	1 cup	4 cups
Hawaiian pineapple rings, with juice	10	40

Mix tea with apricot preserves, and mix water with arrowroot. Combine and bring to a boil. Cut top of ham into diamond shapes. Place in 350° F. oven, baste with some of the sauce, and bake for 30 minutes. Add pineapple juice to the pan, and baste ham with remaining sauce. Bake 30 minutes longer. Larger hams will need 45 minutes. Baste at 10-minute intervals. Remove ham and slice. Arrange slices with glazed pineapple rings on a platter covered with sauce.

Plum Pudding

INGREDIENTS   YIELD: 8 to 12 servings

3 oz. butter

8 oz. breadcrumbs

1 lb. raisins

2 oz. almonds

1 lb. currants

1 lemon (zest and juice)

2 eggs

¼ cup milk

2 tbsp. brandy

2 tbsp. rum

1 apple, peeled, cored, and shredded

3 oz. sugar

dash nutmeg

salt to taste

Mix butter and breadcrumbs. Chop all dry ingredients, add lemon, and mix together. Add beaten eggs with milk, brandy, rum, and shredded apple. Combine with remaining ingredients. Place in buttered mold, cover with paper, and steam (place molds in boiling water) or bake in water at 420° F. for 3½ to 4 hours. This pudding can be kept for several weeks in the refrigerator, covered. Serve hot with apricot sauce.

Hot Apricot Sauce

Mash apricots and mix with rum. Bring to a boil and strain. Serve hot.

Somerset Salad

INGREDIENTS	For 4–6	For 8–12
bacon strips, diced	4	8
mushrooms	5	10
sugar	dash	½ tsp.
vinegar	2 oz.	4 oz.
olive oil	2 oz.	4 oz.
salt	to taste	to taste
spinach leaves	1 lb.	2 lb.
walnut pieces	1 tbsp.	2 tbsp.
Holland cheese, diced	2 tbsp.	¼ cup
black pepper, freshly ground	to taste	to taste

Saute diced bacon strips till crisp. Add mushrooms, sugar, vinegar, oil, and salt. Bring to a boil; stir. Pour over fresh spinach leaves and toss. Add walnut pieces, cheese, and freshly ground black pepper. See Color Plate 7.

English Chiffon Pie Classic

INGREDIENTS	One 9-Inch Pie	Two 9-Inch Pies
sugar	2 tbsp.	4 tbsp.
butter, melted	½ cup	1 cup
graham cracker crumbs	2 cups	4 cups
Twinings spiced tea	2 tbsp.	4 tbsp.
water, boiling	2 cups	4 cups
sugar	½ cup	1 cup
unflavored gelatin	2 tbsp.	4 tbsp.
egg yolks	2	4
heavy cream, whipped	1 cup	2 cups
egg whites, beaten	2	4
Grand Marnier	1 oz.	2 oz.
orange slices	17	34

Mix smaller quantity of sugar with butter and crumbs. Press evenly over the sides and bottom of pan. Chill. Mix tea with boiling water; mix sugar and gelatin, and stir in hot tea until gelatin dissolves. Beat egg yolks and add to gelatin mix. Chill. Fold in whipped cream, and then egg whites. Pour into pie shell and chill till firm. Garnish with additional whipped cream mixed with Grand Marnier and orange slices.

The Classic English Tea Table

Afternoon tea in England is as much a social occasion as a pause for refreshment. This classic is served in an elegant silver tea service accompanied by a vase of fresh flowers, a "jug" or second teapot of hot water, a bowl of sugar, a pitcher of milk (never cream, which is too heavy for tea), a dish of thinly-sliced lemon, and porcelain tea cups and saucers. The connoisseurs' accompaniment to afternoon tea is good conversation. The traditional blends are Formosa oolong, jasmine, lapsang souchong, and Russian caravan.

Tea is 5,000 Years Old

Be a tea-taster and try the various basic teas—green, brown, and black. While all tea as we know it today has been fired and heat dried, green tea, in use for 5,000 years (and still the ceremonial tea of Japan), is made of leaves that are not fermented before firing. It's called green gunpowder. China black and brown teas (Formosa oolong) have been used for 1,500 years. Try a cup of Assam, first harvested in 1839, a Darjeeling cultivated subsequently, and a Ceylon or orange pekoe, available since 1875. Finish with the new, flavored Ceylons, such as lemon or spiced tea.

The three tea groups, black, brown, and green, all have subvarieties, but black tea has the most. China blacks are usually considered the most delicate. There is also the Prince of Wales or Russian caravan, its tarry flavor a result of jasmine, and the lapsang souchong from the Fukien province of China. Advanced tasters can savor the nuances of three Darjeeling blends: Darjeeling, Queen Mary, and vintage Darjeeling. On the day you think you'd like a cup of Irish Breakfast or oolong tea, and not just a cup of tea, then you will be a connoisseur. And when you're in London, visit Tom's Coffee House on the Strand, founded by Thomas Twining in 1706.

The Characteristics of Good Tea
A well-made pot or cup of tea should have aroma, flavor, bright color, and strength. If you buy good tea and prepare it correctly, your tea will always have those four essential characteristics. The recipe for good tea making depends on:

1. the way you measure the leaf,
2. the time you allow for infusion,
3. the procedure when using large teapots,
4. the correct use of milk, and
5. the water effect.

Hot Tea
To make hot tea, warm a teapot while fresh water is being boiled. Tea should be placed in the teapot, allowing one teaspoonful for each person plus one extra teaspoonful to increase the strength. As soon as the water boils it should be poured over the tea in the teapot. The tea should be stirred and the teapot lid replaced. To obtain full flavor and strength, the tea should remain in the teapot for 3 minutes for a small leaf (5 minutes for a large leaf) before pouring into cups or glasses. Milk or lemon may then be added, if required.

Teabags may be used instead of loose tea, in which case allow one bag for each person, and an extra teabag for strength.

Iced Tea
Make a pot of tea as for a hot brew, but use four times as much tea. Then strain the tea into an equal measure of cold water, allowing no tea leaves into the liquid. Pour the tea over ice cubes in large glasses. Fresh lemon juice, mint, or sugar may be added, if desired.

Restaurant Tea
Start with a good tea. Use the correct amount by using preweighed packs, immersible tea bags, or an accurate tea measure. Preheat the teapot with boiling water, and empty thoroughly. Place tea in the pot. Use freshly boiled water. Time the brewing accurately for the size of the pot. Allow tea to stand 5 to 6 minutes, then stir the tea in the pot to ensure uniform strength. Remove the tea bags or leaves.

Serving	Drams/Oz.	Grams	Brewing Time
Per pot for one	3½ drams	6.5	5 minutes
Pot for two	6 drams	10.5	5 minutes
½ gallon pot	13 drams	23	6 minutes
1 gallon pot	1½ oz.	42	7 minutes
3 gallon pot	3½ oz.	99	14 minutes
5 gallon pot	6¾ oz.	191	14 minutes

NOTE   1 ounce = 16 drams = 28.35 grams.

Varieties of Tea
China black—medium black leaf from the Chinese mainland.
Lapsang souchong—large leaf China tea with a tarry, smoky flavor.
Formosa oolong—large leaf from the island of Formosa; fragrance likened to the aroma of ripe peaches.
Ceylon breakfast—golden liquor, blend of Ceylon.
Queen Mary—Darjeeling blend, supplied to the late Queen Mary of England.
Irish breakfast—northern Indian; rich blend favored by the Irish, with a strong thick brew.

Indian breakfast—Assam blend teas, with a malty character.
Earl Grey—oriental blend, popular internationally.
English breakfast—full-bodied English favorite; a blend of small leaf Ceylon.
Orange pekoe—Ceylon blend.
Darjeeling—muscatel flavor, from the Himalayan foothills.
Lemon—medium leaf Ceylon.
Prince of Wales—considered the burgundy of China teas; a blend of
    Keemun black teas.
Jasmine—exotic tea scented with actual jasmine flowers.
Rose hip—blended with hibiscus flowers; best if flavored with rum.
Mint—made from the leaves of mitcham mint; best with honey and lemon.
Camomile—pleasant and soothing; lemon gives a complementary tang.
Linden—with a flavor of lime flowers; ideal with a little brown sugar.
Verbena—with a slice of orange; noted in history for medicinal qualities.
Vintage Darjeeling—exclusive, expensive blend of the choicest Darjeeling;
    selected once a season at their prime.
Russian caravan—a favorite of the Russian aristocracy; blend of quality
    China and Taiwan oolong teas.
Gunpowder green tea—historic tea of China; unfermented green tea, with a
    curled leaf similar in appearance to gunpowder.
Spiced tea—Ceylon pekoe blend; leafed teas with cut cloves and dried
    orange peel. Exotic flavors of the East.

Greece

The golden age of Greek civilization spread throughout the Mediterranean—olive groves lend an oriental flavor—Greek fish soup rivals the bouillabaisse of France. Greece is a country that dazzles the culinary traveler.

> *Spartan Tureen*
>
> *Piraeus Salad*
>
> *Lamb Athenaeus*
>
> *Dolmathes Acropolis*
>
> *Demetrius Cheesecake*
>
> *Cafe Metaxa*

Spartan Tureen

INGREDIENTS   YIELD: 6 to 8 servings

1 tsp. olive oil
2 onions, sliced
½ leek, chopped
2 carrots, diced
juice of ½ lemon
juice of one garlic clove
1 tsp. parsley, chopped
dash of saffron
1 bay leaf
dash of turmeric
(Cont.)

Prepare fish in bite-size portions. Saute in olive oil, onions, leek, and carrots. Add remaining seasonings, tomatoes, clams and mussels, and white wine; bring to a boil. Add remaining seafood, and fish stock or water. Simmer for 20 minutes, and place in tureen.

black pepper, freshly ground, to taste

salt to taste

2 tomatoes, peeled and diced

4 clams, washed

8 mussels, washed

1 cup white wine

4 oz. red snapper

4 oz. mackerel

4 oz. cod

4 oz. turbot

2 6-oz. lobster tails, cut in half

fish stock or water, to cover

Piraeus Salad

INGREDIENTS   YIELD: 6 to 8 servings

1 garlic clove, crushed

sea salt to taste

2 anchovies, fillet

4 tomatoes, cut in sections

3 medium green peppers

2 scallions, chopped

12 artichoke hearts, quartered

4 tbsp. olive oil

3 tbsp. vinegar

1 cup feta cheese

12 pitted, ripe olives

2 tbsp. lemon juice

½ tsp. oregano

black pepper, freshly ground, to taste

lettuce leaves

watercress

Rub garlic in salad bowl with salt; add anchovies until mixture is smooth. Add tomatoes, green pepper, scallions, artichoke hearts, oil, and vinegar, and toss with remaining ingredients. Serve on lettuce leaves surrounded with watercress.

Lamb Athenaeus

INGREDIENTS   YIELD: 30 servings

1 whole baby lamb, or parts

Marinade

10 garlic cloves, crushed

2 cups wine vinegar

2 cups olive oil

2 onions, finely chopped

2 tbsp. oregano

1 cup white wine

1 tbsp. salt

2 tbsp. black pepper, freshly ground

Originally roasted on a spit in northern Greece, this dish can be made with parts of lamb on an outdoor grill.

Mix all ingredients for marinade and brush lamb on all sides. Place on spit, over open fire. Turn slowly, and brush on marinade during entire roasting. For medium rare, smoke for 6 to 7 hours.

Dolmathes Acropolis

INGREDIENTS   YIELD: 6 to 8 servings

14 grape leaves or fig leaves

yogurt to cover leaves

Filling

2 onions, finely chopped

2 tbsp. olive oil

2 lb. lamb meat, ground

1 cup rice

juice of one garlic clove

2 cups water

3 tbsp. walnuts

dash of cinnamon

¼ cup red wine

salt to taste

black pepper, freshly ground, to taste

Saute onions in olive oil. Add ground meat and brown. Add rice and remaining ingredients, and bring to a boil. Simmer for 25 minutes until all liquid is absorbed. Cool. Divide filling among leaves; roll and place in buttered dish. Bake at 375° F. for 35 minutes. Pour yogurt over and bake 10 minutes longer.

Demetrius Cheesecake

INGREDIENTS   YIELD: One 9-Inch Cake

Filling

1 tbsp. sugar

¼ cup honey

salt to taste

2 tbsp. flour

1 lb. cream cheese, softened

zest of one lemon

4 eggs, separated

1 cup sour cream

Crust

1 cup graham crackers

3 tbsp. crushed almonds

2 tbsp. sweet butter

1 tbsp. sugar

Topping

shaved chocolate

confectioner's sugar

Grease 9-inch cake form. Mix crackers, almonds, butter, and sugar and press on bottom of cake form.

Combine sugar, honey, salt, and flour. Add cream cheese and zest of lemon. Blend well. Stir in egg yolks and sour cream. Beat egg whites until stiff and fold into mixture. Place on top of cracker crust. Bake at 325° F. for 1½ hours. Cool for one hour. Remove from cake form. Place shaved chocolate on top, and sprinkle with confectioner's sugar.

Cafe Metaxa

To 1 cup of espresso coffee, add ½ oz. Metaxa. Top with 2 tsp. whipped cream, and sprinkle with cinnamon. Yields one serving.

Italy

Seven famous hills—the River Tiber—the small republic of San Marino. Pasta al dente is a classic of the Roman Empire but Marco Polo might have a hard time explaining where spaghetti originated.

Fettucini Romano

Salada Palermo

Fegato Veneto

Gnocchi San Remo

Zabaglione Caruso

Caffe Contessa Maria

Fettucini Romano

INGREDIENTS   YIELD: 4 servings

Fettucini

3 cups flour, sifted

3 eggs

2 tbsp. water

salt to taste

Sauce

½ cup butter, melted

1 tsp. basil

juice of 1 garlic clove

1 cup parmesan cheese

Make a well in the center of the flour. Add eggs, salt, and water. Knead till dough forms ball, then remove from board. Cover and let rest for one hour. Divide into 3 sections. Roll each section paper thin. Let dry for one half hour. Cut into ¼-inch strips. Place on waxed paper and sprinkle with flour. Drop in boiling, salted water. Boil for 7 minutes, and drain well. Mix butter, basil, and garlic. Pour over fettucini, and sprinkle with parmesan. Bake for 3 minutes at 425° F.

Salada Palermo

INGREDIENTS   YIELD: 4 servings

3 eggplants, peeled and diced

4 tomatoes, sliced

4 figs

2 tbsp. sugar

salt to taste

4 tbsp. wine vinegar

2 apples, peeled and sliced

4 tbsp. olive oil

juice of 1 garlic clove

2 tbsp. pistachio nuts

3 sweet peppers

1 cup seedless grapes

juice of 1 lemon

bunch of dandelion greens

Mix diced eggplant, tomatoes, figs, sugar, salt, and vinegar. Let rest for ½ hour. Add remaining ingredients. Toss and serve with dandelion greens surrounding.

Fegato Veneto
Calves Liver, Venetian Style

INGREDIENTS YIELD: 4 servings

3 onions, thinly sliced
3 oz. butter
1½ lb. calves liver, sliced thin in julienne
2 oz. white wine
4 oz. demi glaze
black pepper, freshly ground, to taste
dash of oregano

Saute onions in butter. Add calves liver and saute 2 minutes, until medium rare. Add white wine and demi glaze. Bring to a boil, season, and serve immediately.

Gnocchi San Remo

INGREDIENTS YIELD: 4 servings

2 lb. Idaho potatoes
½ cup milk
2 tbsp. butter
1 cup flour
2 eggs, beaten
salt to taste
¼ cup parmesan cheese

Boil potatoes, peel, and put through a strainer. Bring milk and butter to boil. Add flour and stir. Remove from pan; add eggs, potatoes, salt, and parmesan cheese, and mix together. Knead on a floured board. Roll out, and cut into 1x3-inch sticks. Cook gnocchi in boiling salted water until they rise to the top. Place in serving dish, and sprinkle with more parmesan cheese.

Zabaglione Caruso

INGREDIENTS YIELD: 4 servings

6 egg yolks
¼ cup sugar
½ cup marsala
¼ cup brandy
zest of 1 orange
2 pints fresh raspberries

In top of double boiler, beat egg yolks and sugar. Mix in marsala and brandy, and beat well until mixture thickens. Do not boil. Add orange zest. Divide fresh raspberries into serving glasses and pour sauce over. Serve immediately.

Caffe Contessa Maria

INGREDIENTS YIELD: 4 servings

6 sugar cubes
zest from 1 orange
1 cinnamon stick
2 cloves
2 oz. Grand Marnier
2 oz. Remy Martin
4 cups espresso
1 cup whipped cream
dash of ground cinnamon

Place sugar, orange zest, cinnamon stick, and cloves in large silver bowl. Add Grand Marnier and Remy Martin. Bring to boiling point, ignite, and slowly pour in espresso. Ladle into fireproof glasses. Top with whipped cream and sprinkle with ground cinnamon.

Japan

Centuries of culture and simple, elegant cuisine—adventurous travelers try sashimi (raw fish) or yakitoro (boiled fish)—enjoy a little cup of sake (rice wine) before your dinner.

Sashimi Tokyo

Shiitake Soup

Shrimp Tempura

Yakitori

Sukiyaki Classic

Jasmine Tea

Sashimi Tokyo

INGREDIENTS   YIELD: 8 to 12 servings

2 tbsp. sea bass, thinly sliced
1 cup soy sauce
1 tbsp. gingerroot, shredded
2 tbsp. mustard
2 tbsp. sour cream
juice of 3 lemons
1 tbsp. shallots, finely chopped
salt and cayenne pepper, to taste
Chinese cabbage leaves, to garnish

Cut sea bass into thin strips and chill thoroughly. Mix soy sauce with gingerroot, mustard, sour cream, lemon juice and shallots, and season. Arrange sea bass with toothpicks on cabbage leaves. Serve sauce in separate round dish on the same plate.

NOTE   During the classic age, man fed himself with natural food. In that tradition, this delicacy is a perfect appetizer.

Shiitake Soup

INGREDIENTS   YIELD: 8 to 12 servings

½ gal. beef consomme
½ lb. shiitake (sliced mushrooms)
4 scallion stems, chopped

Bring beef consomme to a boil. Add shiitake and chopped scallions prior to serving.

Shrimp Tempura

INGREDIENTS   YIELD: 8 to 12 servings

5 lb. prawns
milk
10 eggs, beaten
½ cup water
2 cups wheat flour
salt and pepper, to taste
vegetable oil, for frying

Sauce
soy sauce mixed with honey
grated horseradish
and ginger

Peel shells of prawns, split the backs open, wash, and soak in milk. Beat together eggs, water, flour, and seasoning. Heat oil to 350° F. Dip prawns in egg mixture, covering them all over. Fry in hot oil till golden brown. Serve with sauce.

Yakitori

INGREDIENTS   YIELD: 8 to 12 servings

1¾ lb. chicken meat, cubed

½ lb. chicken livers

1 cup water chestnuts, cubed

1 cup bamboo shoots

1½ cups soy sauce

¼ cup mustard

1 tsp. ginger powder

juice of 1 lemon

salt and pepper, to taste

Arrange alternately on a bamboo stick, chicken, livers, water chestnuts, and bamboo shoots. Marinate in mixture of soy sauce, mustard, ginger, lemon juice, salt, and pepper. Grill over open fire and brush with sauce. Serve with rice and sake.

Sukiyaki Classic

INGREDIENTS   YIELD: 8 to 12 servings

¼ lb. butter

¼ cup soy sauce

2 tsp. sugar

3 lb. beef tenderloin, thinly sliced

¾ cup sake

3 cups spinach leaves

3 onions, sliced

1 head Chinese cabbage, cut

10 bamboo sprouts

1 lb. mushrooms, sliced

At the table, melt butter in a skillet. Add soy sauce and stir in sugar. Place strips of meat in pan and cook to individual taste. Add sake a little at a time. Arrange individual vegetables around the pan. Cook until wilted but crisp. Add more sake as needed to keep liquid in pan. Serve with boiled rice and beaten raw egg in separate small bowls. See Color Plate 3.

South Pacific

A continent and small islands—coconuts and laughing birds—volcanos and orchids. Captain James Cook explored the South Sea Islands on an exotic journey to the sun. Mangoes, pineapples, and papayas flavor the cuisine of the South Pacific.

Tahitian Papaya Soup

Hawaiian Paradise Casserole

Flaming Spinach Salad Aloha

Fiji Coconut Chateau

South Sea Cafe

Tahitian Papaya Soup

INGREDIENTS   YIELD: 4 servings

5 papayas, peeled and cored

3 tbsp. honey

juice of 1 lemon

2 oz. brandy

2 tbsp. sour cream

2 tbsp. sliced almonds, toasted

Peel and dice one papaya into small cubes. Mash remaining papayas in blender. Add honey, lemon juice, and brandy. Strain and divide among serving cups. Top each with sour cream and sprinkle with toasted almonds.

Hawaiian Paradise Casserole

INGREDIENTS   YIELD: 4 servings

Casserole

3 tbsp. salted butter

1 onion, finely chopped

5 oz. fresh mushrooms, quartered

4 8-to-10 oz. boneless chicken breasts, cut into large chunks

16 shrimps, peeled and deveined

1 tsp. curry powder

1 14 oz. can Hawaiian pineapple chunks in own juice, drained

2 fresh tomatoes, peeled and diced

2 cups water

1 cup long grain rice

1 tsp. salt

1/8 tsp. black pepper, ground

2 oz. sliced almonds, toasted

Sauce

juice of drained pineapple

juice of 1 lemon

1/8 cup white vinegar

5 tbsp. spiced mustard

2 oz. Grand Marnier

To prepare casserole, melt butter in heavy skillet, and saute onions and mushrooms for 5 minutes. Add chicken and shrimp, and stir for several minutes. Add curry powder, pineapple chunks, and remaining ingredients. Place in large casserole. Bake at 350° F. for 1 hour, and sprinkle with toasted almonds.

To prepare sauce, combine all ingredients and bring to a boil.

Flaming Spinach Salad Aloha

INGREDIENTS   YIELD: 4 servings

1 lb. fresh spinach leaves

1 cup mangoes, diced

1 cup pineapple, diced

1 cup papaya, diced

1/2 cup pineapple juice

1 oz. pineapple rum

1 oz. 151 proof rum

1 oz. vinegar

salt, to taste

2 oz. olive oil

black pepper, freshly ground, to taste

Place spinach leaves in bowl with fresh fruit and seasonings. Heat pineapple juice, vinegar, and oil, and pour over salad. Add rum and ignite. Toss salad.

Fiji Coconut Chateau

INGREDIENTS   YIELD: 4 servings

7 egg yolks
3 tbsp. sugar
4 cups plum wine
2 coconuts, cut in half
dash of ground cinnamon
2 tsp. shredded coconut, toasted
fresh South Sea flowers

In top of double boiler, whisk egg yolks, sugar, and plum wine until creamy. Pour into the halved coconut shells, and sprinkle with cinnamon and coconut. Arrange flowers (leis) around the coconuts.

South Sea Cafe

INGREDIENTS   YIELD: 4 servings

1 slice orange peel
1 whole clove
3 sugar cubes
1 cinnamon stick
4 oz. Remy Martin
1 oz. Tia Maria
4 cups espresso

Place orange peel, clove, and sugar in chafing dish, and heat. Place cinnamon stick and cognac in heated ladle, ignite, and pour slowly over sugar until it dissolves. Add Tia Maria and espresso. Serve immediately.

Spain and Portugal

Granada, the last capital of the Moorish kingdom—the explorations of Christopher Columbus—the ports of Cadiz, Barcelona, Lisbon—and the classic paella.

Sopa Columbus

Paella Valenciana

Andalusian Salad

Breast of Chicken Au Porto

Orange Seville

Porto

Sopa Columbus

INGREDIENTS   YIELD: 4 servings

1 onion, finely chopped
2 eggplants, peeled and diced
3 tomatoes, peeled and diced
2 tbsp. olive oil
½ pumpkin, peeled and diced
juice of 1 garlic clove
dash of caraway seed, crushed
8 cups beef stock
1 cup smoked sausage, sliced
1 cup croutons
salt and pepper, to taste

Saute onions, eggplant, and tomatoes in oil. Add pumpkin, garlic, and caraway seeds. Add beef stock and bring to a boil. Simmer for 30 minutes, season, and add remaining ingredients.

Paella Valenciana

INGREDIENTS   YIELD: 4 servings

1 onion, finely chopped

3 tbsp. olive oil

2 lb. chicken, cut bite size

2 green peppers, chopped

1 tsp. saffron

2½ cups rice

5 cups chicken stock

20 mussels, cleaned

10 clams, cleaned

10 shrimp, peeled and deveined

2 tomatoes, peeled and diced

juice of 2 garlic cloves

salt to taste

black pepper, freshly ground, to taste

2 scallion stems, chopped

Saute onions in oil. Add chicken pieces and cook for 10 minutes. Add green pepper, saffron, and rice. Add chicken stock, bring to a boil, and simmer for 10 minutes. Add remaining ingredients, except for scallions. Stir, cover, and bake at 375° F. for 10 minutes until rice is cooked. Sprinkle with chopped scallions.

Andalusian Salad

INGREDIENTS   YIELD: 4 servings

2 garlic cloves

salt and pepper, to taste

1 head romaine, washed

10 mushrooms, sliced

3 oz. lemon juice

2 oz. wine vinegar

4 oz. walnut oil

1 bunch watercress

3 oranges, peeled and cut in sections

dash of sugar

½ tsp. tarragon, chopped

Mix salt and garlic, and rub in salad bowl. Add chopped romaine and mushrooms. Add lemon juice, vinegar, and oil. Toss with remaining ingredients.

Breast of Chicken Au Porto

INGREDIENTS   YIELD: 4 servings

¼ cup shallots, diced

3 oz. butter

salt, to taste

black pepper, freshly ground, to taste

4 boneless breasts of chicken

¼ cup celery, diced

2¼ cup carrots, diced

2 oz. cognac

(Cont.)

Saute shallots in butter. Season chicken breasts, and add celery and carrots. Bake for 15 minutes at 400° F. Flame with cognac, and add demi glaze and porto. Simmer for 15 minutes. Add garlic juice and heavy cream.

1 cup demi glaze

2 cups porto

juice of 2 garlic cloves

¼ cup heavy cream

Orange Seville

INGREDIENTS   YIELD: 4 servings

4 oranges

1 cup whipped cream

2 cups vanilla custard

1 oz. rose water

16 crystallized mint leaves

1 cup whipped cream, for decoration

8 fresh rose buds, for decoration

Cut oranges in half, empty shells, and dice orange sections. Set shells aside. Fold whipped cream into custard, and mix with rose water and diced orange sections. Fill orange shells and place two mint leaves in each. Fill pastry bag with whipped cream. On each serving plate, surround orange with cream. Place a fresh rose bud next to it, or in center of orange.

Switzerland

A land divided into Cantons—in some of the valleys a Latin dialect is still heard—the scene of one of my first ventures in gourmet cooking.

Classical Gourmet Punch

Fondue Netstal

Pot-Au-Feu Bonne Menagere

Emince a la Fridolin

Rosti

Turkish Coffee

Classical Gourmet Punch

INGREDIENTS   YIELD: 6 to 8 servings

2 bottles red burgundy

juice of 4 oranges

2 cloves

juice of 4 lemons

1 pt. rum

1 piece sugar loaf

Bring the burgundy, orange juice, cloves, and lemon juice to a boil in a copper bowl. Lay the mulling tong, with sugar loaf, over the bowl. Pour some of the previously warmed rum (151 proof) over sugar to soak, then light. Continue to ladle the rum over the burning sugar until used up. Serve in prewarmed cups or glasses. *Never* pour rum from the bottle. See Color Plate 8.

Fondue Netstal

INGREDIENTS   YIELD: 6 servings

1 garlic clove
5 cups neuchatel white wine
1 lb. gruyere cheese, grated
½ lb. emmentaler cheese, grated
¼ lb. appenzeller cheese, grated
2 oz. kirschwasser
1 tsp. cornstarch
juice of 1 lemon
white pepper, ground, to taste
dash of nutmeg
dash of paprika
1 loaf French bread, cut in cubes

Rub the inside of pan with the garlic clove and remove. Add white wine and place over heat. Add cheese to wine by stirring with a wooden spoon. Bring to a boil. Add kirschwasser mixed with cornstarch, lemon juice, and seasoning. Transfer to fondue bowl. Regulate the flame so the fondue continues to boil. Stir when dipping the bread.

Pot-Au-Feu Bonne Menagere

INGREDIENTS   YIELD: 4 servings

2 lb. beef flanken, quartered
1 medium onion, whole
4 cloves
1 gal. beef consomme
¼ cup celery, julienne
2 carrots, julienne
¼ cup leeks, julienne
1 cup cabbage, cut into squares
4 pork sausages
3 raw potatoes, quartered
3 strips bacon, diced
1 bay leaf
salt and pepper, to taste
2 tbsp. chives, chopped
¼ cup grated parmesan cheese

Boil beef flanken, onion, and cloves, in consomme for 2 hours. Remove beef and set aside. Add vegetables and sausages and simmer for 20 minutes. Add potatoes, bacon, bay leaf, seasoning, and beef. Simmer until meat is soft. Remove onion and cloves. Serve with grated cheese on the side. See Color Plate 7.

Eminence a la Fridolin
Geschnetzeltes a la Fridolin

INGREDIENTS   YIELD: 3 servings

1 lb. pork, thinly sliced

½ lb. sirloin steak, thinly sliced

¼ lb. calves kidneys

2 oz. butter

2 tbsp. chopped parsley

4 shallots, finely chopped

10 mushrooms, thinly sliced

salt and pepper, to taste

1 cup demi glaze

1 cup heavy cream

Saute pork, sirloin, and kidneys in butter for 5 minutes. Sprinkle with chopped parsley, and remove from pan. Saute shallots and mushrooms, and season. Combine with meat, add demi glaze, and bring to a boil. Add heavy cream. Serve with Rosti. See Color Plate 5.

Rosti

Saute 3 cups of shredded, cooked potatoes and 4 strips of diced bacon in butter. Season with salt and pepper. Spread with Swiss cheese (optional). Sprinkle with chopped parsley. See Color Plate 5.

Turkish Coffee

YIELD: 4 servings

To prepare Turkish coffee, ⅔ pint water, 8 teaspoons ground Turkish coffee or espresso, and 4 teaspoons of sugar are required. A real coffee mill, a Turkish coffee pot, and a stockli rechaud are required. Set the fresh, cold water on the heat, and shake the freshly ground coffee and sugar into it just before it boils. Stir with a spoon and bring to a boil. Remove from heat and let stand for a short while. Pour into cups.

2. Spectacular Specialties of Five Continents

Europe

During the journey of the Orient Express in 1892, the lives of the passengers were endangered only by too much food and wine—the grand candlelit dinner was a black tie affair.

THE ORIENT EXPRESS CLASSIC

Hors-d'Oeuvre Parisienne

Consomme Oriental

Paupiettes de Veau Constantinopal

Pommes Dauphine

Endive Massenet

Fromages

Crepes Napoleon

Cafe Noir

Hors-d'Oeuvre Parisienne

Caviar—Place caviar in original jar on crushed ice or socle surrounded with slices of lemon and lime. Garnish with tidbits of toast, chopped egg whites, egg yolks, and mint leaves.

Lobster—Boil tails with seaweed. Cool, peel, slice, and place on Boston lettuce leaves. For a sauce, use mayonnaise mixed with freshly grated horseradish, lemon juice, and orange zest.

Oysters—Marinate with white wine, olive oil, and chopped capers.

Pate de Foie Gras—Dip spoon in hot water, and cut oval pieces. Arrange in center, surrounded with chopped aspic.

Mushrooms—Saute sliced mushrooms in olive oil with diced tomatoes, pepper, salt, chopped parsley, and lemon juice. Cool and place on lettuce leaves.

Crab meat—Use lump meat mixed with mayonnaise and whipped cream. Serve on chopped spinach leaves and decorate with sliced truffles.

Celeriac—Peel, slice in julienne, and marinate with lemon juice, prepared mustard, salt, pepper, and olive oil.

Aubergines—Slice eggplant in long strips. Combine with garlic juice, a little white wine, olive oil, lemon juice, dash of thyme, one bay leaf, coriander, diced tomato, salt, and pepper. Cover and bring to a boil. Cool and marinate.

Consomme Oriental

INGREDIENTS   YIELD: 8 servings

8 cups beef consomme

1 cup cooked rice, with saffron

1 oz. sherry

¼ cup carrots, peeled and diced

¼ cup celeriac, peeled and diced

¼ cup red beets, peeled and diced

Cook each vegetable separately in salt water and strain. Mix with rice. Bring consomme to a boil. Add sherry and pour over mixture.

Paupiettes de Veau Constantinopal

INGREDIENTS   YIELD: 6 servings

½ lb. veal shoulder

1 tsp. parsley, chopped

1 lb. calves brain (skinned)

4 egg whites

3 tbsp. heavy cream

salt to taste

white pepper to taste

6 5-oz. veal cutlets, pounded

4 oz. butter

¼ cup white wine

1 cup demi glaze

3 tomatoes, cut in half and grilled

For farce, finely grind, or place in chopper, the veal shoulder, parsley, calves brain, egg whites, heavy cream, salt, and pepper.

Divide farce among veal cutlets. Roll tightly and brown in butter on each side. Add white wine and reduce for several minutes. Add demi glaze and simmer for 10 minutes, until done. Place on serving platter and surround with grilled tomatoes and pommes dauphine.

Pommes Dauphine

Peel 6 large potatoes, cut in quarters, and boil in salt water. Strain and mash through a fine sieve. Add two whole eggs, a dash of nutmeg, and 1 tbsp. butter. Place in casserole and cook, stirring constantly, until mixture separates from pot. Mix in ⅓ cup un-sweetened chou paste. Divide into portions. Roll, and fry in hot oil.

Endive Massenet

Place Boston lettuce leaves on a platter. Cut Belgian endive lengthwise and arrange in a circle. In center, place chopped artichoke buttons with julienne of green and red pepper. Top with toasted sliced almonds and sprinkle with curry powder. Top with Italian dressing and sprinkle with freshly ground black pepper.

Crepes Napoleon

INGREDIENTS   YIELD: 8 servings

Crepes

5 eggs

3 tbsp. water

2 tsp. confectioner's sugar

salt to taste

¼ cup all-purpose flour

Combine eggs, water, sugar, and salt. Beat thoroughly, and add sifted flour. Beat until smooth. Brush omelet pan with oil. Heat and prepare very thin crepes.

Vanilla Cream

1½ cups milk

¼ vanilla bean

2 eggs, separated

1 oz. cornstarch

5 oz. confectioner's sugar

Bring milk and vanilla bean to a boil. Cool, and add egg yolks, cornstarch, and 3 oz. of sugar. Whisk and bring to a boil. Remove from heat. Whip egg whites with remaining sugar until firm. Mix into cream.

   Fold crepes and arrange on a platter. Pour vanilla cream over and sprinkle with shaved chocolate.

Africa

Many kings have crossed the North African desert with their trains of camels—oases have been the setting for feasts celebrated without cutlery—the result is a great cuisine.

THE SULTAN'S CLASSIC

Hummus Soup

Pyramid Salad

Marinated Roast Quail, Sultan

Okra Rice

Fruits from the Bazaar

Mint Tea

Hummus Soup

INGREDIENTS   YIELD: 6 servings

2 oz. butter

1 egg

3 tbsp. chickpeas, chopped

salt, to taste

4 oz. farina

boiling water

8 cups chicken consomme

1 tsp. chives, chopped

Beat butter with eggs. Add chickpeas, salt, and farina. With a teaspoon, make balls. Place in boiling salted water, and simmer balls for 20 minutes in covered pot. Remove balls and add to boiling chicken consomme. Sprinkle with chopped chives.

Pyramid Salad

INGREDIENTS   YIELD: 6 servings

4 oz. celeriac, peeled and diced

4 oz. carrots, peeled and diced

4 apples, peeled and diced

2 oz. walnuts, chopped

juice of half a lemon

dash of Worcestershire sauce

2 cups aspic, melted

3 cups mayonnaise

dash of sugar

salt and pepper, to taste

Garnish

Figs, dates, dried apricots, lettuce leaves, orange wedges, quartered hard-boiled eggs, and mint leaves.

Cover celeriac and carrots with water, add lemon juice, and blanch for 4 minutes. Cool. Mix remaining ingredients and place in a pyramid form (four-cornered, pointed mold). Place in refrigerator and chill well. To serve, place form for a second in hot water; turn over on lettuce leaves arranged on a platter. Arrange fruit garnish on the four sides of pyramid. Place quartered eggs at the four corners with mint leaves.

Marinated Roast Quail, Sultan

INGREDIENTS   YIELD: 6 servings

6 quail

melted butter

2 oz. brandy

2 cups demi glaze

¼ cup heavy cream

Marinade

2 onions, sliced

½ carrot, sliced

5 mushrooms, sliced

3 tbsp. vinegar

dash of thyme

1 bay leaf

(Cont.)

Combine all ingredients for marinade. Bring to a boil and simmer for 20 minutes. Cool. Pour over quail and refrigerate, covered, for 24 hours. Remove quail, brush with butter, and roast for 30 minutes at 325° F. Pour brandy over and ignite. Add demi glaze, and bring to a boil. Stir in heavy cream. Arrange with okra rice.

1 tbsp. peppercorns
1 tsp. juniper berries
2 cups red wine
juice of 1 lemon

Okra Rice

INGREDIENTS   YIELD: 6 servings

1 small onion, finely chopped
1 lb. okra, cut in ½ inch pieces
2 oz. butter
1 cup rice
2½ cups water
dash of saffron
salt to taste

Saute onion and okra in butter. Add rice and stir until glossy. Add water, saffron, and salt. Bring to a boil and bake at 350° F. for 35 to 40 minutes.

Fruits from the Bazaar

Arrange mixed nuts in the center of an oval silver tray. Surround with dried apricots, pears, figs, raisins, oranges, dates, peaches, prunes, plums, nectarines, apples, and currants. Garnish with fresh mint leaves or palm leaves.

Asia

From the heat of the Gobi Desert to the arctic cold, man lived a million years before Genghis Khan crossed the pages of history—the Feast of Lanterns ends the New Year.

THE GENGHIS KHAN CLASSIC

Shangri-La Soup

Pomegranate Salad

Lotus Pork

Duck Shanghai

Hunan Rice

Stir Fried Vegetable

Mandarin Lily

Tea Hangzhou Xihu Longjing

Shangri-La Soup

INGREDIENTS   YIELD: 8 servings

1 cup julienne chicken breast

½ cup bean sprouts

1 tbsp. soy sauce

8 cups chicken consomme

½ cup sliced bamboo shoots

2 pieces dried tangerine peel (soaked), sliced

10 mushrooms, sliced

2 scallions, sliced

Place chicken, bean sprouts, and soy sauce in saucepan and cover with some chicken stock. Simmer for 25 minutes. Add bamboo shoots and sliced tangerine peel. Add remaining chicken consomme. Bring to a boil, and add mushrooms and scallions.

Pomegranate Salad

INGREDIENTS   YIELD: 8 servings

8 pomegranates

3 ripe pears

½ lb. seedless white grapes

1 cup honeydew melon balls

1 cup fresh raspberries

¼ lb. fresh cherries, pitted

2 oz. brandy

¼ cup white wine

¼ cup confectioner's sugar

juice of 1 orange

mint leaves

Cut off the top of the pomegranates. Core the center and separate seeds. Squeeze juice of the cored meat into bowl. Cut remaining fruit. Combine with juice of orange, brandy, wine, and sugar. Chill well. Fill the pomegranates and place on a serving dish. Surround with mint leaves.

Lotus Pork

INGREDIENTS   YIELD: 8 servings

2½ lb. lean pork loin

2 tbsp. oil

1 lb. mushrooms, sliced

4 scallion stems, chopped

2 lb. fresh lotus root, peeled and sliced

2 oz. sherry

2 tbsp. soy sauce

salt and pepper, to taste

½ cup brown sauce

Slice pork loin thin. Heat oil and stir fry pork for 5 minutes. Add mushrooms, scallions, and lotus root. Stir fry for 3 more minutes. Add sherry, soy sauce, salt, and pepper. Top with brown sauce. Cover and simmer for 5 minutes.

Duck Shanghai

INGREDIENTS   YIELD: 8 servings

pepper, to taste

¼ cup soy sauce

1 tsp. ground ginger

2 4-lb. ducklings

1 onion, sliced

4 scallions, chopped

2 green peppers, sliced

2 tbsp. butter

16 shrimp, peeled and deveined

⅛ cup wine vinegar

2 tbsp. sugar

1 cup white wine

1 tbsp. cornstarch

8 oz. pineapple chunks

Mix pepper, half of the soy sauce, and ginger, and brush duckling. Place on roasting rack in oven at 400° F. for 2½ hours, basting frequently with the drippings, until crisp. Cool. Remove meat from bones, and cut in bite-size portions. Stir fry the onions, scallions, and green pepper in butter. Add the duckling, shrimp, remaining soy sauce, vinegar, and sugar, and stir for 5 minutes. Mix the wine and cornstarch and pour over. Bring to a boil and serve. Top with pineapple chunks.

Hunan Rice

INGREDIENTS   YIELD: 8 servings

1 onion, finely chopped

2 tbsp. peanut oil

2 cups long grain rice, soaked in water for 20 minutes

3 cups water

salt, to taste

2 eggs, lightly beaten

½ small Chinese cabbage, shredded

¼ cup soy sauce

white pepper, ground, to taste

Saute onions in 1 tbsp. peanut oil. Add strained rice, water, and salt. Bring to a boil and simmer for 25 minutes. Heat remaining peanut oil and add beaten eggs. Stirring constantly, add rice, cabbage, and soy sauce. Brown lightly and season with pepper.

Mandarin Lily

INGREDIENTS   YIELD: 8 servings

2 cups milk

½ tsp. vanilla extract

1 tbsp. cornstarch

3 egg yolks

1 tsp. confectioner's sugar

2 cups whipped cream

1 tsp. rose water

8 mandarins

ground cinnamon, to sprinkle

8 ladyfingers

Mix milk, vanilla, and cornstarch. Bring to a boil and cook until thickened. Beat egg yolks and add to hot milk with sugar. Cool and mix with whipped cream and rose water. Cut mandarin peels into leaf shapes. Separate mandarin sections and place in a glass dish. Pour sauce over and sprinkle with cinnamon. Arrange mandarin peels with ladyfingers around bowl for garnish.

America

North, South, East, and West—always an inventive cuisine—its basic simplicity is a delight.

THE AMERICAN CLASSIC

Clam Chowder

Avocado Salad

Carpetbagger Steak

Wild Rice

Pineapple Corn

Strawberry Shortcake

Coffee

Clam Chowder

INGREDIENTS   YIELD: 8 servings

24 clams, large chowder
1 cup onions, diced
4 tbsp. flour
4 oz. butter
1 cup celery, diced
1 cup carrots, diced
2 cups raw potatoes, diced
dash of thyme
1 bay leaf
½ cup white wine
1 cup heavy cream
salt and freshly ground pepper, to taste

Rinse clams well, wash, and place in pot. Cover with water and boil until clams open. Strain. Remove clams and discard shells. Trim away brown parts and cut in quarters. Brown onions and flour in butter. Add 2 quarts of clam stock. Add celery, carrots, potatoes, and seasoning. Simmer for 45 minutes. Add white wine and clams, and bring to a boil. Finish with heavy cream. Season to taste.

Avocado Salad

INGREDIENTS   YIELD: 8 servings

4 anchovy fillets
salt to taste
3 egg yolks
6 tbsp. wine vinegar
6 tbsp. olive oil
1 romaine lettuce, in bite-size pieces
2 scallions, julienne
1 cup croutons
6 avocados, peeled and sliced
black pepper, freshly ground, to taste

In salad bowl, mash anchovy fillets with salt. Add egg yolks, and beat with vinegar and oil. Toss with romaine, scallions, croutons, avocado, and pepper.

Carpetbagger Steak

INGREDIENTS   YIELD: 8 servings

8 14-oz. shell steaks, trimmed of all fat

4 shallots, finely chopped

1 oz. butter

8 small shrimp, peeled, deveined, and cut in half

8 oysters, shucked

2 oz. green peppercorns in vinegar, drained

salt to taste

2 oz. brandy

¼ cup demi glaze

Slit each steak along the side to make a pocket. Saute shallots in butter with shrimp. Cool. Fill each pocket with one oyster and the shrimp mixture. Sew up the slit. Press in the peppercorns and salt. Saute in butter for 3 minutes on each side. Add brandy and ignite. Add demi glaze. Place on serving platter. Garnish with wild rice.

Wild Rice

INGREDIENTS   YIELD: 8 servings

1 onion, finely chopped

¼ cup red pimiento, chopped

2 oz. butter

1½ cups wild rice

3½ cups water

1 oz. sherry

salt and pepper, to taste

Saute onions and pimiento in butter. Add wild rice. Add water, bring to a boil, and bake at 350° F. for 45 minutes, or until done. Add sherry, salt, and pepper.

Pineapple Corn

INGREDIENTS   YIELD: 8 servings

1 tbsp. butter

2 tbsp. flour

¾ cup milk

2 cups corn

salt to taste

4 eggs, separated

1 cup drained pineapple tidbits

Melt butter. Add flour, stir in milk, and bring to boil. Add corn, salt, and egg yolks. Beat egg whites until stiff. Combine all ingredients. Place in buttered casserole and bake at 375° F. for 25 minutes.

Strawberry Shortcake

INGREDIENTS   YIELD: 8 servings

2¼ cups all-purpose flour

2 tbsp. sugar

salt to taste

2 tbsp. baking powder

¾ cup butter, sweet

¾ cup milk

3 pints ripe, large strawberries

3 oz. Grand Marnier

1 pint heavy cream, whipped

confectioner's sugar

Grease cake pan with butter. Combine flour, sugar, salt, and baking powder. Mix in butter. Add milk and mix to a dough. Knead lightly. Place in cake pan and bake for 15 minutes at 400° F. Cut into portions. Place on serving dishes. Soak half the sliced berries in the Grand Marnier. Divide among each dish. Top with whipped cream. Divide remaining berries on top. Sprinkle with powdered sugar.

Coffee

The best coffee beans, the finest brewing, the various types of waters, and the presentation itself, all contribute to this American classic. There are many regional differences, from cafe au lait of the North to the strong, black coffee of the South. But whether the occasion is an intimate supper at home, or an evening at that special dining spot, nothing complements an expertly prepared meal like a flavorful, full-bodied cup of coffee.

Much has been written concerning the romance of coffee and the proper brewing methods. We offer only a limited study of interest to the coffee lover.

Coffee Varieties

There are approximately fifty varieties of coffee that fall into three general groups. There are Brazils, named after the country of origin. Milds (not to be construed as meaning mild) come from Central America, including Columbia, Guatemala, and Mexico. Robustos are from Africa and are named for the countries of origin, for example, Congos and Ivory Coast. Still other African coffees are named after the district of growth.

The coffee blender attempts to achieve a uniform blend by skillfully interchanging available coffees. Green coffees are first prepared in very small quantities in a test roaster, then ground and brought to the testing table. The testing procedure is rather simple: a penny-weight of freshly ground coffee is placed in a tasting cup and properly heated water is added; the taster smells the aroma and then tastes for flavor and body by slurping a spoonful of the brew far back into the mouth, being careful not to swallow. This procedure is repeated until all of the test coffees have been tasted. Then the tester, who has noted the characteristics of the various coffees, must combine them harmoniously to achieve that perfect cup of coffee.

However, no matter how much skill is utilized in preparing the blend, you, the consumer, have the final say in determining just how fine or how bad the brew will be.

Brewing

There is nothing more gratifying to a host or hostess than the words, "This is a great cup of coffee." And there is no reason why they should not be heard time after time if a few simple brewing rules are followed.

1. Equipment must be clean.
2. Use fresh, cold water.
3. Water must be at proper temperature.

4. Use the proper grind for your equipment.
5. Use a proper water/coffee ratio.
6. Allow proper brewing time.
7. Never repour brewed coffee over the grinds.

Whether you are preparing coffee for a few friends or for a banquet, the above rules apply. Rules 1 and 2 are straightforward. The proper water temperature should be 200° F., give or take 5°, when it comes into contact with the coffee; coffee should be served at 185° to 190° F. A proper grind allows water to pass through the coffee bed in the correct time, with little or no sediment. The correct formula requires two gallons (never more than two and one-half gallons) of water for each sixteen ounces of coffee. Our readers will have to determine the correct water/coffee ratio based on the size of their equipment. The results will be worth the effort.

When brewing, allow:

1 to 4 minutes for a fine grind
4 to 6 minutes for a drip grind
6 to 8 minutes for a regular grind

The reason for the different times is simply that the finer the grind, the faster the water saturates the coffee and extracts the desirable characteristics. If we allowed six to eight minutes (needed for a regular grind) for the fine grind, we would end up with undesirable bitterness and astringency due to overextraction of acids and oils. Finally, never repour. Repouring filters out the good qualities originally extracted.

Whether you are the proprietor of an intimate dining spot or feeding large groups, I suggest a brush-up course in coffee-brewing methods, which have been upgraded due to extensive research. Most fine coffee companies have experienced sales personnel who will assist in training your staff in preventive maintenance, sanitation, and proper brewing procedures. Remember that the last thing your customer usually has in your establishment is a cup of coffee. If it is fine, it can help to counteract any weaknesses in the meal; if it is inferior, the opposite can occur.

In conclusion, if you follow these few simple suggestions and find that you and your customers are still not satisfied with the results, it is time to try other blends until you can honestly say, "This is a great cup of coffee."

Australia

Pioneers over a camp fire preserved fish from the Gold Coast—English settlers modified their traditional dishes to reflect a new continent.

THE BUSHMAN CLASSIC

Kangaroo Soup

Barbecued King Prawns

Fillet of Venison Bushman

Golden Peach with Berries

Tropical Fruit Salad

Queensland Custard

Tea Victoria

Kangaroo Soup

INGREDIENTS   YIELD: 8 servings

1 kangaroo tail, skinned
3 tbsp. barley
10 cups beef consomme
2 onions, finely chopped
2 carrots, peeled and diced
2 celery stalks, diced
1 tsp. butter
1 bay leaf
1 oz. sherry
salt to taste
white pepper, ground, to taste
1 tsp. chives, chopped

Cut kangaroo tail (if unavailable, substitute oxtail) into chunks. Place in roasting pan and roast at 375° F. for two hours. Remove the meat from the tail and cut in ¼-inch pieces. Simmer barley in beef consomme for 1½ hours. Saute onions, carrots, and celery in butter for 5 minutes. Add beef and barley stock, chopped kangaroo tail, and bay leaf, and simmer for 45 minutes. Remove bay leaf. Add sherry, salt, and pepper to taste. Sprinkle with chives.

Barbecued King Prawns

INGREDIENTS   YIELD: 8 servings

32 prawns, peeled and deveined
¼ cup oil
1 onion, finely chopped
2 garlic cloves, finely chopped
1 tsp. butter
2 tsp. mustard
1 tsp. chili powder
juice of 2 lemons
¼ cup vinegar
1 tbsp. sugar
1 tbsp. Worcestershire sauce
¾ cup tomato ketchup
white pepper, ground, to taste

Toss prawns in oil and place on barbecue (open fire or broiler). Saute onions and garlic in butter. Add remaining ingredients and bring to boil. Simmer for 5 minutes. Place sauce in center of platter surrounded with prawns.

Fillet of Venison Bushman

INGREDIENTS   YIELD: 8 servings

32 strips lard, ¼ × 2 inches
8 5-oz. venison fillets
2 oz. butter
1 oz. brandy
2 cups game sauce
peaches, to garnish
lingonberries, to garnish

(Cont.)

Lard four strips into each venison fillet. Combine marinade, pour over fillets, and marinate for 48 hours. Remove and saute fillets in hot butter 3 minutes on each side. Pour brandy over and ignite. Add game sauce and simmer for 5 minutes. Place on serving dish and surround with peaches and lingonberries.

Marinade
1 cup red wine
1 bay leaf
1 tbsp. juniper berries
dash of thyme
juice of 1 lemon
1 tsp. black peppercorns
1 onion, chopped

Golden Peach with Berries

INGREDIENTS   YIELD: 8 servings

8 peaches, cut in half
½ cup red wine
2 oz. brandy
16 tbsp. blackberries
confectioner's sugar

Peel peaches and boil in red wine. Remove and soak in brandy for one hour. Fill each half with blackberries and sprinkle with confectioner's sugar.

Tropical Fruit Salad

INGREDIENTS   YIELD: 8 servings

2 papayas
2 mangoes
1 pineapple
10 Chinese gooseberries
2 oz. rum
2 oz. praline liqueur
mint leaves, to garnish

Peel all fruit. Cut papayas, mangoes, and pineapple into bite-size pieces; slice gooseberries. Place in bowl with rum and liqueur and chill. Serve in champagne glasses garnished with mint leaves.

Queensland Custard

INGREDIENTS   YIELD: 8 servings

⅓ cup sugar
5 eggs
salt to taste
3 cups milk
2 oz. praline liqueur
2 tbsp. almonds
2 oz. butter
2 pt. fresh raspberries
2 cups whipped cream
dash of nutmeg

Beat sugar, eggs, and salt. Add milk and praline liqueur. Strain. Add almonds, stirring constantly. Place liquid in buttered mold. Poach in water, covered, for 35 minutes. Chill. Turn mold upside down, and decorate with raspberries and whipped cream. Sprinkle with nutmeg.

Tea Victoria

Two cups black leaf China tea with 1 cinnamon stick and juice of half lime. Yields one serving.

3. The Art of Classic Chinese Cuisine

China

The mountains of Tsing Hai, the river Yangtze—strange plants and buds used for a cuisine that was recorded on silk—classics of regional cooking adapted to today's kitchens.

Lotus Buds

Mongolian Mushroom Soup

Wonton Consomme

Lobster Kwangtung

Chicken Shanghai

Sweet and Sour Chicken Liver

Salad Chungking

Hong Kong Dust

Jasmine Tea

Lotus Buds

INGREDIENTS   YIELD: 6 to 8 servings

½ lb. crab meat

½ lb. lobster meat

½ lb. shrimp, peeled and deveined

15 water chestnuts, finely chopped

5 shallots, finely chopped

1 tsp. sherry

dash of ginger root, freshly grated

2 egg whites, beaten stiff

1½ tsp. cornstarch

salt and pepper, to taste

sesame seeds, for rolling

oil, for deep frying

Finely chop crab meat, lobster meat, and shrimp. Add water chestnuts and shallots. Mix with sherry and ginger root, and add egg whites. Add cornstarch and seasoning. Make ¾-inch balls and roll in sesame seeds.

Heat oil and deep fry balls for 3 minutes, or until golden brown.

Mongolian Mushroom Soup

INGREDIENTS   YIELD: 6 to 8 servings

20 dried black mushrooms

8 cups beef stock

4 eggs, whisked

1 scallion, sliced

½ cup bamboo shoots, sliced

dash of soy sauce

Cover mushrooms with water and soak for one hour. Remove. Bring liquid to boil with beef stock, and pour over mushrooms. Add eggs, scallion, bamboo shoots, and soy sauce.

Wonton Consomme

INGREDIENTS   YIELD: 6 to 8 servings

½ lb. ground beef
1 tsp. soy sauce
1 tsp. ginger root, freshly grated
1 cup chopped spinach leaves
salt and pepper, to taste
16 wonton squares
8 cups beef consomme
1 scallion stem, chopped

Mix ground beef, soy sauce, ginger, and spinach leaves with salt and pepper. Place in wonton squares. Fold in triangles and pinch edges to seal. Drop in boiling, salted water and boil for 6 minutes. Remove. Bring beef consomme to boil. Add wontons and scallion.

Lobster Kwangtung

INGREDIENTS   YIELD: 6 to 8 servings

2 lb. lobster meat
½ cup fish stock
1 slice fresh ginger root, minced
dash of sugar
2 tbsp. sherry
1 tbsp. cornstarch
¼ cup cold water
1 oz. soy sauce
1 tsp. sesame oil
1 onion, finely sliced
1 cup bean sprouts
½ cup celery, sliced
½ cup bamboo shoots
½ lb. mushrooms, sliced
juice of 1 garlic clove
2 scallion stalks
salt to taste
black pepper, ground, to taste

Cut lobster meat into bite-size portions. Combine fish stock with ginger root, sugar, and sherry. Mix cornstarch with water and soy sauce. Stir fry lobster meat in oil for 2 minutes. Add onions, bean sprouts, celery, bamboo shoots, and mushrooms. Stir fry for 3 minutes, then add fish stock. Bring to a boil, and add cornstarch mixture and remaining ingredients. Simmer for 3 more minutes. Season to taste.

Chicken Shanghai

INGREDIENTS   YIELD: 6 to 8 servings

2 lb. breast of chicken, cut in strips
1 tsp. sesame oil
2 carrots, peeled and cut in strips
2 Chinese white turnips, peeled and cut in strips
2 onions, sliced
2 cups celery stalks, cut in strips
½ cup water
1 clove star anise

Stir fry chicken strips in oil. Add carrots, turnips, onions, and celery strips and cook for 3 minutes. Add water and remaining ingredients. Bring to a boil and simmer for 15 minutes, covered.

(Cont.)

2 scallions, chopped
2 tbsp. sherry
¼ cup soy sauce
½ lb. snow peas
1 tsp. sugar
1 slice fresh ginger root
½ Chinese cabbage
salt and pepper, to taste

Sweet and Sour Chicken Liver

INGREDIENTS   YIELD: 6 to 8 servings

2 lb. chicken livers
3 tbsp. vegetable oil
5 tbsp. soy sauce
4 tbsp. wine vinegar
3 tbsp. sugar
1 tsp. tomato paste
4 tbsp. orange juice
1 tsp. cornstarch
5 tbsp. water

Saute chicken livers in hot oil until brown. Add soy sauce, vinegar, sugar, tomato paste, and orange juice. Bring to the boiling point. Mix water and cornstarch. Add to liver and simmer for 3 minutes.

Salad Chungking

INGREDIENTS   YIELD: 6 to 8 servings

1 lb. bean sprouts
1 cup bamboo shoots, sliced
½ Chinese cabbage, sliced thin
1 tsp. sugar
3 tbsp. soy sauce
2 tbsp. sesame oil
salt and pepper, to taste

Blanch bean sprouts in water, remove and cool. Mix with bamboo shoots and Chinese cabbage. Mix sugar, soy sauce, and sesame oil, and toss with salad. Add salt and pepper.

Hong Kong Dust

INGREDIENTS   YIELD: 6 to 8 servings

3 cups whipped cream
1 tsp. plum wine
1 lb. chestnut puree
15 walnuts
10 kumquats
¼ cup crystallized ginger

In large bowl, mix whipped cream with plum wine. Pour in serving glasses (champagnes). Top each portion with chestnut puree and decorate with walnuts, kumquats, and crystallized ginger.

More Chinese Classics

Chow Fried Rice

INGREDIENTS	For 12	For 24
onions, finely chopped	2	4
green peas	1 cup	2 cups
bamboo shoots	1 cup	2 cups
sesame oil	4 oz.	8 oz.
salt and pepper	to taste	to taste
chicken, cooked and diced	2 cups	1 qt.
cooked rice	2 qt.	4 qt.
eggs, scrambled	4	8
soy sauce	¼ cup	½ cup
sugar	2 tsp.	1⅓ tbsp.

Stir fry onions, green peas, and bamboo shoots in sesame oil for 10 minutes. Season. Add chicken, rice, and scrambled eggs. Toss and add remaining ingredients.

Spinach Shanghai

INGREDIENTS	For 12	For 24
fresh spinach leaves	4 lb.	8 lb.
sesame oil	⅔ cup	1⅓ cups
garlic juice	2 tbsp.	4 tbsp.
chicken stock	2 cups	1 qt.
soy sauce	1½ tbsp.	3 tbsp.
salt and pepper	to taste	to taste

Wash spinach leaves thoroughly. Heat sesame oil in large pan. Add garlic and spinach leaves, and cook for 2 minutes. Add remaining ingredients, and continue cooking for 2 minutes.

Sirloin Hong Kong Style

INGREDIENTS	For 12	For 24
shell steak	3 lb.	6 lb.
garlic cloves	3	6
butter	2 oz.	4 oz.
mushrooms, sliced	10	20
sherry	½ cup	1 cup
demi glaze	2 cups	4 cups
soy sauce	⅓ cup	⅔ cup
ginger	1 tsp.	2 tsp.

Rub steak with garlic. Saute in butter on both sides. Remove. Saute mushrooms, and add sherry and remaining ingredients. Bring to a boil, pour over steak, and bake at 375° F. for 10 minutes, or until medium rare. Garnish and serve with marinated red cabbage and cucumber slices.

Sweet and Sour Pork

INGREDIENTS	For 4	For 24
pork, cut into strips	1 lb.	6 lb.
salt and pepper	to taste	to taste
onions, sliced	½	4
sesame oil	1 tsp.	3 tbsp.
pineapple juice	½ cup	3 cups
vinegar	2 tbsp.	1 cup
soy sauce	1 tbsp.	⅔ cup
sherry	2 oz.	½ cup
brown sugar	1 tsp.	1 cup
cornstarch	1 tsp.	6 tsp.
green peppers, julienne	1	6
tomato, cut in wedges	1	4
pineapple chunks	½ cup	3 cups
cooked rice	1 cup	6 cups

Season pork strips with salt and pepper. Saute onions in sesame oil, add pork strips, and brown. Add pineapple juice, vinegar, soy sauce, sherry, and brown sugar. Cover and simmer for 30 minutes. Stir in cornstarch, mixed with some cold water, until thickened. Add green pepper, tomato, and pineapple chunks, and simmer for 15 minutes. Place cooked rice on serving plate and top with sweet and sour pork. See Color Plate 4.

Ho Salad

INGREDIENTS	For 4	For 24
fillet of beef, strips	6 oz.	2 lb.
soy sauce	1 tsp.	2 tbsp.
vinegar	1 tbsp.	¼ cup
olive oil	2 tbsp.	½ cup
salt and pepper	to taste	to taste
cabbage, shredded	8 oz.	3 lb.
tomato, cut in wedges	1	6

Marinate beef strips in soy sauce, vinegar, and oil for 10 minutes. Season. Saute beef and chill. Arrange shredded cabbage, surrounded with tomato topped with beef on platter. Serve with mustard sauce mixed with mayonnaise. See Color Plate 4.

Kwangtung Shrimp

INGREDIENTS	For 4	For 24
raw shrimp	1¼ lb.	7 lb.
mushrooms, sliced	5	3 cups
onions, finely chopped	¼ cup	1½ cups
sesame oil	1 tbsp.	½ cup
pea pods, cut	8 oz.	3 lb.
water	4 tbsp.	2 cups
cornstarch	¼ tsp.	3 tbsp.
sugar	dash	1 tbsp.
soy sauce	1 tsp.	¾ cup
ground pepper	to taste	to taste

Saute shrimp, mushrooms, and onions in oil. Add pea pods. Mix water with cornstarch, and add remaining ingredients. Season and serve with white rice. See Color Plate 4.

Lo Mein

INGREDIENTS	For 4	For 24
pork shoulder, cut in julienne	12 oz.	4 lb.
sesame oil	½ tsp.	2 tbsp.
onions, sliced	½ cup	6 onions
bamboo shoots	1 cup	4 cups
water chestnuts	⅓ cup	1½ cups
celery, sliced	⅓ cup	2 cups
soy sauce	2 tsp.	1 cup
ginger	dash	2 tsp.
salt and pepper	to taste	to taste
water	½ cup	3 cups
cornstarch	1 tsp.	½ cup
buttered egg noodles	½ lb.	2 lb.

Stir fry pork in oil till brown. Add onions, bamboo shoots, water chestnuts, celery, soy sauce, ginger, and seasoning. Stir fry for 5 minutes. Add water mixed with cornstarch. Stir fry buttered egg noodles. Pour mixture over. See Color Plate 4.

Marco Polo Beef

INGREDIENTS	For 4	For 24
sirloin of beef, cut in slices	1 lb.	6 lb.
salt and pepper	to taste	to taste
sesame oil	1 tbsp.	⅔ cup
water	1 cup	6 cups
cornstarch	½ tsp.	2 tbsp.
onions, finely chopped	1	6
garlic juice	1 clove	5 cloves
soy sauce	dash	2 tbsp.
oyster sauce	2 tbsp.	¾ cup
mustard	¼ tsp.	1 tbsp.

Season beef and saute in oil. Mix water with cornstarch, and add with remaining ingredients. Simmer for 5 minutes. Serve over buttered noodles. See Color Plate 4.

Almond Orange Festival

INGREDIENTS	For 4	For 24
orange gelatin	2 oz.	12 oz.
boiling water	¾ cup	1 qt.
cold water	¾ cup	1 qt.
cream cheese	5½ oz.	2 lb.
almond extract	dash	3 tbsp.
sliced peaches	to garnish	to garnish
maraschino cherries	to garnish	to garnish

Dissolve gelatin in boiling water. Add cold water. In blender, combine cream cheese with almond extract and gelatin. Blend at low speed. Fill mold and chill until firm. Unmold and garnish with peaches and maraschino cherries. See Color Plate 4.

Rice Crunch

Cook 1 cup white rice until very soft. Place in pan and chill well. Cut into squares and fry till golden brown. See Color Plate 4.

4. American Classics, a Nouvelle Cuisine

Alabama

Its gulf coast seafood attractions are bon secour oysters and lump crabmeat—speckled trout abound in the lakes—a meal can be a gourmet's delight under trees covered with centuries-old Spanish moss—blackberries, pecans, and catfish.

Bon Secour Classic
Baked Oysters

INGREDIENTS	For 6	For 24
bon secour oysters	30	10 dozen
cloves of garlic, crushed	8	20
red peppers, finely diced	4	16
cooked spinach leaves, chopped	½ cup	2 cups
butter	8 tbsp.	2 cups
breadcrumbs, freshly made	1 cup	4 cups
salt and black pepper, freshly ground	to taste	to taste
Tabasco sauce	1 tsp.	1 tbsp.
sauce mornay	1 cup	4 cups
parmesan cheese	¼ cup	1 cup
parsley	for garnish	for garnish

Open oysters to half shell. To prepare stuffing, saute garlic, red peppers, and spinach in butter. Add breadcrumbs and saute until mixture is binding. Season with salt, pepper, Tabasco sauce, and cool. Top each oyster with mixture and sauce mornay, and sprinkle with parmesan cheese. Bake at 375° F. for 30 minutes. Garnish with parsley.

Arkansas

Jackson, Stone, and Fulton counties—white river trout—the western bonanza land—sugar cured hams, smoked slowly over glowing embers of native hickory.

Arkansas Classic
Baked Ham

INGREDIENTS	For 12 to 14	For 30
smoked ham, precooked	10-lb.	20-lb.
mustard	2 tbsp.	4 tbsp.
whole cloves	20	40
sugar	¼ cup	½ cup
red wine sauce	2 cups	4 cups
raisins	¼ cup	½ cup

Trim fat from ham and cut top in diamond shapes. Brush with mustard, stud with cloves in the points, and cover with sugar. Bake for 1¼ hours at 350° F. Slice. Place slices in casserole, cover with red wine sauce and raisins, and simmer for 5 minutes. Serve with sweet potatoes.

California

The gold coast of America—superior grapes and wines—olives, oranges, dates, fish, and artichokes are the best from the West.

Gold Coast Classic
Dungeness Crabs Garni

INGREDIENTS	For 3	For 24
water	to cover	to cover
juice of lemon	3	10
carrots, cut	2	8
celery stalk, cut	1	4
onions, cut	2	8
bouquet garni	1	1 large
Dungeness crabs, approx. 1¼ lb. each	3	24
coast sauce	1 cup	8 cups
gold sauce	1 cup	8 cups
classic sauce	1 cup	8 cups
salt and pepper	to taste	to taste

In large kettle, bring water, lemon juice, carrots, celery, onions, and bouquet garni to a boil. Place crabs in liquid, boil for 20 minutes, and remove. Remove top shell and clean inside. Reserve milky substance for gold sauce. Crack legs into pieces and refrigerate. To serve, arrange legs around upturned crab shell in center of platter and fill each with a sauce. Garnish with fresh raw vegetable stalks and greens.

Coast Sauce
Mix ½ cup mayonnaise with a dash of vinegar, sugar, lemon juice, cayenne pepper, tarragon, chopped chives, whipped cream, and Tabasco.

Gold Sauce
Mix milky substance with mustard, mayonnaise, lemon juice, curry powder, and chopped watercress.

Classic Sauce
Mix mayonnaise with lemon juice and plenty of caviar.

Colorado

The crown jewel of the Rockies—ghostly silver mining towns and the dude ranches of today—buffalo, antelope, cattle, and rainbow trout—gourmets on horseback.

Crown Jewel
Flaming Buffalo Steaks

INGREDIENTS	For 6	For 24
8 oz. buffalo steaks	6	24
strips of lard	12	48
black pepper, freshly ground	to taste	to taste

Lard steaks, and season with salt and pepper. Saute in hot oil for 3 minutes on each side. Add juniper berries and brandy and ignite. Add red wine, demi glaze, and lemon juice. Bring to a boil. Remove steaks. Add sour cream to the sauce and strain over steak. Serve with baked apples.

(Cont.)

olive oil	4 oz.	2 cups
juniper berries, chopped	2 tbsp.	½ cup
brandy	2 oz.	8 oz.
red wine	4 oz.	2 cups
demi glaze	4 oz.	2 cups
juice of lemon	1	4
sour cream	½ cup	2 cups

Florida

The Everglades and the Keys—the coral reefs and the Maclay Gardens—citrus trees, celery, and fish are Sunshine State classics.

Pompano Classic
Pompano in Wine Sauce

INGREDIENTS	For 6	For 25
shallots, chopped	¼ cup	2½ cups
butter	¼ cup	½ lb.
mushrooms, sliced	¼ cup	2½ cups
5 oz. pompano fillets	6	25
white wine	2 cups	2 qt.
flour	2 tbsp.	1½ cups
salt and white pepper, ground	to taste	to taste
bouquet garni	1	1 large
chervil	1 tsp.	2 tsp.

Saute shallots in 1 tsp. of butter. Add mushrooms. Place pompano on top, add white wine, and simmer for 20 minutes, covered. Heat butter and add flour. Pour remaining liquid from fillets over, and whisk. Bring to boil and season. Add bouquet garni. Strain over fillets and add chervil.

Georgia

In the classic South, quail hunting and salt water fishing, peanut plantations, America's historic Savannah, and coach lamp dining in Atlanta. These are the pioneer places of Georgia. Nuts, peaches, watermelons, snapper.

Quail Hunting Classic
Breast of Quail in Grape Leaves

INGREDIENTS	FOR 6	For 24
quail breasts	6	24
salt and pepper	to taste	to taste
bacon slices	6	24
grape leaves	6	24
butter	4 oz.	1 lb.
brandy	1 oz.	4 oz.
porto	1 cup	4 cups
peach halves	6	24

Season breasts with salt and pepper. Wrap in bacon and grape leaves. Brush with butter and roast at 350° F. for 25 minutes. Add brandy and porto, and bring to boil. Fill peaches with pecans, top with honey, and bake for 10 minutes. Make a rice ring on serving platter. Place breasts in center with sauce. Arrange peaches around the ring and garnish with mint leaves.

(Cont.)

pecans	6 tsp.	½ cup
honey	6 tsp.	½ cup
cooked rice, for ring	2 cups	8 cups
mint leaves	for garnish	for garnish

Hawaii

The "Imu" ceremony of the roasted pig—the luau—mahi-mahi and Pacific blue marlin—the delicate, sweet taste of the macadamia nut and the pineapple, guava, papaya, passion fruit, coconut, mango, and coffee—Aloha.

Pineapple, coffee, macadamia nuts, seafood, sugar, coconuts, squid, marlin, and swordfish are from these islands.

Aloha Macadamia Pie

INGREDIENTS	One 9-inch Pie	Two 9-inch Pies	
Crust			
flour	1 cup	2 cups	Combine flour, salt, and coconut, and blend well. Add shortening and water. Knead for dough. Roll out and line pie forms. Bake at 450° F for 12 minutes. Cool.
salt	dash	1 tsp.	
coconut, grated	⅓ cup	⅔ cup	
shortening	⅓ cup	⅔ cup	
water	⅛ cup	⅓ cup	
Filling			
vanilla pie filling	4 oz.	8 oz.	Mix vanilla filling with milk. Bring to a boil. Add crushed pineapple and nuts, stirring until mixture thickens. Simmer for 5 minutes. Cool slightly. Fill pie shell. Chill well. Add garnish. See Color Plate 2.
milk	2¼ cups	4½ cups	
crushed pineapple	1 cup	2 cups	
macadamia nuts, chopped	½ cup	1 cup	

Garnish
Whipped cream, pineapple chunks, and marzipan decoration. Fried macadamia rolls glazed with melted brown sugar.

Idaho

Sun Valley in the winter and camping in the summer—the natural wonders still survive—lumberjack festivals—barbecued trout, potatoes, onions, and beef.

Lumberjack Classic
Grilled Trout

INGREDIENTS	For 5	For 25
12-oz. trout	5	25
butter	4 oz.	1 lb.
juice of lemon	1	5
basil	dash	1 tsp.
salt and pepper	to taste	to taste
butter	5 oz.	1½ lbs.
mustard	¼ cup	1¼ cups
capers, chopped	5 tbsp.	1 cup

Brush trout on all sides with butter and lemon. Season with basil, salt, and pepper. Grill outdoors on each side. Heat butter, and whisk in mustard and capers. Pour over trout on serving platter. Serve with a roasted potato.

Iowa

Fertile farmlands—corn and hogs—riverboats once carried settlers along the Mississippi and Missouri Rivers.

Pioneer Classic
Chicken Pot

INGREDIENTS	For 4–6	For 24
3-lb. chickens, quartered	5	20
bouquet garni	1	1 large
onions, sliced	2	8
butter	1 tbsp.	½ lb.
celery, sliced	6 stems	24
carrots, peeled and sliced	6	24
mushrooms	¼ lb.	1 lb.
water or chicken stock	to cover	to cover
scallions, chopped	3 stems	12
turnip, sliced	1	4
large potatoes, peeled and sliced	2	8
chives, chopped	1 tbsp.	½ cup
salt and white pepper, ground	to taste	to taste

In salted water, bring chicken pieces and bouquet garni to boil. Saute sliced onions in butter till golden brown. Add celery, carrots, and mushrooms, and cook for 5 minutes. Add chicken stock and remaining ingredients, and simmer for one hour. Remove chicken pieces and reduce remaining liquid to half. Remove bouquet garni. Serve in soup pot, sprinkled with additional chopped chives.

Louisiana

Mardi Gras, jazz, and antebellum plantations—Creole cooking, jambalaya omelets, gumbo, and cafe-au-lait—the old French market in New Orleans—okra, sugar, shrimp, and crabs.

Mardi Gras Classic
Chicken Rice Casserole

INGREDIENTS	For 6	For 24
onions, diced	¼ cup	1 cup
butter	5 tbsp.	1 cup
chicken pieces	4 lb.	16 lb.
salt and black pepper, freshly ground	to taste	to taste
basil	dash	1 tsp.
thyme	dash	1 tsp.
bay leaf	1	3
tomatoes, peeled and diced	4	16
ham, diced	½ cup	2 cups
long grain rice	1 cup	4 cups
okra, chopped	¼ cup	1 cup
chicken stock	2½ cups	2 qt.

Saute onions in butter. Add chicken and seasoning, and stir for 5 minutes. Add tomatoes, ham, rice, okra, and chicken stock. Place in casserole and bake at 375° F. for 1¼ hours.

Maine

A land of mountains and rugged coasts—Cumberland County and crystal lakes—windjammers and seafarers—lobster, clams, game, berries, and vegetables.

New England Classic
Boiled Lobster

INGREDIENTS	For 2	For 20
onion, sliced	1	2
celery, sliced	1 stalk	3 stalks
carrot, sliced	1	3
fresh seaweed	½ lb.	3 lb.
bouquet garni	1	1 large
water	2 gal.	to cover
salt	to taste	2 tbsp.
3-lb. Maine lobster	2	20
parsley sprig	for garnish	for garnish
clarified butter	½ cup	5 cups
juice of garlic	1 clove	5 cloves

Combine onion, celery, carrot, seaweed, bouquet garni, and water. Add salt and boil for ½ hour. Place lobsters in water and boil for 25 minutes. Remove, split open, and place on serving platter. Garnish with parsley, and serve with butter mixed with garlic juice.

Massachusetts

A land of legends—Paul Revere and the Boston Tea Party—the golden age of American literature—the shot heard round the world—the Boston Symphony Orchestra—cod, flounder, and shad.

Tea Party Classic
Baked Cod Fillet

INGREDIENTS	For 4	For 24
5-oz. cod fillets	4	24
salt and white pepper, ground	to taste	to taste
butter	2 oz.	½ lb.
basil	1 tsp.	2 tbsp.
white wine	½ cup	3 cups
garlic cloves	2	12
shallots, finely chopped	2 tbsp.	¾ cup
capers	2 tsp.	4 tbsp.
black olives, chopped	2 tbsp.	¾ cup
tomatoes, peeled and diced	2	12

Season cod fillets, brush with butter, and bake at 350° F. for 15 minutes. Add basil and white wine, and simmer for 10 minutes. Saute garlic and shallots in butter. Add capers, olives, tomatoes, and 2 oz. of wine stock. Bring to a boil. Place cod on serving platter, and pour mixture over. Garnish with parsley. Accompany with new potatoes.

Michigan

A fisherman's delight, the largest specimens average 50 pounds—farms and factories—the home of the automotive industry—fish, vegetables, dairy, and fruit.

Rainbow Trout Classic
Stuffed Rainbow Trout

INGREDIENTS	For 4	For 24
12-oz. rainbow trout, boned	4	24
shallots, finely chopped	2 tbsp.	1 cup
butter	2 tbsp.	1 cup
crabmeat	12 oz.	4½ lb.
cream sauce	2 tbsp.	1 cup
dill, chopped	2 tbsp.	1 cup
salt and pepper	to taste	to taste
lard	8 slices	48 slices
white wine	8 oz.	5 cups
flour	1 tbsp.	½ cup
pistachios	1 tbsp.	¼ cup
herb butter	4 oz.	1½ lb.

Bone the trout, cutting from the backbone. Saute shallots in 1 tbsp. butter. Add crabmeat, cream sauce, 1 tsp. dill, and seasoning. Cool. Stuff trout, cover with lard, and tie. Saute on both sides. Add white wine and simmer for 25 minutes. Remove and discard lard. Heat remaining butter, add flour, and whisk in liquid from trout. Strain, season, add remaining dill, and pour over trout. Sprinkle with pistachios, and divide herb butter by placing on each trout. Garnish with fresh dill sprigs.

Minnesota

Wilderness canoe areas—the sunflower and the prairie—Viking ancestry and the legend of Paul Bunyan—honey, poultry, and dairy.

Sunflower Classic
Cornish Hens with Eggplant

INGREDIENTS	For 4	For 24
cornish hens	4–6	24
oregano	dash	2 tbsp.
salt and pepper	to taste	to taste
butter	4 oz.	1 lb.
eggplants	2 medium	8 medium
onion, finely chopped	1 medium	4 medium
tomatoes, peeled and diced	4	16
mozzarella cheese slices	4	16
potatoes, peeled and sliced	4	16
cauliflower head	1	4
triangle croutons, golden brown and dipped in chopped parsley	12	48

Season cornish hens with oregano, salt, and pepper. Brush with butter and roast at 350° F. for 40 minutes. Cut eggplant in half lengthwise and scoop out center. Saute meat of eggplant in butter with onions and tomatoes. Season. Place filling in shell, cover with mozzarella, and bake for 20 minutes. Line sliced potatoes in casserole and season. Brush with butter and bake for 40 minutes. Boil cauliflower in salted water. On a serving platter, arrange eggplant in center. Surround with cauliflower rosettes. Arrange cut cornish hen around cauliflower, and surround everything with sliced potatoes and triangle croutons.

Mississippi

The fertile land of the Delta and the Gulf Coast—Spanish and French influences, Huck Finn on a Mississippi riverboat—bales of cotton—nuts, vegetables, and seafood.

Queen's Classic
Oysters With Pernod

INGREDIENTS	For 4	For 20
shallots, finely chopped	½ cup	2 cups
fennel, chopped	2 tbsp.	½ cup
butter	5 tbsp.	1 lb.
pernod	1 tsp.	½ cup
blanched spinach, chopped	1½ cups	2 qt.
juice of garlic cloves	1	6
breadcrumbs	¼ cup	1¼ cups
salt and white pepper, ground	to taste	to taste

Saute shallots and fennel in butter. Add pernod, spinach, garlic juice, and breadcrumbs. Season. Divide mixture over oysters. Top each with cream sauce, chives, and parmesan cheese. Bake at 450° F. for 10 minutes. Finish under broiler for 3 to 4 minutes, until lightly colored.

(Cont.)

oysters in half shell	2 dozen	10 dozen
cream sauce	1 cup	5 cups
chives, chopped	2 tbsp.	½ cup
parmesan cheese	¼ cup	1¼ cups

Missouri

The Pony Express and Mark Twain—The Lake of the Ozarks region—the Gateway Arch—squirrel, quail, and turkey hunting—vegetables, poultry, and pork.

Pony Express Classic
Stuffed Pork Chops

INGREDIENTS	For 6	For 20
6 oz. pork chops	12	40
spinach leaves, chopped	½ cup	2 cups
butter	3 tbsp.	½ cup
nutmeg	dash	½ tsp.
salt and pepper	to taste	to taste
caraway seeds, finely chopped	1 tbsp.	¼ cup
brandy	1 oz.	3 oz.
brown sauce	1 cup	1 qt.

Make pockets in the pork chops. Saute spinach leaves in 1 tbsp. butter, and season with nutmeg and salt and pepper. Fill pockets and sew up. Season chops and saute in butter, on each side, till golden brown. Add finely chopped caraway seeds and brandy, and ignite. Add brown sauce and simmer for 15 minutes. Remove threads. Serve with risotto.

Montana

Wild flowers, virgin forests, lakeside campfires—the legends of the Blackfeet, Sioux, and Cheyenne—cattle ranches and wheat—game, dairy, and vegetables.

Campfire Classic
Turkey on a Spit

INGREDIENTS	For 15–20	For 40
24–26 lb. turkey	1	2
juice of lemons	4	8
black peppercorns	1 tsp.	1 tbsp.
oil	½ cup	1 cup
parsley, chopped	¼ cup	½ cup
oregano	2 tbsp.	4 tbsp.
vinegar	¼ cup	½ cup
red wine	2 cups	4 cups

Mix all ingredients. Brush turkey on all sides and marinate for 24 hours. Place on spit and roast over an open fire, brushing with marinade. Turn occasionally while roasting.

Nebraska

Land of the pioneer—sand hills, lakes, and prairies—huge rock formations—the battles of the mighty Sioux—beef, grain, and sheep.

Adventure Classic
Fillet Mignon Bouquetere

INGREDIENTS	For 2–4	For 20
fillet mignon, center cut	2½ lb.	7½ lb.
peppercorns	2 tsp.	½ cup
salt	to taste	to taste
butter	1 tsp.	¼ lb.
brandy	2 oz.	¼ cup
red wine	4 oz.	2½ cups
tarragon	1 tsp.	2 tbsp.
demi glaze	4 oz.	2½ cups
heavy cream	¼ cup	1 cup

Rub center cut fillet with salt and peppercorns. Saute in butter on each side. Bake at 375° F. for 25 minutes. Remove. Pour brandy over and ignite. Add red wine, tarragon, and demi glaze. Bring to a boil, add heavy cream, and simmer for 5 minutes. Arrange on a serving platter surrounded with vegetable garniture.

Vegetable Garniture

Fresh asparagus spears, grilled tomatoes, cauliflower au gratin, small potato rosettes, and artichokes topped with hollandaise sauce.

Nevada

Lake Tahoe, Las Vegas, and Reno—Basque sheep herders introduced their seafood recipes—the Comstock Lode—beef, poultry, wheat, and game.

Basque Classic
Seafood in Rice

INGREDIENTS	For 4–6	For 24
various seafood, bite-sized (carp, catfish, pike, bass)	5 lb.	20 lb.
olive oil	2 tbsp.	¼ cup
vinegar	1 tbsp.	3 tbsp.
juice of lemon	1	3
cloves of garlic, crushed	4	10
salt and pepper	to taste	to taste
butter	4 oz.	1 lb.
onion, finely chopped	1	4
rice	1 cup	4 cups
fish stock	2½ cups	½ gal.
bay leaf	1	3
saffron	dash	1 tsp.
coriander	dash	½ tsp.
parsley, chopped	1 tbsp.	4 tbsp.

Marinate seafood in olive oil, vinegar, lemon juice, garlic, salt, and pepper for one hour. Saute in butter for 20 minutes. Saute onions in butter. Add rice, fish stock, bay leaf, saffron, coriander, salt, and pepper, and bake for 45 minutes at 375° F. Form a rice ring. Place fish in center, and sprinkle with chopped parsley.

New Hampshire

Bows and arrows, woodcock, pheasant, deer, and fox—the scenic splendor of rivers, lakes, and mountains—covered bridges and colonial homes—dairy, fruit, and game.

Woodcock Classic
Flaming Woodcock

INGREDIENTS	For 2	For 20
shallots, finely chopped	2	20
butter	5 oz.	1 lb.
sage	dash	1 tbsp.
goose liver	8 oz.	5 lb.
truffles	1 tsp.	¼ cup
woodcocks	2	20
bacon	to cover	to cover
brandy	2 oz.	8 oz.
demi glaze	6 oz.	2 qt.

Saute shallots in 2 oz. of butter. Season with sage. Add goose liver and cook for 2 minutes. Add truffles. Stuff woodcocks, cover with bacon, and tie. Roast in casserole at 375° F. in remaining butter, for 12 to 15 minutes. Add brandy and ignite. Add demi glaze and bring to a boil. Serve in same casserole.

NOTE   To tie, twist neck so that the beak sticks into the leg.

New Jersey

The Garden State with its golden sand and blue waters—Cape May and the great falls of Patterson—Miss America and Atlantic City—industry and truck-crop farms—vegetables, fruit, dairy, and poultry.

Cross Road Classic
Meatloaf Bouquetere

INGREDIENTS	For 4–6	For 20–24
onion, finely chopped	1	4
butter	1 tsp.	2 tbsp.
white bread, soaked in water	5 slices	20 slices
ground beef	5 lb.	25 lb.
whole eggs	5	10
V-8 juice	¼ cup	¾ cup
marjoram	to taste	1 tsp.
salt and pepper	to taste	to taste
potatoes, mashed	1 cup	4 cups
nutmeg	to taste	½ tsp.
egg yolks	2	8
tomatoes, grilled	6	24
peas	¼ cup	1 cup
asparagus tips	18	72
parmesan cheese	⅛ cup	1 cup

Saute onion in butter. Squeeze all liquid from soaked bread and grind together with meat. Add whole eggs, V-8 juice, marjoram, salt, and pepper. Form a loaf and bake at 375° F. for 45 minutes. Slice and place on serving platter. Mix mashed potatoes with nutmeg and egg yolks. Using a pastry bag, shape around the platter. Place grilled tomatoes, topped with peas and buttered asparagus tips, around the platter. Sprinkle meat with parmesan cheese and place under a salamander. Garnish with watercress and bacon strips.

(Cont.)

COLOR PLATE 1. *Right:* Brazilian Lagosta Cocktail (p. 94) and Canja (p. 105). *Below, top to bottom:* Couscous (p. 6), Mediterranean Rice Classic (p. 5), and Sahara Salad (p. 6).

COLOR PLATE 2. *Left:* Aloha Macadamia Pie
(p. 49). *Below:* India Chicken Classic (p. 105).
COLOR PLATE 3. *Right:* Sukiyaki Classic
(p. 19). *Far Right:* Szechuan Chicken Classic
(p. 105). *Below, right, top to bottom:* Tsugaru
Classic (p. 99) and Kama Boko Classic (p. 94).

COLOR PLATE 4. *Top to Bottom:* Sweet and Sour Pork (p. 43), Ho Salad (p. 43), Lo Mein (p. 44), Kwangtung Shrimp (p. 44), Almond Orange Festival (p. 45), and Rice Crunch (p. 45).

watercress	for garnish	for garnish
bacon strips, crisply fried	6	24

New Mexico

Home of the Mescalero Apache—Indian and Spanish influences—space-age industries and Spanish haciendas—grains and sheep.

Rio Grande Classic
Leg of Lamb on a Spit

INGREDIENTS	For 8–10	For 16–20
salt and pepper	1 tsp.	2 tsp.
garlic, crushed	12 cloves	24 cloves
leg of lamb, 14–16 lb.	1	2
vinegar	½ cup	1 cup
red wine	½ cup	1 cup
Tabasco	1 tsp.	2 tsp.
oil	2 tbsp.	4 tbsp.
rosemary	1 tsp.	2 tsp.

Rub salt, pepper, and garlic into lamb. Combine vinegar, red wine, Tabasco, oil, and rosemary. Brush lamb. Roast lamb over open spit fire, brushing with liquid. Turn every 15 minutes until desired doneness, medium to rare.

New York

The Adirondacks, Niagara Falls, Lake Placid—West Point and wineries—the theaters, fashions, and finances of New York City—wine, poultry, dairy, beef, and game.

Entrecote Classic
Flaming Sirloin Steak

INGREDIENTS	For 4	For 20
10-oz. sirloin steak	4	20
sea salt	to taste	to taste
green peppercorns, in brine	4 tsp.	½ cup
butter	1 tbsp.	¼ lb.
brandy	2 oz.	½ cup
red wine, N.Y. State	2 oz.	1¼ cups
demi glaze	4 oz.	2½ cups
heavy cream	2 oz.	1¼ cups

Remove all fat from steaks. Season with sea salt, and press green peppercorns on each side of steak. Brown in butter for 5 minutes on each side. Add brandy and ignite. Add red wine and demi glaze. Bring to a boil. Remove steak and place on serving platter. Reduce sauce to half. Add heavy cream and pour over entrecote.

Big Apple Kebob Classic

The largest kebob in the Mediterranean Sea and Middle Eastern cooking is ground lamb or mutton highly seasoned with saffron, pressed together on a spit,

(Cont.)

and turned while roasting in front of a hot fire. This delicacy, served with a mixed green salad and finished with a flaming Mediterranean coffee, is worth trying, and may some day become the classic in The Big Apple. See Color Plate 7.

Flaming Mediterranean Coffee

INGREDIENTS   YIELD: 6 to 8 servings

1 peel of orange
1 peel of lemon
1 cinnamon stick
1 tsp. sugar
3 whole cloves
4 oz. dark rum
1 oz. Sabra liqueur
4 cups hot, strong, black coffee

In chafing dish, place orange and lemon peels, cinnamon stick, sugar, and cloves. Heat slowly. Add dark rum and ignite. While flaming, add Sabra liqueur and gradually add black coffee.
   Put in demitasse cups and serve immediately.

North Dakota

Wagon trains crossed the prairie—trappers roamed the land—a favorite of Theodore Roosevelt—sugar, wheat, and game.

Wagon Train Classic
Pheasants in Sauce

INGREDIENTS	For 5	For 20
lard, sliced in strips	1 lb.	4 lb.
young hanging pheasants	5	20
salt and white pepper, ground	to taste	to taste
paprika	dash	2 tbsp.
oil	3 tbsp.	¾ cup
brandy	2 oz.	1 cup
white wine	½ cup	2 cups
demi glaze	1 cup	1 qt.
heavy cream	½ cup	2 cups

Insert lard in pheasants. Tie and rub seasoning and paprika all around. Place in oiled roasting pan. Roast for 35 minutes at 375° F. Remove excess fat. Pour brandy over and ignite. Add white wine, reduce by simmering to half, and add demi glaze. Bring to a boil, basting pheasant occasionally. Roast for 15 more minutes, or until done. Remove pheasant. Add heavy cream, bring to boil, and strain over pheasant.

Ohio

Yellow perch, chinook salmon, and bluegill sunfish—wonderland for hunters—steel and glass industries—vegetables, fish, and fruit.

Early Settlers Classic
Marinated Sauerbraten

INGREDIENTS	For 10–14	For 24–28
rump beef, 7 lb.	1	2

Marinade

wine vinegar	1 cup	2 cups
water	2 cups	1 qt.
onion, chopped	1	2
whole cloves	5	10
bay leaves	1	3
peppercorns	10	20
carrot, sliced	1	2
celery stalk, sliced	1	2
lemon, cut in half	1	2
juniper berries	5	10

Sauce

flour	¼ cup	½ cup
butter	¼ cup	½ cup
cooking liquid	4 cups	2 qt.
gingersnaps	10	20
lingonberries	½ cup	1 cup
apples, sliced	2	4
salt and white pepper, ground	1 tsp.	2 tsp.
sour cream	¼ cup	½ cup

To marinate, combine all ingredients with beef. Cover and let stand for 3 to 5 days. Remove meat. Bring liquid to a boil. Saute beef in hot oil on all sides. Add to liquid and simmer for 3 hours, or until meat is tender. Remove.

For sauce, brown flour in butter. Add cooking liquid and remaining ingredients. Simmer for ½ hour, and strain over sliced meat. Serve with potato dumplings.

Oklahoma

Festivals are a way of life—Indian ceremonies called powwows—the Dust Bowl is being reclaimed—oil rigs are everywhere—beef, nuts, and poultry.

Powwow Classic
Wild Rice Casserole

INGREDIENTS	For 4–6	For 24
wild rice	1 cup	4 cups
water	3 cups	12 cups
poultry seasoning	1 tsp.	1 tbsp.
salt	to taste	to taste
white pepper, freshly ground	to taste	to taste
chicken, cut bite sized	3 lb.	12 lb.
butter	2 tbsp.	½ cup

Boil wild rice in salted water till soft, approximately 1½ hours. Add water if necessary. Remove and strain. Saute seasoned chicken pieces in butter until golden brown. Add onions and brown. Add green peppers and sherry. Place with rice in casserole. Add almonds and bake at 350° F. for 20 minutes.

(Cont.)

onions, medium, chopped	2	8
green peppers, diced	2	8
sherry	2 oz.	8 oz.
almonds, chopped	2 tbsp.	½ cup

South Dakota

Mt. Rushmore in the Black Hills—the Homestead Act and gold dust dreams—home of the Sioux—cattle, corn, and fish.

Gold Dust Classic
Sliced Fillet of Beef, Sorrel

INGREDIENTS	For 4–6	For 24
fillet of beef, sliced	2 lb.	8 lb.
salt and pepper	to taste	to taste
butter	3 oz.	12 oz.
mushrooms	5 oz.	1¼ lb.
demi glaze	5 oz.	3 cups
heavy cream	3 tbsp.	¼ cup
sorrel, chopped	1 tbsp.	3 tbsp.
rice ring, cooked with corn	3 cups	12 cups
watercress	for garnish	for garnish

Season beef with salt and pepper, and saute in butter until medium rare. Add mushrooms and demi glaze, and bring to a boil. Add heavy cream and sorrel. Form rice ring. Place meat in center and garnish with watercress.

Texas

From the Santa Elena Canyon to the Alamo—long-horned cattle and seafood from the Gulf of Mexico—the caverns of Sonora and the giant yuccas near Sierra Blanca—a land of contrasts—beef, poultry, dairy, and shrimp.

Longhorn Classic
Prime Ribs

INGREDIENTS	For 10–12	For 20–24
prime rib roast, 12–15 lb.	1	2
salt	to taste	to taste
black pepper, freshly ground	to taste	to taste
crushed garlic	2 tbsp.	4 tbsp.
carrots, diced	2	4
celery, diced	2 stalks	4 stalks
onions, chopped	2	4
water	2 cups	4 cups
longhorn sauce	2 cups	1 qt.

For longhorn sauce, allow 1 cup of cream sauce per rib roast with 2 tbsp. fresh horseradish. Bring to a boil. Add ½ cup heavy whipped cream and dash of Tabasco.

For roast, rub rib roast with salt, pepper, and crushed garlic. Place in 450°F. oven for 30 minutes. Add carrots, celery, and onions, and roast for 30 minutes more at 350° F. Add water and reduce heat to 300° F. Roast for 2 more hours, or until meat thermometer shows desired doneness. Strain juice, and pour over meat. Serve longhorn sauce on the side.

Utah

Butch Cassidy and the Sundance Kid—the Great Salt Lake—Brigham Young and his followers—dairy, beef, and fish.

Sundance Classic
Tournedos With Truffle Sauce

INGREDIENTS	For 4	For 24
5-oz. tournedos of beef	4	24
salt	to taste	1 tsp.
black pepper, freshly ground	to taste	to taste
butter	2 oz.	1½ cups
madeira sauce	6 oz.	4½ cups
rosemary	dash	1 tsp.
truffles, chopped	1 tsp.	2 tbsp.
fried eggs	4	24
tomatoes, cut in half and broiled	2	12
watercress	for garnish	for garnish

Season beef. Saute in butter for 3 minutes on each side. Add madeira sauce, rosemary, and truffles. Simmer for 3 more minutes. Remove and place on serving platter. Top each with a fried egg. Surround with broiled tomato and watercress. Serve with sauteed potatoes.

Virginia

Colonial Williamsburg, where patriots plotted the course of history—Jamestown, the first English settlement in the New World—the Shenandoah Valley and Blue Ridge Mountains—Smithfield ham, and pork.

Shenandoah Grits Classic
Grits in a Ring

INGREDIENTS	For 4–6	For 20–24
grits	1 cup	4 cups
water	3½ cups	2½ qt.
sharp cheese, grated	¼ lb.	1 lb.
Smithfield ham, diced	¼ lb.	1 lb.
apples, peeled and sliced	2	8
milk	½ cup	2 cups
shrimp, peeled	2 lb.	8 lb.
garlic, crushed	2 cloves	8 cloves
butter	1 tbsp.	¼ cup
salt and white pepper, ground	to taste	to taste
white wine	¼ cup	1 cup
parsley, chopped	1 tsp.	to sprinkle

In double boiler, stir grits into boiling salted water and cook for 40 minutes. In buttered rice ring dish, alternate cooked grits, cheese, ham, and apple slices. Add milk and bake at 300° F. for 30 minutes. Cool. Turn over on serving platter and keep warm. Saute shrimp and garlic in butter. Season. Add white wine and reduce liquid. Pour in center of grits ring. Sprinkle with chopped parsley.

Washington

The northwest corner of the United States—Mt. Rainier and Puget Sound—timber country—Walla Walla sweets are the delicious huge onions—game, dairy, salmon, vegetables, fruit, and shellfish.

Walla Walla Classic
Onion in Onion

INGREDIENTS	For 4	For 24
Walla Walla onions	4	24
butter	2 tbsp.	¾ cup
mushroom buttons	¼ lb.	1½ lb.
dill, chopped	1 tbsp.	¼ cup
salt and pepper	to taste	to taste
cream sauce	¼ cup	1½ cups
pearl onions	½ cup	3 cups
parmesan cheese	2 tbsp.	¾ cup

Peel Walla Walla onions and cut off tops. Empty centers and chop very finely. Bake at 375° F. for 5 minutes. Remove onions, saute in butter. Add mushroom buttons, dill, salt, and pepper till translucent. Add cream sauce and fill centers of onions. Place pearl onions on top. Sprinkle with parmesan cheese, and bake at 450° F. for 10 minutes.

Wyoming

Yellowstone National Park and the Grand Tetons—Buffalo Bill and Cheyenne—the Equality State—lamb, beef, poultry, fruit, and vegetables.

Buffalo Bill Classic
Lamb Skewer

INGREDIENTS	For 8	For 24
lamb kidneys, cut in cubes	1 lb.	3 lb.
bacon	16 slices	48 slices
lamb, cut in cubes	8 lb.	24 lb.
green peppers, cut in squares	4	12
onion, quartered and separated	1	3
cherry tomatoes	16	48
mushroom caps	16	48
vinegar	2 tbsp.	½ cup
olive oil	4 tbsp.	¾ cup
juice of garlic clove	1	3
rosemary	dash	1 tsp.
black pepper, freshly ground	to taste	to taste
salt	to taste	to taste

Wrap lamb kidney cubes in bacon. Alternate on skewer with lamb, peppers, and onions. Place a cherry tomato and mushroom cap at both ends. Marinate in remaining ingredients for two hours. Roast on a grill, brushing occasionally with marinade, until done.

5. The Classic Buffet

The Make-Up of a Classic Buffet

The classic buffet is a feast for the eyes as well as the palate. It consists of:

Hors-d'Oeuvre Froid	Cold Appetizer
Potage	Soup
Hors-d'Oeuvre Chaud	Warm Appetizer
Poisson	Fish
Grosse Piece	Main Course
Entree Chaude	Hot Entree
Entree Froide	Cold Entree
Sorbet	Sorbet
Roti	Roast
Salade	Salad
Legume	Vegetable
Entremets	Sweets
Savoury	Savoury
Dessert	Dessert

The more modern menu offers:

Hors-d'Oeuvre Froid	Cold Appetizer
Potage	Soup
Hors-d'Oeuvre Chaud	Hot Appetizer
Poisson	Fish
Grosse Piece	Main Course
Legume	Vegetable
Salade	Salad
Dessert	Dessert

In preparing a modern buffet menu, it is important to consider the different types of functions, such as, weddings, special anniversaries, birthdays, business affairs, luncheons, or dinners. You must also take into account the clientele: women, men, families, younger or older persons. The price of the planned function, the time of the year, seasonal availability of foods, and specialties of the house are also important considerations. Finally, room size and the production of the kitchen and the personnel are factors that affect the buffet.

The first step is to determine the main course and then select the appetizer and dessert. Never ask, "What would you like to start?"—a common mistake made by sales staff.

The following is a list of selections appropriate for a modern classic menu:

Cold Appetizer—caviar, lobster, foie gras, oysters; egg dishes; combined salads; aspic decorated dishes; fish, meat, vegetable, or fruit dishes.
Soups—consomme; cream or puree soups; regional, exotic, or national soups.
Fish—shellfish; fresh-water or salt-water fish.
Hot Entree—egg dishes; mushroom, sweetbreads, kidney, or fowl dishes.
Main Course—fowl, meat, or game, carved to order, with side dishes.
Cold Entree—pates, galantines, or shrimp dishes.

Sorbet—sherbets in fruit with liquor, on ice.
Roasts—lamb, veal, fillet of beef, or pork roasts.
Salads—tomato; romaine, Belgian endive; vegetable salads; mixed variety.
Vegetable—asparagus, spinach, mushrooms, peas, broccoli, or salsify.
Sweets—creams, puddings, ice cream; puff paste, savarin.
Savoury—cheeses, small toasts.
Dessert—fresh fruit, compotes; pastries, petits fours.

The modern caterer presents food in its natural state, form, and shape. This must be taken into consideration when selecting a platter, bowl, or mirror. Leave two inches of the rim showing as a border for food presented by itself.

Centerpieces

Every buffet should have a centerpiece; the larger the buffet, the more pieces. Ice carvings or sculptures are the best. Naturally, the smaller the buffet, the smaller the sculptures. If butter is used, it should be placed close to the meat or fish. Larger pieces can be displayed with compatible objects. For example, a dancing ballerina with a scarf; a fish, with a net and sea shells surrounding it, or a fruit arrangement with different colored leaves, depending on the season.

A spotlight can be used as long as there is no heat damage. A rotating colored lamp gives excellent results with centerpieces. These items can be used over and over again, providing they are handled carefully and stored properly. The layout of the buffet determines the location of the centerpiece. The number of guests determines the size of the buffet.

A centerpiece of food does not have to be edible. It can be birds in plumage, or a shortening or tallow sculpture. However, stuffed, decorated langouste, turkey or ham with mousse and aspic can make the perfect centerpiece on a mirror. The appetizing appearance of a buffet, with the proper arrangement of food and sauces, can make an affair a great success.

Classic Cold Sauces

The chaud-froid aspic sauce is basically for cold dishes (appetizers, game, fowl, fish) or to cover larger centerpieces. Various ingredients give color: spinach for green, tomato puree for red, demi glaze for brown, paprika, curry, and others. For dark meat, a demi glaze with aspic is appropriate; for white meat, a veloute or supreme sauce. The modern and fast solution is aspic mixed with mayonnaise, but this is not a chaud-froid classic.

Basic Sauces

White aspic sauce—a veloute or bechamel from the prepared entree, mixed with aspic.
Brown aspic sauce—a reduced demi glaze (strained, cooled, and all fat removed), mixed with aspic.
Game aspic sauce—a game sauce, reduced as demi glaze, with aspic.
Fish aspic sauce—a fish veloute, mixed with aspic.
Fowl aspic sauce—a supreme sauce, mixed with aspic.

Other Classic Sauces

Dill sauce—hard-boiled egg yolk mixed with soaked white bread, and squeezed through a fine sieve. Whip raw egg yolk with sugar, salt, vinegar, and oil, like mayonnaise. Combine, and add chopped dill.

Currant sauce—currants mixed with lingonberries and red wine, ginger, lemon juice, and orange juice. Boiled and cooled, with julienne of lemon rind added.

Chinese gooseberry sauce—gooseberries peeled and squeezed through a fine sieve. Mixed with white wine, sugar, and lemon juice.

Mint sauce—mint leaves, finely sliced. Add hot white wine and vinegar, sugar, salt, and pepper.

Fine herb sauce—finely chopped shallots, cucumbers, capers, and chives, mixed with mustard, anchovy paste, vinegar, oil, salt, and pepper.

Sauce roma—mayonnaise mixed with finely chopped watercress, spinach, tarragon, lemon juice, and garlic juice.

Sauce tartare—finely chopped pickles, capers, and parsley, mixed with lemon juice, mustard, salt, and pepper. Onions should be used only if not stored for over a day.

Sauce Essex—finely chopped chervil, tarragon, chives, hard-boiled egg yolk, and pistachios, mixed with mayonnaise and lemon juice.

Sauce perigord—mayonnaise mixed with julienne of truffles, finely chopped capers, tarragon, parsley, and lobster meat.

Sauce chantilly—mayonnaise, lemon juice, and whipped cream.

Sauce fennel—mayonnaise mixed with boiled and cooled julienne fennel, yogurt, mustard, worcestershire, and cayenne.

Sauce classical gourmet—mayonnaise mixed with chopped cucumber, shallots, capers, chives, mustard, lemon juice, tomato puree, diced shrimp, and red caviar.

Salmon sauce classic—salmon squeezed through a fine sieve. Mix with lemon juice combined with mayonnaise, whipped cream, and ground white pepper.

Sauce Mayonnaise

INGREDIENTS	4 Cups	10 Gallons
egg yolks	4	2 qt.
vinegar	3 tbsp.	2 cups
mustard	1 tbsp.	½ cup
Worcestershire sauce	1 tbsp.	¼ cup
juice of lemon	1	½ cup
salt and pepper	to taste	to taste
olive oil	3½ cups	9 gal.

Whip egg yolks with vinegar, mustard, Worcestershire sauce, lemon juice, salt, and pepper. Slowly add oil until mixture is well emulsified and stiff.

NOTE   Add a touch of hot water to smooth. This binds sauce for better storage.

Salads and Dressings

Salads of simple greens, vegetables, fish, fowl, or fruit, or in combination, have become America's national specialties. Served as an appetizer or entree, it is the size that differentiates salads. If an accompaniment to the main course, keep them simple with a dressing. For buffets, the most popular are gelatin salads.

Salad must be fresh daily; leaves must be firm and crisp. The character of a salad changes with the dressing. Its flavors are derived from the different herbs and various sauces—chutney, chili, Worcestershire, or the all-American ketchup. Decorations make them colorful.

Caribe Salad

INGREDIENTS	For 4	For 24
saffron rice, boiled	2 cups	12 cups
raisins	1 tbsp.	½ cup
mayonnaise	½ cup	3 cups
curry	½ tsp.	3 tsp.
white pepper, ground	to taste	to taste
juice of lemon	1	5
red peppers, diced	¼ cup	1½ cups
coconuts, halved	4	24
mangoes, sliced	2	12
mint leaves	8	48
lettuce leaves	8	48
avocados, sliced	2	12

Combine saffron rice with raisins, mayonnaise, curry, pepper, lemon juice, and red peppers. Divide in centers of halved coconuts. Place sliced mangoes and mint leaves around. Place on lettuce leaves garnished with avocado slices.

South Pacific Salad

INGREDIENTS	For 4	For 24
Hawaiian pineapples, halved lengthwise	2	12
cottage cheese	4 scoops	24 scoops
papayas, diced	2	12
raspberries	½ cup	3 cups
Chinese gooseberry sauce	1 cup	6 cups
palm leaves	4	24
mint leaves	to garnish	to garnish

Scoop out centers of halved pineapples. Dice meat. Place in center, one scoop of cottage cheese, surrounded with diced pineapple, papaya, and raspberries. Pour gooseberry sauce over cottage cheese. Place pineapples on palm leaves and decorate with mint leaves.

Chinese Salad

INGREDIENTS	For 4	For 24
Chinese cabbage, shredded	1 head	6 heads
Bermuda onion, sliced	1	6
red pepper, sliced	1	6
pistachios, chopped	1 tbsp.	6 tbsp.
teriyaki sauce	1 tbsp.	6 tbsp.
black pepper, freshly ground	to taste	to taste
fine herb sauce	¼ cup	1½ cups

Combine cabbage, onion, red pepper, pistachios, teriyaki sauce, and pepper. Add fine herb sauce and toss lightly.

Boston Lobster Salad

INGREDIENTS	For 4	For 24
lobsters	2	12
celery, diced	1 cup	6 cups
lime rind, grated	1	6
sauce perigord	1 cup	6 cups
fresh ginger, grated	½ tsp.	2 tbsp.
toasted almonds, sliced	1 tsp.	2 tbsp.
Boston lettuce leaves	8	48
watercress	to garnish	to garnish

Boil lobsters and chill. Cut in half, dice meat, and reserve shells. Mix meat with celery, lime rind, and sauce perigord. Divide among lobster shells. Sprinkle with grated ginger and toasted almonds. Arrange on lettuce leaves with watercress.

Flaming Florida Orange Salad

INGREDIENTS	For 4	For 24
Florida oranges	8	48
coconuts, halved	4	24
sugar	½ cup	3 cups
Jamaican rum	½ cup	3 cups
mint leaves	to garnish	to garnish

Peel and slice oranges. Place in coconut shells and sprinkle with sugar. Warm rum. Divide among filled coconuts and ignite. Serve immediately. Garnish with mint leaves.

Avocado Salad Classic

INGREDIENTS	For 4	For 24
grapefruit juice	4 tbsp.	1½ cups
white wine	½ cup	3 cups
gelatine	2 oz.	12 oz.
avocados	8	48
salt	to taste	to taste
cayenne pepper	to taste	to taste
Boston lettuce leaves	8	48
mangoes, sliced	2	24
hard-boiled eggs, quartered	4	48
tomatoes, cut in wedges	2	12
watercress	to garnish	to garnish
sauce chantilly	1 cup	6 cups

Heat grapefruit juice and wine. Dissolve gelatine. Mash avocados and combine. Season with salt and pepper and place in mold. Chill well. Arrange lettuce leaves on a platter. Dip mold in warm water for a second and turn upside down on platter. Garnish with mangoes, eggs, tomatoes, and watercress. Top with sauce chantilly.

Swedish Salad

INGREDIENTS	For 4	For 24
cooked beef tongue	1 lb.	6 lb.
celeriac, julienne	½ cup	3 cups
sauce Essex	1 cup	6 cups
apples	4	24
romaine leaves	8	48
mint leaves	to garnish	to garnish

Cut beef tongue into julienne. Mix with celeriac and ⅔ of sauce Essex. Cut tops off apples, core, and empty meat. Add to meat mixture. Divide filling among apples set on romaine leaves. Top apples with remaining sauce. Garnish with mint leaves.

Tomato Salad

Eight medium tomatoes sliced thinly, topped with 1 cup finely chopped onions, 1 tsp. garlic juice, 2 oz. wine vinegar, 1 oz. olive oil, ½ tsp. sugar, salt, and freshly ground white pepper to taste. Yields 4–6 servings.

Celeriac Salad

Peel 2 knolls of celeriac, cut in julienne, and boil in 2 cups of water and 1 tbsp. vinegar for 2 minutes. Cool and drain. Marinate in 2 oz. vinegar, 2 oz. olive oil, julienne of 6 green olives, 1 tsp. sugar, 1 tsp. mustard, and juice of 1 lemon. Season with salt and pepper to taste. Yields 4–6 servings.

String Bean Salad

Two lbs. freshly cooked string beans, combined with 2 large onions cut in julienne, juice of 2 garlic cloves, 1 tsp. mustard, julienne of 1 medium red pimiento, 1 tsp. green peppercorns, ½ cup of sherry wine vinegar, juice of 1 lemon, and ⅓ cup of olive oil. Season with sea salt and freshly ground black pepper. Yields 4–6 servings.

Asparagus Salad

Two bunches fresh asparagus spears, cooked and peeled, cut into 2-inch pieces, marinated in ½ cup white wine, 1 tsp. wine vinegar, ¼ cup olive oil, 1 tsp. sugar, 2 tsps. chopped chives, salt, and freshly ground black pepper to taste. Yields 4–6 servings.

Cucumber Salad

Peel 5 cucumbers. Cut in half lengthwise, discard seeds, and slice thinly. Combine with ⅓ cup vinegar, juice of 2 lemons, juice of 6 cloves of garlic, 3 finely chopped onions, and ⅓ cup olive oil. Season with salt and ground white pepper. Yields 4–6 servings.

Hot Potato Salad

Ten large red potatoes, cooked and peeled, cut into thin slices, and seasoned with sea salt and freshly ground white pepper. For marinade, saute 3 strips of bacon, diced, and combine with ½ cup of hot beef consomme, 1 oz. white vinegar, 3 sliced scallions, and 2 oz. olive oil. Toss lightly. Keep warm. Yields 4–6 servings.

Cabbage Salad

One medium head of white cabbage, shredded or thinly cut. Combine with 1 tsp. caraway seeds, ½ cup of sherry wine vinegar, 1 tbsp. sugar, 1 tbsp. freshly shredded horseradish, ¼ cup olive oil, juice of 1 lemon, and 2 oz. water or white wine. Sea salt and freshly ground white pepper to taste. Yields 4–6 servings.

Classical Gourmet Dressing

INGREDIENTS	4 Cups	2 Gallons
strawberry vinegar	1½ cups	3 qt.
walnut oil	1½ cups	3 qt.
water	¾ cup	3 pt.
sugar	2 tbsp.	¼ cup
tarragon, finely chopped	1 oz.	4 oz.
onion, finely chopped	1	6
mustard	2 tsp.	¼ cup
tomato paste	2 tsp.	¼ cup
lemon juice	2	6
salt	¼ tsp.	1 tsp.
black pepper, freshly ground	¼ tsp.	1 tsp.

Mix all ingredients in blender for 5 minutes at medium speed. Excellent for any kind of green salad.

Pepe Dressing

Combine 2 oz. of chutney, chopped, with ½ cup of mayonnaise, and ½ cup of yogurt. Season with salt and pepper, and ½ tsp. curry powder. Blend with juice of 1 lemon. Excellent for seafood and fruit salads. Yields 4–6 servings.

Gourmet Dressing

Combine ½ cup tarragon vinegar with 2 tbsp. honey, 1 tbsp. mustard, dash cayenne pepper, and 1 tbsp. sesame seeds. Blend with 1 cup of olive oil. Season with sea salt, and freshly ground black pepper to taste. Excellent for plain tossed salad, fruit dips, and cold fish dishes. Yields 4–6 servings.

Classic Curry Dressing

Combine ½ cup of sherry wine vinegar with ½ cup of olive oil, 2 tbsp. mustard, 1 tbsp. sugar, 2 tbsp. Worcestershire sauce, 2 tbsp. curry powder, ½ cup of finely chopped chutney, 2 oz. brandy, sea salt, and freshly ground white pepper. Blend at medium speed for 2 minutes. Excellent for vegetables or Belgian endive. Yields 4–6 servings.

Sake Dressing

Combine ½ cup of sake with ½ cup of mayonnaise, juice of 2 limes, ½ cup of yogurt, 1 tsp. powdered ginger, salt, and freshly ground white pepper. Excellent for pineapples or vegetables. Yields 4–6 servings.

Apple-Pecan Classic

INGREDIENTS	For 4	For 24
apple gelatin	4½ oz.	2½ cups
boiling water	¾ cup	1¼ qt.
apple juice	10 oz.	46 oz.
apples, sliced in sections	1	4
celery, chopped	¼ cup	1½ cups
pecans, chopped	¼ cup	1 cup
apples, chopped	1 cup	4 cups

Dissolve gelatin in boiling water and add apple juice. Chill until slightly thickened. Decorate mold with apple slices and fill half full with gelatin. Chill. Add celery, pecans, and chopped apples to remaining gelatin. Chill until firm. Hold mold in warm water for several seconds, then turn over on round platter. Decorate with apple slices and pecans. Fill center with a mixture of mayonnaise, sugar, whipped cream, and lemon juice. See Color Plate 5.

California Fruit Salad

INGREDIENTS   YIELD: 1 serving

3 lettuce cups

3 oz. pineapple chunks

4 fresh orange sections

4 grapefruit sections

4 apple wedges, unpeeled

3 oz. grapes, washed

3 slices of cantaloupe

½ banana, sliced

1 scoop cottage cheese

1 fresh strawberry

mint sprig

poppy seed dressing

Place lettuce cups on large plate. Put one scoop of cottage cheese in center, topped with fresh strawberry. Surround with slices of cantaloupe, grapefruit sections, orange sections, banana slices, pineapple chunks, apple slices, grapes, and mint sprig. Serve dressing on the side.

Pate, Galantine, Terrine, and Mousse

In the classic culinary art, these items are indispensable. *Pate,* also called pate en croute, consists of game, fish, pork, fowl, liver, or meat, finely ground (farce), and seasoned with brandy, spices, and herbs. It is also mixed with lard and layers of tongue, meat, or liver strips. A pate is placed in a pastry crust, decorated, and baked (with a hole in the crust). After it is cooled, it is filled with melted aspic. *Terrines* use the same mixture as a pate. They are placed in earthenware dishes, lined with slices of salted pork lard, and covered. The most classic of all is foie gras. For *galantines*, place the skin of fowl on cheese cloth. Fill with a mixture, either layers of meat, or truffles. Roll gently onto skin. Sew skin roll and simmer in appropriate stock. Cook in same, remove cloth and threads. Chill. Cover with chaud froid sauce, decorate, and cut into thin slices. A *mousse* is made from the liver of geese, ducks, or chicken; or from fish or meat. This is mixed with veloute and heavy cream. Placed in timbales or souffle dishes, the mousse is decorated and filled with aspic.

Pastry Dough for Pate

INGREDIENTS

1 lb. all-purpose flour

salt to taste

5 oz. lard or 6 oz. butter

1 egg, beaten

about ½ cup water

Mix flour, salt, and lard till it reaches a crumbly consistency. Add egg and sprinkle with water. Knead dough till firm. Chill for 2 to 3 hours.

Lining the mold

Roll dough out ¼ inch thick. Grease pan with lard. Place dough on all four sides. Fill pan and cover top with dough. Decorate.

Pate en Croute, Acropolis Classic

The pate dough is placed in forms, and filled with alternating layers of pike and lobster mousse with truffles. It is baked, chilled, and filled with aspic. It is decorated with truffles, pears stuffed with marinated chanterelles, baby swans of pate au choux, and a piece montee, of tallow, decorated with olives and crystallized mint leaves. The three pates are presented on a mirror.

Pike Mousse

Take 10 shallots and chop finely. Saute in butter, and grind with 2 lb. of raw pike meat. Combine with 3 egg whites, and ¼ cup heavy cream. Season with salt and ground white pepper. Add 1 chopped truffle and 2 oz. white wine. Mix thoroughly.

Lobster Mousse

Grind 2 lb. of lobster meat finely, and combine with 3 egg whites, and ¼ cup heavy cream. Season with a dash of dry mustard, and 4 drops of Worcestershire sauce. Salt and pepper to taste.

Place alternately in pate form lined with dough. Cover top and make two holes. Bake at 350° F. for 1½ hours. Remove and fill with melted aspic. Cool and fill again with melted, cool aspic. Refrigerate for two hours.

Classic Salmon Pate

INGREDIENTS   YIELD: 12 to 14 servings

2½ lb. raw salmon
salt and white pepper, ground to taste
3 egg whites
1 cup heavy cream
pastry dough
½ lb. raw salmon strips
1 tsp. truffles, chopped
1 cup aspic, cooled

Grind skinned and boned salmon twice. Season. Add egg whites mixed in heavy cream. Place in form laid with pastry dough. In center, place salmon strips and truffles. Cover, and make two holes on top. Decorate with remaining dough in leaf or fish designs. Bake for two hours, at 350° F. until top is brown. Remove. When almost cold, fill holes with cool aspic. Chill overnight. To remove from mold, place mold in hot water for two minutes. Turn over and slide out. Cut into portions, and serve with sauce chantilly.

Classic Veal Galantine

INGREDIENTS   YIELD: 10 to 14 servings

small breast of veal
2 lb. veal for farce
½ lb. lard
2 tbsp. pistachio nuts
½ lb. chicken liver, soaked in milk
1 lb. beef tongue, diced
1 tsp. truffles, chopped
2 oz. cognac
2 eggs
1 cup heavy cream
poultry seasoning to taste
salt and white pepper, ground, to taste
rosemary to taste
veal stock to cover

Remove all bones from breast. Cut breast to make a pocket. Finely grind veal and lard. Add pistachio nuts, chicken liver, beef tongue, truffles, cognac, eggs, heavy cream, and seasoning. Fill pocket and sew up. Roll in cheese cloth. Cook in veal stock for 3 to 4 hours. Cool in stock, remove, and chill. Cover with chaud froid sauce. Cut and decorate with cooked vegetables.

Classic Goose Liver Terrine

INGREDIENTS   YIELD: 12 to 16 servings

1 lb. salt pork fat, sliced thin and cooked
1 medium onion, finely chopped
½ lb. lard
2 lb. goose liver
2 oz. cognac
2 oz. madeira
½ tsp. truffles, chopped
2 eggs, beaten well
salt and white pepper, ground, to taste
½ cup aspic, flavored with madeira

Before slicing the pork fat, boil it for 20 minutes. Cool and slice thinly (to prevent shrinking). Line terrine mold. Saute onion in lard till golden brown. Cool and grind very finely. Add goose liver and grind twice, till very fine. Add remaining ingredients (except aspic). Place in terrine mold, and cover with pork fat. Top with terrine cover. Place in boiling water to just below the rim or bake in low oven till firm. Cool. Remove from mold by dipping in hot water. Remove pork fat, replace in terrine mold, and fill with madeira aspic. Cool.

Classic Ham Mousse

INGREDIENTS   YIELD: 12 4-oz. servings

2½ lb. lean, smoked ham

salt and white pepper, ground, to taste

½ cup cream sauce

3 tbsp. melted aspic

½ cup whipped heavy cream

12 barquettes (boats from pastry dough)

12 truffle slices

12 sprigs of dill

Grind smoked ham very finely. Season and mix with cream sauce, aspic, and whipped cream. Pipe mixture into the barquettes with a pastry bag. Decorate with truffles and dill. Brush additional aspic lightly on top.

Rock Cornish Hen Earl of Essex

INGREDIENTS   YIELD: 5 servings

5 cornish hens, 12 oz. each

salt and white pepper, ground, to taste

3 7-oz. foie gras

3 oz. butter

1 cup shallots, finely chopped

2 tsp. currant jelly

3 cups port wine

zest from 1 orange

1 oz. brandy

½ cup heavy cream

1 tsp. cornstarch

Season cornish hens with salt and pepper. Stuff with foie gras. Tie legs with string. Brown in butter on each side over medium heat. Roast in 350° F. oven for 20 minutes. Remove strings. Remove hens, add chopped shallots and simmer for 3 minutes. Add currant jelly and port wine. Reduce to ½ over medium heat. Place hens in a casserole and strain sauce over hens. Add orange zest. Pour brandy over and ignite. Stir in heavy cream mixed with cornstarch, and bring to boil. Top each hen with one slice of foie gras. Garnish with mushroom caps, turned carrots, turned turnips, cauliflower, and truffles. If desired, garnish platter with baby goose made of pate a chou. See Color Plate 6.

Poularde Montagne

INGREDIENTS   YIELD: 7 servings

4–5 lb. large chicken (poularde)

water, for poaching

1 carrot, sliced

½ cup celery, diced

2 onions, sliced

salt, to taste

½ gal. mayonnaise

1 gal. aspic, melted

4 truffles

toast, cut to shapes

3 lb. foie gras

8 egg whites, cooked

Poach poularde in water with carrot, celery, onions, and salt for 45 minutes. Remove, cool, and peel off skin. Set on rack of refrigerator, and chill well. Mix mayonnaise with 1 cup of warm aspic. Cover poularde by ladling over only once. Chill again. Put truffles in blender with ½ cup melted aspic and blend for 20 minutes, scraping the sides of the blender occasionally. When ready, pour on flat surface and place in refrigerator. Chill well. Cut shapes of toast, cover with mounds of foie gras, refrigerate, and cover with melted aspic. Cover the bottom of a silver platter very thinly with aspic. Chill. Use various cutters to cut truffles in designs. Cut egg whites in half-moon designs. Dip toothpick in cool melted aspic and decorate poularde and foie gras. Again chill well and cover all items with cool melted aspic. Arrange on a platter and surround poularde with diced aspic.

II
Hotellerie
on Board the
Luxury Ship
Laconia

6. Breakfast at Sea

The sea breezes, the shining, glittering sun, the exotic islands, the moon at night, the calypso music in the south—these are the images I remember. November of 1963 saw the end of the luxury ship *Laconia*. Only a smoking wreck was left, along with memories of food preparation in the style of an empire.

Eggs

During my voyage at sea, and my visits to the different ports and cultures, I discovered innumerable preparations for eggs. By way of information, eggs are graded according to the particular standards of a country and are categorized as jumbo, extra large, large, medium, small, and pee wee. The color of the shell does not affect the flavor, the nutritive value, or the performance of cooking. The color of the yolk can vary from light to dark. A high quality egg, when broken on a plate, will have a well-centered yolk standing out of the white. Poor quality eggs have a flat yolk and a watery and thin white. High quality eggs are necessary for poaching and frying; lower quality eggs will do for other uses. Eggs should always be cooked at moderate temperatures.

Fried Eggs Renaissance

Melt 1 tbsp. butter. Fry two eggs sunnyside. Transfer to a hot platter. Brown remaining butter and pour over eggs. A French delicacy. Yields 1 serving.

Fried Eggs Laconia

An English muffin cut in half and toasted. Top each half with a slice of grilled Canadian bacon and a fried egg on each bacon. Sprinkle with toasted almonds. Serve with asparagus tips, tomato concassier, and a parsley sprig on the side. A British delicacy. Yields 1 serving.

Pearl of the Pacific

Two eggs poached in water with vinegar. Place in broiled, halved papaya. Top with hollandaise sauce, sprinkle with toasted, shredded coconut, and set on top of a palm leaf. A South Pacific delicacy. Yields 1 serving.

Mermaid Omelet

YIELD: 6 servings

9 eggs

⅓ cup milk

½ tsp. salt

3 tsp. butter

one scallion and 6 shrimp, sauteed in
butter

Beat eggs with milk and salt. Melt butter in large frying pan and pour in mixture. Cook over low heat until set. Fill with sauteed shrimp and scallions, and roll up omelet. Serve on large platter surrounded with toasted white bread triangles. A Danish delicacy.

Omelet San Marco

YIELD: 1 serving

3 eggs

2 tbsp. milk

dash of salt

dash of pepper

1 tbsp. zucchini, chopped

2 tsp. butter

1 tsp. parmesan cheese, grated

Beat eggs with milk, salt, and pepper. Saute zucchini in butter, and pour egg mixture over. Cook until set. Sprinkle with parmesan cheese. Place under salamander until golden brown. A Venetian specialty.

Omelets Around the World

Basic Omelet Mixture

Three eggs beaten with 2 tbsp. milk, and a dash of salt and ground white pepper. Yields 1 serving.

Omelet Viennese (Austria)—saute in butter, finely chopped onions, and chicken livers; add red wine.

Omelet Swiss Style (Switzerland)— filled with neuchataler cheese, topped with Swiss cheese au gratin.

Omelet Scorpio (Greece)—saute in olive oil, diced eggplant, tomatoes, onions, olives, and feta cheese.

Omelet Black Forest (Germany)— saute in butter, cepes, and diced shallots; add wine. Pour over omelet.

Omelet Valencia (Spain)—saute in butter, diced tomato, garlic cloves, onions, sliced pepperoni, and chopped parsley. Pour egg mixture over. Do not roll the mixture.

Omelet Suchumi (Russia)—thin slices of sturgeon and caviar.

Omelet Chung Yeung (China)—saute in butter, bean sprouts, bamboo shoots, and water chestnuts; add soy sauce.

Omelet Yakimono (Japan)—saute in butter, scallions, diced chicken, and peas; add teriyaki sauce.

Omelet Bruxelles (Belgium)—fill with artichoke bottoms, tomatoes, and chives; top with mornay sauce, au gratin.

Omelet Nova Scotia (Canada)—fill with slices of Nova Scotia salmon and chives.

Omelet Guadalajara (Mexico)—fill with avocado slices, chopped pimiento, and sliced bananas.

Omelet Copacabana (South America)—saute in butter, diced onions, diced lamb shoulder, diced potatoes, green peppers, and red pimiento; simmer in white wine.

Omelet Villa Cisnero (Africa)—fill with tangerine slices, dried apricots, figs, and tomatoes.

Fried Eggs (Oeufs Sur Le Plat) Around the World

Melt butter in a pyrex dish with salt. Cook eggs slowly until done. Place small amount of garnish next to egg yolk.

Oeufs Sur Le Plat Perigord (France)—saute in butter, chicken livers with demi glaze and truffles.

Oeufs Sur Le Plat Eleuthera (Bahamas)—saute in butter, diced chicken breast, avocados, and guavas (tropical fruit).

Oeufs Sur Le Plat Maldonado (Uruguay)—saute in butter, diced fillet mignon, shallots, and green pepper; add red wine.

Oeufs Sur Le Plat Laconia—broiled tomato half stuffed with sauteed spinach and anchovies; topped with parmesan cheese.

Oeufs Sur Le Plat Viking (Sweden)—a slice of ham and radish; topped with gruyere cheese.

Oeufs Sur Le Plat Budavalasz (Hungary)—sliced hot Hungarian sausages with pepperoni.

Oeufs Sur Le Plat Madras (India)—diced mutton with curry sauce on toasted bread.

Oeufs Sur Le Plat Shalimar (Kashmir)—diced chicken marinated in yogurt. Baked and served on toast.

Oeufs Sur Le Plat Aberdeen (Hong Kong)—crabmeat and asparagus spears with ginger sauce.

Oeufs Sur Le Plat Oceania (South Pacific)—sauteed prawns with curry sauce and baked bananas.

Poached Eggs (Oeufs Poches) Around the World

Break egg into a cup. Bring water and vinegar to boiling point. Cook unsalted approximately three minutes. Place in warm salted water until serving time.

Oeufs Poches Cairo (Egypt)—two broiled tomatoes topped with saffron rice, eggs, and tomato hollandaise.

Oeufs Poches Bombay (India)—place eggs on top of curry rice with raisins. Top with curry sauce.

Oeufs Poches Cadiz (Spain)—diced tomatoes and onions sauteed in olive oil; add demi glaze. Serve on toast.

Oeufs Poches Athena (Greece)—diced eggplant and olives topped with sauce mornay au gratin.

Oeufs Poches Rothschild (France)—place on croutons with gooseliver, truffles, and sauce madeira.

Oeufs Poches Viennese (Austria)—place on croutons with slices of prosciutto and paprika sauce. Top with julienne of prosciutto.

Oeufs Poches Lisbon (Portugal)—place on croutons with asparagus tips and cream sauce.

Oeufs Poches Anchorage (Alaska)—saute king crab meat in butter; cover eggs with hollandaise sauce.

Oeufs Poches Hilo (Hawaii)—grill pineapple rings. Center eggs and top with curry sauce and toasted shredded coconut.

Oeufs Poches Puerto Espana (Trinidad)—place on croutons with oyster sauce au gratin.

Soft-Boiled Eggs

Have eggs at room temperature.
Bring water to boil and simmer eggs
for 6 minutes. Remove to cold
water for several seconds to prevent
further cooking.

Scrambled Eggs

Beat eggs with milk or cream. Place
in hot butter, stirring until flakes
form. Keep creamy. These eggs can
be combined with mushrooms,
vegetables, fish, meat, or any
variety of fowl.

Baked Eggs

Heat oil. Break eggs into a bowl
and season with salt and pepper.
Place in hot oil, holding egg whites
together with spoon. Bake for two
minutes. Garnish as for poached
eggs.

Shirred Eggs

Butter a ramequin and put in a little
cream. Break egg into ramequin and
bake until done. Ramequin can be
lined with ham, bacon, noodles,
rice, vegetables, potatoes, et cetera.

7. Soups

The various types of soup include stocks, consommes, cream soups, puree soups, vegetable soups, fish soups, fruit soups, and crustacean soups.

Basic Procedures

In order to create a consomme, a basic clear stock has to be made. Whether it is chicken, meat, or fish, the specific bones must be used for the base. For a clear beef stock or bouillon, bring beef bones and cold water to a boil and simmer for one hour. Add burned onions, raw carrots, celery, parsley, and bouquet garni. Simmer slowly for several hours. The longer it simmers the stronger the base will be. If a piece of meat is added it will enhance the flavor. (Use chicken bones for a clear chicken stock.) Strain through cheese cloth.

Bring the clear beef stock to a boil and add a small amount of ground beef mixed with egg white and water. Simmer for one hour, strain, and season. For a double strength consomme, use twice as much ground meat. This applies to fish or any other base. A cold consomme has to be reduced more, chilled, and all the fat removed from the top. Various ingredients suggest the name; for example, Consomme Froid Valencia has madeira and diced tomato as ingredients.

Cream soups are thick soups, finished with cream and egg yolk. They are called potages veloutes in French. Potage cremes, which are finished with cream only, have a small amount of bechamel added to the basic stock.

Puree soups are rich in starches, such as lentils or split peas; for less starchy varieties, vegetables, rice, or potatoes are added. Shellfish puree soups, bisques, are included in this category. Today, most purees are made with veloute and thus lose their name.

Vegetable soups combine basic vegetables with water to bring out the flavor of the vegetables.

Fish soups include all the cream, clear, or starchy soups made from fish. They can also have crustaceans as ingredients.

Fruit soups are purees made from fruit, and topped with yogurt or sour cream.

Crustacean soups include all the hard-shelled marine animals, such as, lobster, crabs, and shrimp. They are puree, cream, or clear soups.

Beef Stock or Bouillon

INGREDIENTS	For 12	For 50
beef bones	3 lb.	12 lb.
cold water	¾ gal.	2½ gal.
onion	1	6
celeriac	1	6
celery	1 stalk	½ bunch
carrot	1	6
parsley	5 stems and leaves	1 bunch
bouquet garni	1 small	1 large
tomato	½	2
salt	to taste	to taste

Bring bones and water to boil. Strain and wash bones. Place in kettle with fresh cold water. Simmer for one hour. Cut onion in half, place on stove, and burn till black. Add, with remaining ingredients, and simmer for 4 to 5 hours. Skim excess fat from top. Strain. Season to taste. Never boil.

NOTE   In order to get a stronger beef flavor, a piece of beef is usually boiled with the stock and used for specialty dishes.
   One gallon of stock yields 25 5-oz. portions.

Beef Consomme

INGREDIENTS	For 12	For 50
beef stock	½ gal.	2 gal.
ground meat	½ lb.	2 lb.
egg whites	2	8
water	¼ cup	1 cup

Bring beef stock to boil. Mix ground meat with egg whites and water. Add to stock and simmer for one hour. Strain and salt to taste.

NOTE   For chicken stock, use chicken bones; for fish stock, use fish bones; and for game stock, use game bones.

Consomme Roma—homemade noodles with goose liver and madeira; placed in boiling consomme with chopped chives.
Consomme Berger—consomme with sliced fresh mushrooms, scallions, asparagus tips, and tapioca; finished with madeira.
Consomme Orly—consomme with diced celery, carrots, cauliflower, peas, beans, and sherry.
Consomme Monte Carlo—royale made of eggs whipped with milk and nutmeg, placed in cup, and poached till firm. Cut in small diamond-shaped pieces. Mix with rice and truffles. Madeira added to hot consomme at serving time.
Consomme Madagascar—place rice and curry powder in boiling consomme; sprinkle with chives.
Consomme Contessa—place semolina in boiling consomme and simmer for 10 minutes; add one egg yolk per portion and chopped chives.

Fruit Soup

Fruit soups have a long history. During the early ages, man pureed fruit with mineral waters from springs.

Apricot Kaltschale

Cut 20 fresh apricots in half. Remove pits and bring to boil with ¼ cup sugar, ⅛ cup water. Simmer for 3 minutes. Cool and puree, using blender. Add 2 oz. white wine for proper consistency. Cool in refrigerator, and strain. Break 5 of the pits and chop the kernel finely. When serving, place bowl on ice, top center with yogurt, and sprinkle with the finely chopped kernels. Surround bowl with fresh mint leaves. Yields 2–4 servings.

Raspberry Kaltschale

Cover two pints of fresh raspberries with 2 tbsp. sugar and ¼ cup mineral water, soak for two hours, and press through a fine sieve. Place in iced bowl, garnish with several fresh raspberries and sour cream. Yields 2–4 servings.

Peach Kaltschale

Cut 10 ripe peaches in half and remove seeds. Soak with 4 oz. sugar, juice of 2 lemons, and 1 cup of white wine for one hour. Press through a fine sieve. Combine with 4 oz. vodka, and chill. Divide among chilled champagne glasses. Top each with ½ tsp. cottage cheese, and garnish with fresh mint leaves. Yields 2–4 servings.

Mango Kaltschale

Peel 8 mangoes, cut in half, and remove seeds. Dice mangoes, and set 2 tbsp. aside. Combine remaining with one cup of white wine, juice of 2 lemons, and blend at medium speed for 2 minutes. Press through a fine sieve. Cool and combine with remaining diced mangoes. Serve in two halved coconut shells topped with a slice of banana, and 1 tsp. sour cream. Garnish with fresh mint leaves. Yields 2–4 servings.

Strawberry Kaltschale

Clean 2 pints of ripe strawberries. Soak berries with the juice of 2 lemons, ¼ cup sugar, and ¼ cup mineral water for 1 hour. Press through a fine sieve. Chill and serve in halved cantaloupe melons, topped with 1 tsp. yogurt, and a fresh strawberry. Garnish with a fresh mint leaf. Yields 2–4 servings.

Apple Kaltschale

Peel, core, and dice 10 of your favorite apples. Combine with 4 oz. sugar, juice of 2 lemons, half a cinnamon stick, and ½ cup of white wine. Bring to boil, strain, and cool over ice. Place in bowl, and garnish with diced apples. Place 1 tsp. yogurt on top. Garnish with fresh mint leaves. Yields 2–4 servings.

Lobster Bisque

INGREDIENTS	For 12	For 50
lobster	1	4
butter	3 oz.	12 oz.
shallots	½ cup	1 cup
carrot	1	4
celery	1 stalk	4 stalks
onion	1	4
tomato puree	¼ cup	1 cup
brandy	1 oz.	4 oz.
paprika	dash	1 tsp.
rice	½ cup	2 cups
white wine	½ cup	2 cups
fish stock	¾ gal.	2½ gal.
bouquet garni	1 small	1 large
salt	to season	to season
cayenne pepper	to season	to season

Cut lobster in half and break claws. Saute in butter with shallots till lobster becomes red. Add vegetables. Add brandy and flame. Add paprika, rice, and white wine, and simmer for 20 minutes. Add fish stock and remaining ingredients. Simmer for 30 minutes. Remove meat from lobster tail and set aside. Simmer remaining stock for 2 hours, strain, and add diced lobster meat.

NOTE   Instead of rice, a light roux can be used, by combining flour with butter.

Potage Louis—fish cream soup with sauteed shrimp and lobster. Finished with madeira, diced shrimp and lobster meat, and heavy cream.
Potage Casablanca—fish cream soup with paprika, sherry, and asparagus tips. Finished with heavy cream, whisked egg yolk, and cayenne.
Potage Marseille—fish cream soup with mussels, saffron, and mushrooms. Garnished with dill.
Potage Maria Theresa—carp with diced garden vegetables boiled with a touch of vinegar. Add brown roux and shallots, red wine and juice of lemon, bouquet garni; combine. Season. Garnish with boiled carp roe, whisked in sour cream, and add croutons.

Cream of Asparagus

INGREDIENTS	For 12	For 50
asparagus	10 spears	4 bunches
chicken stock	¾ gal.	2½ gal.
onion, finely chopped	1 medium	3 large
butter	3 oz.	12 oz.
flour	¼ cup	1 cup
milk	1 cup	4 cups
salt and white pepper, ground	to taste	to taste
heavy cream	¼ cup	1 cup
nutmeg, freshly ground	to taste	to taste

Cut asparagus in 1-inch pieces. Set tips aside and simmer remainder in chicken stock. Saute onions in butter till glossy. Add flour, milk, and chicken stock with asparagus. Simmer for two hours at low heat. Strain and season with salt and pepper. Add heavy cream and cooked asparagus tips. Finish with freshly ground nutmeg.

Potage Classic—chicken cream soup finished with white wine, sherry, and diced truffles.
Potage Gourmet—chicken cream soup with artichoke; strained, with paprika and white wine.
Potage Berger—rice cream soup with curry, shallots, and white wine. Strained, with rice and truffles added.
Potage Enzian—cream of tomato soup with diced tomato, diced ham, chives, and vodka.
Potage Morilles—sliced, braised morels with shallots; added to beef veloute with madeira.
Potage Montagne—chicken curry with diced apples, diced chicken, and diced truffles; finished with cognac.
Potage Oriental—basic cream soup with stachys, simmered and strained. Served with diced golden brown croutons.

Potage Puree Classic

INGREDIENTS	For 12	For 50
onions, chopped	2	8
butter	3 oz.	12 oz.
cauliflower, diced	½ head	3 heads
carrots, diced	3	10
celery stalk, diced	1	5
brussels sprouts	2 cups	2 pt.
rice	½ cup	2 cups
tomatoes, quartered	2	8
beef stock	½ gal.	2 gal.
bouquet garni	1 small	1 large
salt and white pepper, ground	to taste	to taste
croutons, diced	6 oz.	1½ lb.
mozzarella cheese	12 slices	50 slices

Saute onions in butter till glossy. Add cauliflower, carrots, celery, brussels sprouts, rice, tomatoes, and beef stock. Add bouquet garni. Simmer for ½ hour, puree, and strain. Add seasoning. Place in individual soup crocks, add croutons, cover with cheese slices, and grill under salamander.

Potage Vienna—lentil puree with bacon and diced celery, carrots, and onions. Also add whole lentils. Seasoned with cayenne, vinegar, sugar, and garlic.

Potage Laconia—green pea puree with julienne of sorrel, sauteed in butter, and finely chopped parsley.

Potage Hunter—game meat braised in red wine. Dice half the meat and puree remainder with game stock. Finish with red wine and sour cream. Add diced meat, and season highly.

Billi Bi Classic

INGREDIENTS   YIELD: 6 to 8 servings

2 onions, finely chopped
1 tsp. butter
1½ cups white wine
1 celery stalk, diced
1 bay leaf
1½ lb. mussels, shelled and cleaned
3 cups heavy cream
1 tsp. cornstarch
1 tsp. water
salt to taste
white pepper, freshly ground, to taste

Saute onions in butter. Add white wine, celery, bay leaf, and mussels. Cover and simmer for 10 minutes. Remove mussels and reduce liquid to half. Add heavy cream and simmer 10 more minutes. Mix cornstarch with some cold water and add to liquid. Bring to boil. Pour over mussels and season to taste.

Boston Clam Chowder

INGREDIENTS   YIELD: 6 to 8 servings

½ bushel clams, washed, boiled, and cut
  in quarters
4 oz. butter
1 lb. onions, diced
½ lb. celery, diced
8 oz. flour
1 qt. milk
1 lb. potatoes, diced
1 tsp. Worcestershire sauce
¼ tsp. white pepper
salt, to taste

Cover clams with water and boil until they open. Remove clams and reduce to half. Melt butter and add onions and celery. Cook for 10 minutes. Stir in flour. Add clam juice and milk and bring to a boil. Add potatoes and remaining ingredients. Simmer for 20 minutes.

Queen Soup Classic

INGREDIENTS   YIELD: 6 to 8 servings

1 lb. chicken breasts, diced
3 cups consomme
2 stalks celery, diced
2 plum tomatoes, peeled and diced
1 cup cooked rice
salt to taste
white pepper, ground, to taste
parsley, freshly chopped

Simmer diced chicken in consomme for 20 minutes. Add celery, tomatoes, and rice. Simmer for 15 more minutes. Season and sprinkle with chopped parsley.

Cucumber Soup Classic

INGREDIENTS   YIELD: 6 to 8 servings

2 cucumbers, peeled
3 cups yogurt
1 cup buttermilk
1 cup beef consomme
salt, to taste
ground white pepper, to taste
2 hard-boiled eggs
paprika, to taste

Core cucumbers and shred finely. Whip yogurt and buttermilk. Add beef consomme, salt, and pepper to taste. Add cucumber and marinate for 2 hours. Place in serving dish, and sprinkle with chopped eggs and paprika. Serve cold.

Fish Soup Paradiso

INGREDIENTS   YIELD: 4 servings

2 lb. cod, cut in portions
1 tsp. olive oil
1 onion, sliced
1 celeriac, cut julienne
1 leek, julienne
¼ cup rice
1 tbsp. flour
8 cups fish stock
2 cloves of garlic
1 small fennel, julienne
1 anchovy, finely chopped
1 tomato, quartered
tarragon, to taste
rosemary, to taste
basil, to taste
salt and pepper, to taste

Saute cod in olive oil and remove. In same oil, saute onions, celeriac, and leek. Add rice and flour. Fill with fish stock and simmer for 30 minutes. Add remaining ingredients and fish. Season and simmer for 10 more minutes.

8. Hors d'Oeuvre

Hors d'oeuvre, or appetizers, are divided into the categories of hot and cold. The purpose of hors d'oeuvre is to offer a combination of delicacies, in small quantities, before the main course to stimulate your appetite. The classic style of service is a wagon, from which the guest selects items to be served by the waiter. Or, they may be displayed at a buffet table. Classic items are caviar on ice, medaillons of lobster, foie gras, supremes of fruit, meats or fish, pates, galantines, or terrines. All are finely decorated.

Classic Hors-d'Oeuvre Froids

Caviar—served on ice, in its original container, with lemon.

Coquilles Zhivago—oysters topped with caviar, surrounded with lobster medaillons.

Lobster—lobster tail, sliced in medaillons, and served on Boston lettuce leaves with foie gras and diced aspic. Lemon and dill sauce accompaniment.

Foie Gras—several teaspoons of foie gras with sieved egg yolk, diced aspic, round toast, and dill sprig.

Fruit—papaya, blueberries, grapes, kiwi fruit, and strawberries, diced and soaked in sugar mixed with Perrier water and white wine. Garnished with mint leaf.

Melon—cut cantaloupe in half, remove seeds, and cut out balls. Mix with honeydew and watermelon balls. Fill shells, pour port wine and sherry over, cover, and refrigerate. Serve on ice, with mint leaf to garnish.

Mushroom—saute sliced mushrooms, diced tomato, and scallions in oil. Add salt, pepper, vinegar, and chopped parsley. Chill.

Crab—place watercress in champagne glass. Top with Virginia crab meat mixed with capers, whipped cream, mayonnaise, and cayenne. Top with sliced, hard-boiled egg and truffle slice.

Artichoke—small artichoke, quartered and blanched in water with vinegar. Marinate with fennel, lemon, thyme, garlic, shallots, coriander, oil, and pepper. Serve chilled.

Cucumber—cut into 1-inch slices, peel and remove seeds. Marinate in dill, vinegar, oil, bay leaf, peppercorns, and lemon juice. Remove from marinade and fill with mousse of ham; glaze with aspic.

Aubergine—sliced eggplant seasoned with garlic, lemon, coriander, thyme, bay leaf, salt, pepper, water, oil, and diced tomato. Bring to a boil, chill, and marinate. Serve ice cold.

Hearts of Palm—fresh marinated, and sliced. Serve with curry and mustard sauce, tomato, and diced green peppers in champagne glass with dill.

Leek—cut leeks in 3-inch lengths. Tie and boil in water with vinegar. Separate, and arrange with sardines and anchovy on lettuce leaves. Brush with Italian dressing, and garnish with tomato wedges and hard-boiled eggs.

Rote Reuben—small beets, baked, peeled, scooped, and filled with julienne of ham, celery, mustard, mayonnaise, and aspic. Decorate with hard egg whites, and surround with diced aspic.

Celeriac—marinate julienne of raw celeriac with oil, mustard, vinegar, lemon juice, salt, and pepper. Decorate with tomato rosettes.

Asparagus—tips of asparagus boiled in salt water, and marinated in lemon juice, dill, vinegar, oil, salt, and pepper. Mix with mushrooms, tomatoes, and garlic. Sprinkle with chopped parsley.

Chanterelle—saute finely chopped shallots in olive oil. Add chanterelles, a dash of paprika, sour cream, and chopped dill. Season with salt and pepper.

Salsify—peel, cut in 1-inch pieces, and cook in lemon water. Saute finely chopped onions in butter, with diced tomato, capers, and chopped fennel. Add salsify.

Herring Salad—diced herring fillet mixed with diced beets and boiled potatoes, celery, apples, capers, onions, mustard, vinegar, mayonnaise, and lemon juice. Serve on lettuce leaf sprinkled with julienne of pickles. Garnish with radish slices and watercress.

Salade Volaille—chicken breast, cooked and diced with diced beef tongue, celery, and julienne of green peppers. Mix with mayonnaise, lemon juice, salt, and pepper. Garnish with egg slices.

Salade Poissons—boneless fish, broken into small pieces, and mixed with julienne of pickles, tarragon, cooked egg whites, mustard, curry, and mayonnaise. Sprinkle with capers.

Stuffed Eggs—hard-boiled eggs, cut lengthwise, and filled with smoked salmon puree mixed with lemon caviar. Decorate with caviar.

Moweneier—gull eggs, hard-boiled. Mix diced boiled carrots, diced apples, walnuts, and celeriac with mayonnaise and curry powder. Place on Boston lettuce leaves. Top with gull eggs, cover with herb mayonnaise and top with dill sprig.

Frog's Legs—poach frog's legs in white wine. Saute diced onions in oil. Add stock, lemon juice, garlic, bay leaf, and bouquet garni. Bring to a boil, simmer, and cool. Marinate frog's legs. Sprinkle with chopped parsley.

Shrimp—barquettes (small pastry boats) filled with shrimp salad mixed with aspic. Decorate with slices of shrimp, and garnish with truffles.

Cheese Truffle

INGREDIENTS	For 20	For 100
pumpernickel	¼ lb.	1¼ lb.
caraway cheese	2 lb.	10 lb.
paprika	dash	1 tsp.
parsley, chopped	1 tsp.	5 tbsp.

Grind pumpernickel into crumbs. Mix caraway cheese with paprika and chopped parsley. Roll out in between waxed paper and cut into desired portions. Roll in pumpernickel. Garnish with parsley sprig.

Artichoke Salad Olympic

INGREDIENTS   YIELD: 4 to 6 servings

15 artichoke hearts
1 cup feta cheese, crumbled
8 black olives, pitted
8 green olives, pitted
2 scallion stems, cut in small pieces
2 onions, sliced
¼ cup sherry wine vinegar
1 tsp. oregano
3 tomatoes, cut in wedges
1 eggplant, peeled and cut in cubes
1 green pepper, sliced
juice of 2 whole lemons
salt, to taste
black pepper, freshly ground, to taste
1 head Boston lettuce, washed and leaves
    separated
¼ cup olive oil
1 bunch watercress

In mixing bowl, combine all ingredients except olive oil and lettuce leaves. Prior to serving, line salad bowl with lettuce. Add olive oil to marinated salad mixture and place in salad bowl. The salad can be served on individual plates and garnished with watercress.

NOTE   Watercress can also be added to the salad bowl instead of being placed on the side.

Romaine Salad

INGREDIENTS   YIELD: 4 servings

salt, to taste
2 garlic cloves
2 anchovy fillets
juice of 2 lemons
1 tsp. sugar
3 tbsp. vinegar
¼ cup olive oil
2 heads romaine lettuce
black pepper, freshly ground, to taste
1 cup croutons
¼ cup parmesan cheese

In wooden bowl, rub salt, garlic, and anchovy till finely pureed. Add lemon juice, sugar, vinegar, and oil, and whisk. Break fresh, washed, romaine into bowl. Toss gently, and season with pepper. Add golden croutons and sprinkle with parmesan cheese.

Classic Hors d'Oeuvre Chauds

Hot appetizers are generally beignets (small fritters), barquettes (small boats), cassolettes, coquilles, quenelles, pastas, small souffles, or toasts with various mixtures au gratin.

Beignet—calves brain pieces, marinated with lemon juice and parsley, dipped in beer batter, and fried golden brown.
Barquette—small boats made from pastry dough. These are filled with sauteed mushrooms, truffles, and chopped shrimp, combined with creamed fish sauce and butter, and seasoned. Decorate with shrimp, and cover with remaining sauce, parmesan cheese, and au gratin.

Cassolette—small ramequins (casseroles) filled with sauteed lobster pieces and shallots, white wine, and yogurt. Season with dill, and garnish with truffle slices.

Grand Express Souffle—Stir egg yolk and parmesan cheese into heavy bechamel sauce. Season with nutmeg, salt, and pepper. Mix in finely chopped spinach leaves and diced cauliflower. Add whipped egg whites and bake in buttered souffle dish for 15 to 20 minutes.

Financiere Toast—slices of white bread, cut into small squares and sauteed in butter till golden brown. Combine mousse of ham with mushrooms and demi glaze for a heavy consistency. Cover toast and sprinkle with chopped egg whites.

Oriental Skewer—marinate diced chicken pieces, tongue, and mushrooms in soy sauce. Arrange on wood skewer, alternating with water chestnuts. Brush with sweet and sour sauce. Dip in beer batter and fry till golden brown. Remove skewer and replace with silver skewer. Brush with additional sweet and sour sauce. (Sauce made from apricots, lemon juice, soy sauce, and Tabasco.)

South Pacific Bouchees—puff paste dough, rolled out thin, and cut in 2-inch circles. Cut out ¾-inch circle in center of half of circles. Brush bottom circles with egg wash; place cut-out circles on top and bake till golden brown. Saute shallots and diced sweetbreads. Add heavy cream, curry powder, and chutney. Season with rum and cayenne powder. Pour mixture in center of bouchees and top with pineapple chunk.

Timbale—in bottom of buttered cup, place one shrimp cut in half. Make a fish farce consisting of finely ground halibut, mixed with egg whites, salt, and ground white pepper. Fill timbales. Place in casserole with boiling water, cover, and poach for 30 minutes. Remove timbales by turning upside down. Cover with sauce. *For sauce,* mix egg yolk with white wine and chopped sorrel. Whip over double boiler till hot; continue whipping till cool, slowly adding melted butter. Cover fish mousse with sauce and top with slice of truffle.

Coquille—a scallop shell filled with sauteed shallots, scallops, salmon, and crab meat combined with lobster sauce. Top with sauce mornay mixed with chopped truffles and brandy, au gratin.

Quenelles—bring to boil 1 cup milk with 2 tbsp. butter, and salt and pepper. Add 8 oz. all-purpose flour. Boil down until mixture separates from pot. Add 3 eggs and 2 tbsp. grated Swiss cheese. Mix thoroughly, form quenelles, and boil in salted water for 15 minutes. Remove, place in oven-proof dish, cover with cream sauce, and sprinkle with grated Swiss cheese and butter flakes. Place under salamander and brown lightly.

Veneziana Pasta—boil 1½ lbs. of spaghetti or any other pasta in plenty of lightly salted water until al dente, up to 5 minutes. Set aside. In 3 tbsp. olive oil saute 2 medium, finely chopped onions, and 2 cloves of crushed garlic for 3 minutes. Add 1 tbsp. finely chopped parsley, 1 tbsp. finely chopped fresh basil, ½ tsp. finely chopped sage, 8 peeled and diced tomatoes, and ¼ lb. finely sliced prosciutto. Season with salt and ground white pepper. And ½ cup of red wine and simmer for 15 minutes. Serve sauce apart from pasta. Yields 4–6 servings.

9. Various Dishes

Preparation of Fish, Meat, Poultry, and Game

Fish

Fish (poissons in French) are divided into two categories, fresh water and salt water. Fresh-water fish, such as eel, trout, sturgeon, pike, carp, salmon, or salmon trout, are best prepared in court bouillon, to enhance the flavor. Court bouillon, the basic fish stock, is a combination of carrots, celery, onions, vinegar, lemon juice, bouquet garni, fish bones, and water that is reduced. When cooking large fish, always start with a cold stock; smaller portions can be started in boiling stock.

Salt-water fish, such as flounder, halibut, turbot, herring, cod, shad, mackerel, haddock, perch, sole, turbot, or squid, have a tastier meat that does not require court bouillon. However, milk should be added, with vegetables and bouquet garni or lemon.

Methods of Cooking

Saute meuniere—smaller fish or portions seasoned with salt and pepper, dipped in flour, and sauteed in butter. Finish with lemon juice, parsley, and remaining butter.

Au bleu—water with vinegar, salt, vegetables, bouquet garni, and lemon. Only live fish, with undamaged skin, should be used to attain the blue color. Simmer only. Sauces for garnishing are served on the side.

Grille—make several cuts on the back, brush with oil, and season. Roll in crumbs or leave plain and cook on hot grill.

Fried—soak in milk, season, and roll in flour or eggs and breadcrumbs. Fry in hot oil until crisp.

Poached—small portions simmered in wine and fish stock. Remaining stock is used for sauces to finish.

Braised—season, and simmer in small amount of stock or wine. Same liquid is poured over the fish during cooking process.

Gratine—with sauce mornay or sprinkled with cheese and butter. Finish under broiler.

Glazed—flamed, using same stock with plenty of butter whipped in.

There are lean fish and fat fish. Whole fish, prepared as portions, have a waste of up to 40 to 50 percent. There are even poisonous fish that can be eaten, if properly prepared by removing the liver and ovaries. These fish are then safe and delicious. Fish are highly perishable. They must be served fresh, or cooked, canned, or frozen when caught. Smoking, marinating, drying, or pickling are other preserving methods.

Meat

Methods of Cooking   *Roasting*—a dry heating process, the meat is seasoned and combined with cut bones and liquid. As a basic formula, dark meat should be pink inside, white meat should be well done. Constant basting gives the best results. Meat roasted on a spit over a direct flame can be marinated or brushed with butter or liquid.
Grilling—portions of meat, seasoned, and grilled in oil or clarified butter.
Braising—meat seasoned and sauteed on all sides in hot oil. Combined with vegetables, tomato puree, wine, bouquet garni, and stock, and covered. After completion of cooking, the sauce should be bound with starch.
Boiling—dark meat is cooked in water. Halfway through the cooking process, add aromates. White meat should be cooked in stock to prevent flavor loss.

Dark meats are beef, lamb, mutton, and game; white meats are veal, pork, and poultry.

Poultry

Chicken, duckling, turkey, goose, quail, squab, and guinea fowl are the most common poultry.

Methods of Cooking   *Roasting*—same as for meat. Young birds should have the breast and the legs wrapped in lard.
Poaching—rub breast with lemon to keep it white during the cooking process.
Braising—Cover breast part with lard, to prevent drying out.
Boiling—poultry should be cooked in white stock to keep the flavor.
Sauteing—with larger birds, saute legs first, then the front parts.

Game

Wild boar, pheasant, wild guinea fowl, hare, partridge, rabbit, woodcock, venison, deer, and bear are all game.
Tenderizing game can be done by hanging it up for several days or up to several weeks. It can also be marinated for several days. The basic methods of roasting, braising, sauteing, grilling, frying, or boiling are the same as for meat. Fruit is the premier accompaniment with game dishes. Larding the different parts keeps the meat juicy.

Fish and Shellfish

Kama Boko Classic
Fish Cakes Garni

INGREDIENTS	For 4	For 24
tuna flakes	1 lb., 8 oz.	9 lb.
fresh breadcrumbs	1 cup	2 qt.
eggs	2	8
onions, finely chopped	½	3
sugar	dash	1 tbsp.
pepper	dash	½ tsp.

Combine all ingredients. Shape into 3-oz. cakes, and fry at 350° F. till golden brown. Serve two per portion. Garnish with cauliflower and marinated beets. See Color Plate 3.

Brazilian Lagosta Cocktail

INGREDIENTS	For 6	For 12
lobster	1 1½-lb.	2 1½-lb.
celery, chopped	1 cup	2 cups
dill, chopped	¼ tsp.	½ tsp.
lemon juice	2 tsp.	1½ tbsp.
vinegar	1 tsp.	1 tbsp.
olive oil	1 tsp.	1 tbsp.
white pepper, ground	dash	to taste
lettuce leaves	12	24
tomatoes, cut in wedges	2	4

Boil lobster with seaweed in lightly salted water. Chill, remove meat, and cut into chunks. Mix with celery, dill, lemon juice, vinegar, olive oil, and pepper, and marinate. Place lettuce leaves in cocktail glasses with crushed ice. Place marinated lobster meat on top with tomato wedge. See Color Plate 1.

Salmon Belvedere

In court bouillon poach an 8 lb. salmon, filled with lobster mousse. Decorate with cucumber slices and pimiento. Garnish with lemon, stuffed eggs, lobster claws, herring, avocados, aspic, and parsley. See Color Plate 6.

Court Bouillon
2 lb. fish bones, 2 gal. water, ½ cup white vinegar, 1 carrot, sliced, 2 onions, finely sliced, 1 stalk celery, chopped, 1 bouquet garni, simmered for two hours and strained.

Lobster Mousse
3 lb. of lobster meat, finely ground, combined with 4 egg whites, ¼ cup of heavy cream, salt, and ground white pepper.

Les Tresors de la Mer
The Treasure of the Sea

INGREDIENTS

3 Alaska king crabs

water, to boil

1 large bouquet garni

salt and pepper, to taste

½ cup shallots

2 oz. butter

1 cup white wine

2 tsp. soy sauce

3 cups aspic

1 tsp. chervil

1 cup mayonnaise

12 barquettes

6 scampi

12 shrimp

3 soft-shell crabs

6 truffles for decoration

6 lb. butter shortening for decoration

Cover Alaska king crabs with boiling water. Add bouquet garni and salt. Simmer for 25 minutes, remove, and chill. From one crab, remove meat and save best parts for decoration. Chop all remaining meat finely. Saute shallots in butter. Add white wine and reduce to half. Cool, and add soy sauce, ½ cup aspic, chervil, and pepper. Mix with chopped crab meat and mayonnaise. Fill barquettes and set aside. Boil scampi, shrimp, and soft-shell crabs in same stock. Remove and chill. Cut shrimp lengthwise and clean. Place truffle decoration on barquettes, with shrimp on top. Arrange scampi with soft-shell crabs. Decorate and cover all items with aspic and chill. On top of a socle, form a rock-shaped shortening piece. Place two king crabs on top pointing to each other. Place entire piece on a mirror. Arrange remaining decorated hors d'oeuvre accordingly.

Lachs—Rosa—Lachs Classic

INGREDIENTS	For 1	For 12
6-oz. salmon fillet	1	12
butter	1 tbsp.	½ cup
white wine	½ cup	2 cups
vegetable juice	½ cup	2 cups
juice of lemon	½	2
bay leaf	1	3
white pepper, ground	to taste	½ tsp.
Sauce		
egg yolks	2	10
stock	1 tsp.	5 tbsp.
clarified butter	¼ cup	2 cups

Brush salmon with butter. Place in 350° F. oven for 10 minutes. Add wine, vegetable juice, lemon juice, bay leaf, and pepper. Bake for 20 minutes. Remove salmon. Bring stock to a boil, reduce to half, and strain. Mix egg yolks with stock. Whip over double boiler till creamy. Whip till cool. Slowly add clarified butter, whipping constantly.

To arrange, place salmon on serving platter. Pour sauce over. Garnish with dill and lemon.

Fillet of Sole La Mer

INGREDIENTS   YIELD: 24 servings

1 onion, diced small

2 green peppers, diced small

2 tbsp. butter

3 tbsp. curry powder

2 cups crushed pineapple

½ lb. cooked shrimp, diced

2 bananas, diced small

1 cup vegetable bouillon

24 sole fillets

1 cup breadcrumbs

salt to taste

2 pt. strawberries

72 pineapple rings

Saute onion and green pepper in butter until transparent. Add curry and blend well. Add pineapple, shrimp, and banana. Add boiling vegetable bouillon, and return mixture to simmer. Add breadcrumbs until mixture thickens. Lightly salt fillets. Place one tbsp. of stuffing in center of each fillet and neatly roll up fillet. Place on greased baking sheet and bake for 10 to 15 minutes in 350° F. oven. Wash strawberries and puree in liquidizer. Drain pineapple rings. When fish is cooked, arrange on bed of pineapple rings. Top with hot strawberry puree before serving.

Florida Red Snapper Classic

INGREDIENTS	For 4	For 24
6-oz. red snapper fillet	4	24
fish stock	½ cup	3 cups
white wine	½ cup	3 cups
salt and white pepper, ground	to taste	to taste
onions, sliced	2	10
carrots, julienne	1 cup	6 cups
celery, sliced	½ cup	3 cups
tomatoes, peeled and diced	2	12
juice of garlic	1 clove	6 cloves
butter	2 oz.	12 oz.

Place fillets in fish stock with wine and seasonings. Simmer for 15 minutes. Saute onions, carrots, celery, tomatoes, and garlic juice in butter. Add to stock and simmer for 15 more minutes. Serve in stock.

Dover Sole Queen Anne

INGREDIENTS	For 4	For 24
English Dover sole	4	24
salt and white pepper, ground	to taste	to taste
juice of garlic	1 clove	3 cloves
flour	1 cup	1 lb.
butter, clarified	4 oz.	2 cups
egg yolks	3	12

Season Dover sole and sprinkle with garlic juice. Dredge in flour and saute in butter till golden brown on each side. Whip egg yolks and wine over double boiler till firm. Add pistachios and season. Arrange sole on serving platter and garnish with fresh mint leaves. Serve sauce separately.

(Cont.)

white wine	1½ cups	2 qt., 1 cup
pistachios, chopped	2 tbsp.	4 tbsp.
mint leaves	for garnish	for garnish

Truite Sonja
Stuffed Trout Sonja

INGREDIENTS   YIELD: 2 servings

2 tsp. shallots, chopped

6 oz. butter

1 celery stalk, cut finely

10 mushrooms, cut finely

2 tbsp. flour

1 egg yolk, beaten well with ⅛ cup heavy cream

10 cooked shrimp, chopped finely

1 truffle, cut finely

juice of ½ lemon

salt and white pepper, ground, to taste

pinch of thyme

2 trout, ready to cook

1½ cups ruby porto wine

⅛ cup heavy cream

3 tsp. capers

1 tsp. parsley, chopped

To prepare stuffing, saute shallots in 3 oz. butter. Add celery and mushrooms, and simmer for 5 minutes. Add flour, stirring constantly. Add egg yolk beaten with heavy cream. Bring to a boil. Add shrimp, and truffle, stirring constantly. Add lemon juice and season. Stuff the trout, and place in buttered casserole. Add wine and bake in oven at 375° F. for 25 to 30 minutes, covered. Add cream. Brown 3 oz. butter, saute capers lightly, and pour over trout.

Serve trout in oval casserole garnished with chopped parsley, and surround with Potatoes Olivette and Tomato Clarmart.

Soft-Shell Crabs Meunier

INGREDIENTS   YIELD: 4 servings

8 medium soft-shell crabs

flour

6 oz. butter

2 cloves garlic, finely chopped

3 tsp. parsley, chopped

juice of 4 lemons

¼ cup chablis wine

black pepper, freshly ground, to taste

Clean crabs and remove tails and sides. Wash and dip in flour on each side. Saute crabs in butter till golden brown. Add garlic, parsley, and lemon juice. Add chablis and pepper, and simmer for 6 to 8 minutes, depending on size.

Place crabs on a silver platter. Pour sauce over and serve with Parisienne potatoes.

Fruits de Mer Assortis Flambes au Pernod
Assorted Seafood Flambe With Pernod

INGREDIENTS   YIELD: 2 to 3 servings

8 oz. Alaska king crab meat

8 oz. bay scallops

8 oz. shrimp, peeled and deveined

1 tsp. shallots, finely chopped

2 oz. butter

1 tsp. flour

1 jigger cognac

½ cup pernod

nutmeg to taste

salt and white pepper, ground, to taste

⅛ cup heavy cream

Cut crab meat into large chunks. Mix with scallops and shrimp, drain, and set aside. Saute shallots in 1 oz. butter but do not brown. Add seafood and simmer for 15 minutes over low heat. Melt remaining butter and mix in flour. Set aside. Add cognac to seafood and ignite. Add pernod, mix in flour, and simmer for 10 minutes. Add seasoning and stir in heavy cream. Serve with saffron rice. Garnish with parsley sprigs.

Alaskan King Crab Chandalar

INGREDIENTS   YIELD: 6 servings

1 cup mayonnaise

¼ cup sherry

juice of ½ lemon

1 tbsp. parsley, chopped

1 tbsp. dill, chopped

2 tbsp. red pimiento, diced

2 tbsp. capers, chopped

salt and white pepper, ground, to taste

1 cup fresh whipped cream

16 oz. Alaskan king crab, cut in ½-inch cubes

12 lettuce leaves

3 avocados, peeled and cut in half

6 dill sprigs, for garnish

6 ripe olives, for garnish

6 lemon wedges, for garnish

Sauce Chandalar
Mix mayonnaise, sherry, lemon juice, parsley, dill, pimiento, capers, seasonings, and whipped cream.

To arrange, mix ⅓ of the sauce with king crab. On each plate, place two lettuce leaves and ½ avocado, filled with crab meat mixture. Pour sauce chandalar over stuffed avocado. Put dill sprig on top, and olive and lemon wedge on the side.

Flaming Eel Brochette Classic

INGREDIENTS   YIELD: 10 servings

3 to 3½ lb. fresh eel, cut in portions and skinned

paprika to taste

curry powder to taste

4 oz. oil

Rub eel portions with paprika and curry powder. Brush with oil and arrange on skewer with mushrooms, peppers, tomatoes, and peaches. Place eel pieces alternately. Marinate in lemon juice for 15 minutes. Grill for 8 to 10 minutes. Brush with butter. Place on silver platter, pour sherry over, and ignite. Serve flaming. Garnish with curried rice and dill.

(Cont.)

20 mushrooms

10 red peppers, quartered

20 cherry tomatoes

20 peach halves

juice of 4 lemons

¼ cup butter, clarified

6 oz. sherry

4 cups curried rice

dill sprigs, for garnish

Meat

Tsugaru Classic
Pork and Apple Cakes

INGREDIENTS	For 4	For 24
ground pork	1 lb., 8 oz.	9 lb.
apples, chopped	1	6
eggs	1	5
onions, finely chopped	1 tbsp.	½ cup
oregano	dash	1 tsp.
salt and pepper mixture	to taste	2 tbsp.

Combine all ingredients. Shape into 3-oz. cakes, and grill over medium heat. Serve two per portion, with fluffy rice, sprinkled with chopped parsley. Accompany with hot mustard sauce. See Color Plate 3.

Pork Chop Classic

INGREDIENTS   YIELD: 10 servings

20 5-oz. pork chops, bone in

salt to taste

black pepper, freshly ground, to taste

flour

6 oz. butter

paprika to taste

4 oz. brandy

2 cups heavy cream

4 carrots, cut thinly in julienne

2 stems leeks, finely sliced

Trim excess fat from chops and season with salt and pepper. Dip in flour on one side. Saute on floured side, in 3 oz. butter, for 6 minutes until brown. Turn and brown for 6 more minutes. Sprinkle with paprika. Pour brandy over and ignite. Add heavy cream and simmer for 5 more minutes. In separate sauce pan, saute carrots in remaining butter for 5 minutes. Add leeks and stir fry for several minutes. Arrange pork chops on serving platter. Divide vegetables on top of each, and pour sauce over. Garnish with risotto.

Flaming Steak Zermatt

INGREDIENTS   YIELD: 4 servings

4 4-oz. steak fillets, trimmed

salt and black pepper, freshly ground, to taste

2 oz. butter

1 onion, sliced

2 red peppers, quartered

2 green peppers, quartered

10 mushrooms, sliced

3 green olives, sliced

4 oz. brandy

1 cup heavy cream

8 oz. herb butter

Season fillets and saute in hot butter 4 minutes on each side. Remove. Add onions, red pepper, green pepper, mushrooms, and green olives. Saute for 4 minutes. Return fillets, pour brandy over, and ignite. Add heavy cream. Place skewer next to each fillet, and top each fillet with 2 oz. herb butter. See Color Plate 7.

Skewer

Place lemon half, pickled onions, black and green olives, stuffed olives, baby corn, large gherkins, raw mushrooms, and potato crisp on skewer.

Herb Butter

Mix chopped chives and a dash of paprika with salted butter.

Entrecote Mirabelle

INGREDIENTS   YIELD: 6 servings

6 16-oz. sirloin steaks

salt to taste

2 tbsp. green peppercorns, in brine

4 tbsp. olive oil

6 lamb kidneys

juice of 4 garlic cloves

½ cup madeira

1 tsp. truffles, chopped

6 tbsp. heavy cream

watercress, for garnish

Rub steaks with salt and press green peppercorns into each steak. Saute in oil for 3 minutes on each side. Remove. Slice lamb kidneys very thin. Saute in same oil for several minutes. Add garlic juice, madeira, and truffles, and bring to a boil. Add heavy cream and pour over steaks. Garnish with watercress.

Fillet Mignon Classic

INGREDIENTS   YIELD: 10 to 12 servings

15 strips of lard

6-lb. whole fillet mignon, trimmed

salt to taste

black pepper, freshly ground, to taste

3 tbsp. olive oil

2 cups demi glaze

½ cup shallots, finely chopped

½ cup red wine

20 morels, soaked

½ cup heavy cream

½ tsp. cornstarch

Insert strips of lard in whole fillet. Rub with salt and pepper, and brush with olive oil. Place in 400° F. oven. Roast for 25 minutes and remove. Place demi glaze in saute pan. Add shallots and saute until golden brown. Add red wine and morels, and simmer for 10 minutes. Add heavy cream mixed with cornstarch. Bring to a boil and simmer for 5 minutes. Pour over fillet mignon on serving platter.

Fillet a la Dutch
Fillet Mignon Holland Style

INGREDIENTS   YIELD: 6 servings

2 oz. butter

½ cup green peppers, sliced

½ cup mushrooms, sliced

½ cup onions, sliced

3 medium tomatoes, peeled and cut into small pieces

½ cup red wine

1½ cups demi glaze (brown sauce)

3 lb. fillet mignon, cut into 2-inch strips

black pepper, freshly ground, to taste

salt to taste

In 1 oz. butter, saute green peppers, mushrooms, onions, and tomatoes for 10 minutes. Add red wine and simmer for 5 minutes. Add demi glaze, bring to a boil, and set aside. Heat remaining butter. Add sliced fillet mignon and brown over very hot flame for 3 minutes, keeping it on the rare side. Add sauce and bring to boil. Season and serve immediately.

On a large platter, arrange a ring of rice with chopped parsley. Place sliced fillet with sauce in center. Arrange 6 sliced peaches, with watercress, on outside of ring.

Renaissance Classic
Roast Rack of Veal, Bouquetere

INGREDIENTS	For 20	For 40
rack of veal	single, 10 lb.	double, 20 lb.
butter	4 oz.	6 oz.
veal bones	1 lb.	2 lb.
celery, diced	1 cup	2 cups
carrots, diced	2	3
onions, diced	2	4
white wine	1 cup	2 cups
glace de viand	½ gal.	1 gal.
sea salt and pepper	to taste	to taste

Cut all excess trimmings from rack of veal. Season and brush with butter. Roast veal bones till golden brown. Add vegetables and rack of veal, and roast for 30 minutes. Add white wine and roast 10 minutes more. Add glace de viand and, glazing occasionally, roast till golden brown (for 1 hour). Remove rack, strain sauce, and season. Arrange a bouquetere of spring vegetables consisting of white radishes, carrots, tomatoes, sauteed mushrooms, and new potatoes, roasted. Place rack in center of silver platter with watercress and bouquetere of vegetables, brushed with butter. Serve sauce on the side.

Escalope de Veau Classic

INGREDIENTS	For 4	For 24
nature part veal, 5-oz. cutlets	4	24
flour	4 oz.	½ lb.
butter, clarified	4 oz.	1 lb.
mushrooms, sliced	8 oz.	3 lb.
juice of lemon	1	4
parsley, chopped	1 tsp.	½ cup
salt and pepper	to taste	to taste

Season cutlets, dredge in flour, and saute in butter. Remove. Add fresh mushrooms and saute for 5 minutes. Add lemon juice. Pour over cutlets, and sprinkle with chopped parsley. Serve with risotto. Garnish with parsley sprig.

Veal Steak Gourmet

INGREDIENTS   YIELD: 4 servings

4 6-oz. veal steaks
salt and pepper, to taste
2 oz. butter
2 apples, cored and cut in half
4 prunes
2 tbsp. cognac
8 oz. demi glaze
1 cup heavy cream
juice of 1 lemon
dash of sugar
½ cup peanuts
4 stuffed olives

Season veal steaks. Saute in butter until brown. Add apples topped with prunes. Cover and let simmer for 5 minutes. Flame with cognac. Remove steaks and apples. Add demi glaze, heavy cream, lemon juice, and sugar. Bring to a boil. Add steaks and apples. Cover with peanuts and olives, and glaze with sauce.

Veal Orloff Classic

INGREDIENTS	For 2	For 20
5-oz. medaillons of veal	2	20
salt	to taste	to taste
white pepper, ground	to taste	to taste
butter	2 tsp.	½ lb.
onions, finely chopped	1	5
mushrooms, diced	5	1 lb.
sauce mornay	4 oz.	5½ cups
truffle slices	4	40
demi glaze	2 oz.	3 cups
madeira	1 oz.	½ cup
mint leaves	2 sprigs	to garnish

Saute seasoned veal medaillons in butter on each side. Remove, place on serving dish, and keep warm. In same pan, saute onions and mushrooms till glazed. Strain, and divide among tops of medaillons. Cover with sauce mornay and glaze under grill. Top with truffle slice. Bring demi glaze with madeira to a boil, and surround each medaillon with madeira sauce. Separate and garnish with mint leaf.

Veal Marsala Classic

INGREDIENTS   YIELD: 4 servings

4 5-oz. veal cutlets, pounded
white pepper, ground, to taste
salt to taste
4 oz. butter
1 lb. fresh mushrooms, sliced
basil to taste
oregano to taste
1 cup marsala

Saute seasoned veal cutlets in butter on both sides, until golden brown. Remove. Add sliced mushrooms and saute for several minutes. Add basil, oregano, and marsala. Return veal cutlets to pan and simmer for several minutes more.

Veal Shank Classic

INGREDIENTS   YIELD: 4 to 6 servings

4 5-lb. veal shanks
salt to taste
black pepper, freshly ground, to taste
4 oz. butter
½ cup shallots, finely chopped
1 cup veal stock
4 oz. brandy

Season veal shanks. Place in roasting pan with butter and shallots. Roast for ½ hour, pour over veal stock. Continue roasting for 1½ hours more, turning and basting occasionally. Remove and strain stock. Slice veal shanks and put on serving platter. Pour sauce over, add brandy, and ignite. Serve flaming.

Wiener Schnitzel

INGREDIENTS	For 4	For 20
5-oz. veal cutlets	4	20
salt	to taste	to taste
white pepper, ground	to taste	to taste
flour	1 cup	3 cups
milk	2 oz.	1 cup
eggs	2	6
breadcrumbs	1 cup	3 cups
butter, clarified	5 oz.	3 lb.

Season cutlets with salt and pepper. Dip in flour, milk and egg mixture, and breadcrumbs. Saute in butter, on both sides, till golden brown. Garnish with 2 lemon slices each and parsley sprig.

Rack of Lamb Chanterelle

INGREDIENTS   YIELD: 4 to 6 servings

2 whole racks of lamb, oven-prepared by butcher
salt to taste
black pepper, crushed, to taste
6 cloves garlic, finely chopped
bones from rack
2 shots cognac
3 cups demi glaze (brown sauce)
⅓ cup heavy cream
8 oz. butter
4 tsp. parsley, chopped
¾ cup breadcrumbs
¼ cup shallots, finely chopped
12 oz. chanterelles
¼ cup chablis

Scrub racks with salt, pepper, and some garlic. Place in casserole in 350° F. oven. Surround with bones and roast for 25 minutes. Take racks out. Strain off fat. Add cognac to bones and ignite. Add demi glaze and simmer for 10 minutes. Add heavy cream and strain. Melt 4 oz. butter, and add garlic and 3 tsp. parsley. Stir over low heat for 3 minutes. Add breadcrumbs and mix well. Take breadcrumb mixture and cover tops of racks of lamb. Bake at 375° F. for 10 more minutes. Set aside till serving time. Saute chopped shallots in 4 oz. butter. Add chanterelles and saute 5 minutes. Add chablis and simmer for 5 more minutes. Add remaining parsley.

Place racks in center of large silver platter. Surround with chanterelles and potatoes a la Parisienne. Use broiled tomato for garnish.

Crown of Lamb Lincoln

INGREDIENTS   YIELD: 8 to 10 servings

⅓ cup brown sugar

1½ onions, finely chopped

2 cups fresh cranberries

6 tbsp. water

juice of lemon

1 double rack of lamb, oven-prepared by butcher

salt and black pepper, freshly ground, to taste

2 tsp. rosemary

¾ cup dry gin

2 cups demi glaze

Stir sugar in heavy casserole till golden brown. Stir in onions, cranberries, water, and lemon juice. Simmer for 20 minutes and strain. Make crown by turning backs of racks together. Tie with string, and rub in salt, pepper, and rosemary. Roast for 25 to 30 minutes at 425° F., medium to rare. Baste roast with cranberry mixture. Pour gin over, and ignite. Add demi glaze. Remove racks and simmer for 5 minutes. Remove string from rack, place on a serving platter, and strain some sauce over meat.

Place Wild Rice Chablisienne in center of racks surrounded by kumquats and watercress. Serve remaining sauce separately.

Leg of Baby Lamb Classic

INGREDIENTS   YIELD: 14 to 18 servings

5 to 6 lb. leg of baby lamb

20 strips pork fat, ¼ × 2 inches

1 tbsp. juniper berries

salt to taste

1 tsp. black pepper, freshly ground

½ cup buttermilk

3 tbsp. soy sauce

4 tbsp. brandy

½ cup red wine

Skin the leg and lard with pork strips inserted around the leg. Press juniper berries around in the meat, and rub with salt and pepper. Brush with buttermilk mixed with soy sauce. Marinate for one hour. Place on a spit and roast for 30 minutes. Mix brandy, red wine, and buttermilk drippings, and brush while roasting. Serve with oven-roasted potatoes.

Braised Lamb Shanks Andrew Jackson

INGREDIENTS   YIELD: 8 servings

2 lamb shanks

salt to taste

black pepper, freshly ground, to taste

4 oz. butter

4 large onions, sliced thin

8 mushrooms, sliced

1 cup white wine (chablis)

juice of 5 garlic cloves

1 tsp. tarragon leaves

4 tbsp. tomato paste

3 cups water

4 tbsp. cornstarch

Season lamb shanks with salt and pepper. Place in roasting pan with melted butter. Roast on each side for 10 minutes. Add onions and mushrooms and brown. Add white wine, garlic juice, tarragon leaves, and tomato paste, and bring to a boil. Add water and simmer for 35 to 45 minutes till shanks are tender. Mix cornstarch with small amount of cold water. Add to liquid and simmer for 5 more minutes. Add salt and pepper, to taste.

Arrange lamb shanks on a silver platter. Serve wild rice, packed in a cup, and turned over to stand up. Surround with sliced peaches and parsley sprigs.

Poultry

Szechuan Chicken Classic

INGREDIENTS	For 4	For 24
salt and pepper mixture	to taste	to taste
chickens, quartered	2	12
soy sauce	2 tbsp.	1 cup
sesame oil	2 tbsp.	¼ cup
ginger	dash	1 tsp.
pineapple, crushed	½ cup	2 cups
coconut, shredded	2 tbsp.	1 cup

Season chicken pieces. Rub with soy sauce, sesame oil, and ginger. Bake at 350° F. for 45 minutes. Heat pineapple in its juice with shredded coconut. Pour over chicken. Serve with white rice. Garnish with carrot curls and parsley. See Color Plate 3.

India Chicken Classic

INGREDIENTS	For 4	For 24
chicken, quartered	1	6
flour	3 oz.	2½ cups
salt and pepper mixture	½ tsp.	1½ tbsp.
butter, clarified	4 oz.	1½ cups
tomato, cut in wedges	1	6
curry sauce	1 cup	2½ qt.

Coat chicken with flour, salt, and pepper. Brush with butter, place in 375° F. oven, bake for 45 minutes. Remove and arrange with sauteed tomato wedges. Pour curry sauce over. Serve with condiment and relish trays. The relish tray should contain pineapple chunks with cream cheese, fresh orange and grapefruit sections soaked in Kirsch, sliced marinated pickle with curry powder, peas and celery salad, sliced cherry tomato, and Boston baked beans. Condiments to serve are shredded coconut, chutney, blanched peanuts, raisins, and chopped cucumbers. See Color Plate 2.

Canja
Brazilian Rice Soup

INGREDIENTS	For 12	For 48
onions, finely chopped	½	2
butter	1 oz.	3 oz.
chicken stock or water	2 qt.	1½ gal.
chicken meat, diced	8 oz.	4 lb.
ham, diced	4 oz.	1 lb.
rice, cooked	½ cup	4 cups
tomato, peeled and diced	1	4
white wine	4 oz.	1 cup
carrots, diced	1	4

Saute onions in butter for several minutes. Add chicken stock or water, and chicken meat. Bring to a boil and simmer for 30 minutes. Add remaining ingredients and simmer for 20 minutes more. Season, and sprinkle with chopped chives. See Color Plate 1.

(Cont.)

pepper	to taste	¼ tsp.
ginger	to taste	⅛ tsp.
salt	to taste	to taste
chives, chopped	1 tsp.	4 tbsp.

Rock Cornish Hen Shenandoah

INGREDIENTS   YIELD: 6 servings

6 cornish hens

salt to taste

white pepper, ground, to taste

1 cup wild rice stuffing

3 oz. butter

1 cup shallots, finely chopped

2 tbsp. currant jelly

4 cups port wine

zest from one orange

1 oz. brandy

½ cup heavy cream

1 tsp. cornstarch

Season cornish hens with salt and pepper. Stuff with wild rice stuffing. Tie legs with string. Brown in butter on each side over medium heat. Place in 350° F. oven. Roast for 20 minutes.

Remove hens and discard string. Add shallots and simmer for 3 minutes. Add currant jelly and port wine. Reduce half over medium heat.

Strain sauce. Add orange zest. Pour brandy over and ignite. Stir in heavy cream mixed with cornstarch. Place hens on serving platter and pour sauce over.

Garnish with mushrooms stuffed with peas, carrots, and turnips.

Wild Rice Stuffing

INGREDIENTS   YIELD: 6 servings

½ cup onions, finely diced

3 oz. butter

1 cup wild rice

salt to taste

black pepper, freshly ground, to taste

3 cups water

¼ cup sherry

3 cups white wine

¼ cup red pimiento, finely diced

Saute onions in butter. Add rice, seasoning, and water, and simmer for 35 minutes. Add sherry, white wine, and pimiento. Simmer over low heat for 40 minutes, until tender.

Coquille de Volaille, Baron Van Brisse

Breast of Chicken in Shell, for the Gourmet

INGREDIENTS   YIELD: 4 servings

4 chicken breasts, boned and skinned

1 cup cream sherry

1 cup Austrian white wine

4 tsp. butter

½ cup shallots, diced

1 cup mushrooms, diced

(Cont.)

Cook chicken breasts in sherry and white wine over low heat for about 25 minutes. Remove chicken and dice ½-inch thick. In 2 tsp. butter, saute shallots, mushrooms, and celery for 10 minutes over low heat. Set aside. Melt remaining butter in heavy skillet. Stir in flour and whip in stock from chicken. Add seasoning, parmesan cheese, and heavy cream. Simmer for 10 minutes and strain. Add vegetables, and chicken, and fill eight 5-inch shells. Sprinkle with additional parmesan cheese and gratinate under salamander. Sprinkle with chopped parsley.

1 cup celery, diced

4 tbsp. flour

white pepper, ground, to taste

salt

parsley, chopped, to taste

½ cup parmesan cheese

1 cup heavy cream

Supreme de Volaille Tuscany
Boneless Breast of Chicken With Leaf Spinach

INGREDIENTS   YIELD: 4 servings

4 chicken breasts, skinned and boned

4 tsp. butter

¼ cup flour

3 cups milk (hot)

nutmeg to taste

salt to taste

white pepper, ground, to taste

4 cups leaf spinach, blanched in boiling
   water

1 cup parmesan cheese

Saute chicken in 2 tsp. butter over low heat until tender, for about 25 minutes. In heavy skillet, melt 2 tsp. butter and stir in flour (do not brown). Whip in hot milk and bring to a boil. Add seasoning and parmesan cheese, and simmer for 15 minutes. Strain. Place leaf spinach, with chicken breast on top, in an oven-proof dish. Strain sauce over. Sprinkle with parmesan cheese and gratinate under salamander.

Bavarian Chicken Classic

INGREDIENTS	For 4	For 20
onion, diced	1 medium	5 medium
green peppers, diced	1	5
butter	4 oz.	¼ lb.
croutons	1 cup	5 cups
whole eggs	3	12
milk	½ cup	2 cups
parmesan cheese	2 tbsp.	6 tbsp.
basil	1 tsp.	5 tsp.
salt and pepper	to taste	to taste
paprika	1 tsp.	5 tsp.
chicken, 2½ lb.	2	10
oil	to brush	to brush

Saute onions and peppers in butter and remove. Add to croutons, egg and milk mixture, parmesan, basil, salt, and pepper. Stuff each chicken with the mixture and tie legs. Rub paprika on the outside of chickens. Season with salt and brush with oil. Roast at 375° F. for 1½ hours, or until done. Serve with lingonberries on the side.

Hainanese Kaifan Chicken

INGREDIENTS   YIELD: 4 servings

4 lb. chicken, chopped

1 oz. green ginger, shredded

1 oz. garlic, chopped

1 oz. fresh Chinese parsley

salt to taste

water

2 oz. pickled cabbage, sliced

12 lettuce leaves, shredded

Rice

1 oz. onion, chopped

1 oz. garlic, chopped

2 oz. chicken fat

2 cups Siam rice

ginger to taste

1½ pt. chicken stock

Saute onions and garlic in chicken fat. Add rice, ginger, and chicken stock. Bring to a boil and bake at 350° F. for 50 minutes.

Combine chicken pieces with green ginger, garlic, parsley, and salt. Cover with water. Bring to a boil and simmer for 45 minutes. Strain and save juice.

Place pickled cabbage and lettuce on a platter. Top with chicken pieces and sprinkle with parsley. Place juice in bowl, and rice and ginger next to it. Serve with soy sauce.

Duckling Singapore

Duck Stuffed With Lotus Seeds

INGREDIENTS   YIELD: 2 servings

1 duckling, 2½ lb.

sea salt to taste

vegetable oil

4 oz. black mushrooms

3 oz. raw pork, chopped

6 oz. lotus seeds

1 oz. green ginger, shredded

3 oz. spring onions, chopped

4 chix egg yolks (preserved)

5 oz. soy sauce

salt and pepper to taste

1 tbsp. sugar

1 oz. sesame oil

MSG to taste

10 oz. green Chinese vegetable (boiled and seasoned)

Wash duck, remove bones, and dry in towel. Rub with sea salt and vegetable oil.

Chop mushrooms, pork, and lotus seeds, and mix with ginger, onions, and egg yolks. Add 3 oz. soy sauce, salt and pepper to taste. Fill duck with stuffing. Tie and roast for ½ hour at 375° F. Remove. Mix remaining soy sauce with sugar, sesame oil, and MSG. Rub into duckling and continue cooking until well done. Arrange with Chinese vegetable for garnish.

Game

Medaillons de Chevreuil Classic
Venison Medaillons Flambe

INGREDIENTS   YIELD: 4 servings

8 3-oz. venison medaillons

2 oz. butter

salt to taste

paprika to taste

1 oz. cognac

1 oz. gin

1 tsp. mustard

1 cup demi glaze

cayenne pepper to taste

½ cup heavy cream

8 pear halves

½ cup vermicelli puree

¼ tsp. truffles, finely chopped

Brown venison medaillons in butter on both sides. Season with salt and paprika. Flambe with cognac and gin. Add mustard and demi glaze, and bring to a boil. Add cayenne and heavy cream. Fill pear halves with vermicelli puree. Heat and place on top of medaillons. Cover with sauce.

NOTE   Vermicelli puree is made by grinding cooked vermicelli with some cream and truffles.

Rabbit Pot Pie Classic

INGREDIENTS   YIELD: 4 servings

2 lb. rabbit meat, boneless

4 oz. butter

2 onions, finely chopped

1 leek stalk, finely sliced

1 bay leaf

½ cup walnuts

1 cup white wine

½ lb. sausage, sliced

1 cup rice

2½ cups water

salt to taste

black pepper, freshly ground, to taste

Cut rabbit meat into portion sizes. Saute in butter until brown. Add onions, leeks, bay leaf, and remaining ingredients. Bring to a boil. Cover and bake at 350° F. for 45 minutes.

Ragout of Venison, Viennese Style, with Austrian Dumplings

INGREDIENTS   YIELD: 4 to 6 servings

2 lb. venison, shoulder or leg, cut in 1-inch squares

2 cups wine vinegar

1 clove garlic, crushed

1 bay leaf

4 juniper berries

5 cups water

juice of ½ lemon

½ tsp. salt

¼ tsp. black pepper, freshly ground

2 cups Austrian red wine

¼ cup celery, finely chopped

¼ cup onions, finely chopped

¼ cup carrots, finely chopped

1 oz. butter

2 tsp. all-purpose flour

2 tsp. sugar

1 cup applesauce

½ cup lingonberries

1 tsp. Worcestershire sauce

3 tsp. sour cream

Combine venison, vinegar, garlic, bay leaf, juniper berries, water, lemon juice, salt, pepper, 1 cup wine, celery, onions, and carrots. Marinate in cool place for 24 hours. Remove venison from pan and bring marinade to a boil. In a heavy skillet, heat butter and brown venison for a few minutes. Add flour, stir constantly, and add hot marinade. Add sugar, applesauce, lingonberries, and Worcestershire sauce. Cook for 20 minutes over low fire. Add sour cream and second cup of wine. Let simmer for 10 minutes or until tender. Remove meat from sauce, place in casserole, and strain sauce over meat. Serve with Austrian dumplings and some additional lingonberries on a side dish.

Austrian Dumplings

INGREDIENTS   YIELD: 4 servings

2 strips bacon, cut fine

½ cup onions, finely chopped

5 white rolls, diced ½-inch thick

2 eggs, beaten with milk

½ cup milk

1 tsp. parsley, finely chopped

½ tsp. salt

¼ tsp. black pepper, ground

½ cup all-purpose flour

1 gal. water with one tsp. of salt, to cook dumplings

Saute bacon with onions until golden brown. Mix cut rolls with eggs and milk, and soak for 2 minutes. Add bacon and onions, parsley, salt, pepper, and flour. Bring salted water to a boil. From the mixture, make four dumplings, squeeze them tightly, and put in boiling water. Cook for 12 minutes. Remove from fire and keep dumplings in water until served, but no longer than 30 minutes.

Fillet of Venison Forestiere

INGREDIENTS YIELD: 4 to 6 servings

4 to 6 venison fillets (or cuts from the saddle of venison)

3 oz. butter

5 shallots, finely chopped

1 cup red wine

2 cups demi glaze (brown sauce)

½ cup lingonberries

dash of thyme leaves

1 cup morels, soaked

salt to taste

white pepper, ground, to taste

1 slice of toast, per serving

2 slices of crisp bacon, per serving

fresh mint leaves to garnish

Saute venison in butter till light brown. Set aside. In same butter, saute shallots till golden brown. Add red wine and demi glaze, and bring to a boil. Add lingonberries and thyme, and cook for 10 minutes at low heat. Strain over venison. Add morels and seasoning, and simmer for 10 minutes.

Serve on toast with bacon. Cover with sauce. Serve with Austrian dumplings and garnish with fresh mint leaves, and serve extra lingonberries on a side dish.

Fillet of Venison Diane

INGREDIENTS YIELD: 4 to 6 servings

4 to 6 venison fillets (or cuts from saddle of venison)

3 oz. butter

½ cup aged brandy

2 cups demi glaze (brown sauce)

½ cup lingonberries

¼ cup heavy cream

nutmeg to taste

salt to taste

white pepper, ground, to taste

2 tsp. truffles, chopped

1 cup chestnut puree

Saute venison in butter till medium rare. Add brandy, and flambe. Add demi glaze and lingonberries. Bring to a boil and simmer for 5 minutes. Strain sauce, add heavy cream and seasoning, and simmer for 5 more minutes. Add truffles.

Place venison on a bed of chestnut puree. Cover with sauce. Serve with spaetzle and lingonberries.

Venison Steak Romanow

INGREDIENTS YIELD: 4 to 6 servings

6 shallots, finely chopped

3 oz. butter

¼ cup vodka

¼ cup port wine

2 cups demi glaze (brown sauce)

juice of ½ lemon

4 tsp. cranberry sauce

3 tsp. sour cream

salt to taste

black pepper, freshly ground, to taste

4 to 6 8-oz. venison steaks (cut from saddle of venison)

¼ cup red caviar

mint leaves for garnish

Saute shallots in 1 oz. butter till golden brown. Add vodka, port wine, and demi glaze, and bring to a boil. Simmer for 5 minutes. Add lemon juice, cranberry sauce, sour cream, and seasoning. Strain. Saute venison steaks in butter. Cover with sauce and simmer for 5 minutes. Just before serving, add red caviar.

Serve on a silver platter covered with sauce. Serve cranberry sauce with mint leaves on a side dish.

Pheasant Marquis

INGREDIENTS YIELD: 2 servings

1 pheasant

1 large slice lard

1 tsp. olive oil

¼ cup carrots, finely chopped

¼ cup celery, finely chopped

¼ cup onions, finely chopped

1 tsp. paprika

2 tsp. flour

¼ cup madeira

½ cup white wine

salt and white pepper, ground, to taste

½ oz. butter

1 jigger cognac

¾ cup heavy cream

1 tsp. truffles, chopped

Rub pheasant with salt and pepper. Cover breast with lard and tie on with string. Roast at 350° F. with olive oil, carrots, celery, and onions for one half hour. Remove lard so breast can brown for 10 minutes. Always pour roasting juice over pheasant while roasting. Remove pheasant. Add paprika and flour to roasting juice. Stir in madeira and white wine. Simmer for 10 minutes. Strain through a fine sieve, season, and bring to a boil. Cut pheasant in half, place in hot butter, and flambe with cognac. Pour sauce over and stir in heavy cream. Bring to a boil and add truffles.

Pheasant is served on a silver platter covered with sauce. A garniture of asparagus spears, with julienne of red pimiento to cover, is served on the side, with mushroom caps and risotto with green peas. Use mint leaves to garnish.

Roast Saddle of Venison
Chef Berger

INGREDIENTS   YIELD: 8 to 12 servings

10 to 12 lb. saddle of venison

1 lb. pork fat, cut into thin strips (about 25)

trimmings from the saddle

2 oz. butter

1 stalk celery, diced

1 carrot, diced

1 onion, diced

jigger of brandy

4 cups red wine

4 tbsp. sugar

1 cup lingonberries

juice of 1 lemon

3 cups demi glaze (brown sauce)

salt and black pepper, freshly ground, to taste

½ cup heavy cream

Saddle of Venison

Trim skin and cut saddle into 12-oz. portions, bone in. Use salt pork, cut in strips ¼ × 3 inches, to lard. Put two strips on each side. Marinate in red wine, wine vinegar, cut onions, carrots, and celery. Add whole black pepper, thyme leaves, bay leaves, whole cloves, and juniper berries. Cover and keep 48 hours in the refrigerator.

Roasting time is 20 to 25 minutes at 395° F. until medium rare. Cover with sauce venison. Serve with 4 oz. spaetzle and 2 oz. lingonberries on a side dish.

Trim and skin the saddle on each side. Make holes in the meat to put strips through approximately every inch. Set aside. Brown trimmings in butter. Add celery, carrots, and onions, and brown for 10 minutes. Add brandy and ignite. Add red wine, sugar, lingonberries, and lemon juice. Simmer for 10 minutes. Add demi glaze and seasoning. Simmer for 1 more hour. Strain through a fine sieve. Bring back to a boil and add heavy cream. Roast saddle for 35 to 45 minutes at 400° F. until medium rare. Add remaining juice to sauce.

On a large silver platter, arrange saddle of venison surrounded with a puree of chestnuts, carrots, potato dumplings, petit pois, and watercress. The sauce is served on the side. Lingonberries are served in a side dish.

Puree of Chestnuts

Use 20 freshly cooked or canned chestnuts. Squeeze through a fine sieve. Mix with 10 oz. butter and ½ cup heavy cream in pot over boiling water until heated. Season with salt and pepper.

Sauce Venison

INGREDIENTS   YIELD: 2½ gallons

6 lb. venison carcass
1 lb. butter
1 lb. carrots, diced ½ inch
1 lb. celery, diced ½ inch
1 lb. onions, diced ½ inch
1 oz. garlic, crushed
6 cups red burgundy wine
1 bay leaf
2 oz. juniper berries
3 qt. water
2 cups wine vinegar
3 cups applesauce
28 oz. lingonberries
1 lb. sugar
3 tsp. Worcestershire sauce
juice of 2 lemons
2 tsp. ginger, ground
1½ lb. all-purpose flour
2 cups sour cream
4 tsp. salt
2 tsp. black pepper, ground

Saute venison carcass in 3 oz. butter, with carrots, celery, onions, and garlic, until golden brown. Add red wine, bay leaves, and juniper berries. Cook for 5 minutes. Add water, vinegar, applesauce, lingonberries, sugar, Worcestershire sauce, lemon juice, and ginger. Cook for 45 minutes. Add roux from remaining butter and flour. Cook for 25 minutes. Add sour cream, season with salt and pepper, and strain through cheesecloth.

Spaetzle

INGREDIENTS   YIELD: 38 servings

3 lb. all-purpose flour
3 tsp. salt
1 tsp. nutmeg
1½ eggs, beaten well, with milk
4 cups milk
1 cup oil

Sift flour, salt, and nutmeg into a bowl. Add eggs mixed with milk gradually. Add oil and mix thoroughly.

For a small quantity scrape small pieces of dough off board with a sharp knife into boiling salted water. Boil 5 to 8 minutes. For a large quantity, press through pan with ½-inch holes. Remove from boiling water into cold water. Drain and saute in salted butter until light brown.

10. Sauces, Side Dishes, and Garnishes

Sauces are the glory of fine cuisine. Gastronomically, around the world, the styles of cooking with sauces reflect the native cuisines.

Sauces

Sauce Demi Glaze
Brown Base Fond

INGREDIENTS   YIELD: 5 gallons

11 lb. beef bones
11 lb. veal bones
1 lb. bacon trimmings
1 lb. carrots, chopped
1 lb. onions, chopped
1 lb. celery, chopped
3 cups tomato puree
15 gal. water
1 bouquet garni (parsley, thyme, bay leaf, peppercorns, garlic cloves)

Brown beef and veal bones with bacon trimmings. Add carrots, onions, and celery and cook till golden brown. Stir in tomato puree. Add water and bouquet garni, bring to a boil, and simmer for 5 hours, or until reduced to two thirds. Strain through fine sieve.

Sauce Espagnole

INGREDIENTS   YIELD: 4 gallons

30 oz. butter
35 oz. flour
5 gal. brown base fond

Melt butter, add flour, brown (roux-brun), and cool. Combine with hot brown base fond. Simmer for 2 hours.

Sauce Demi Glaze

INGREDIENTS   YIELD: 3 gallons

2 lb. beef trimmings and bones
3 oz. bacon trimmings
10 oz. onions, chopped
10 oz. carrots, chopped
1 cup tomato puree
1 bay leaf
1 tsp. peppercorns
2 pt. white wine
4 gal. sauce espagnole
salt to taste

Brown beef trimmings and bones in bacon trimmings. Add onions, carrots, tomato puree, and seasoning. Add white wine and cook for 15 minutes. Add sauce espagnole and simmer for 3 hours. Strain through cheesecloth. Salt to taste.

NOTE   The greater the reduction, the stronger the flavor.

Sauce Veloute
Basic White Sauce

INGREDIENTS   YIELD: 6 gallons

22 lb. veal bones

10 gal. water

1 lb. carrots, chopped

1 lb. onions, chopped

1 lb. celery, chopped

1 bouquet garni (bay leaf, parsley,
  peppercorns, juniper berries)

30 oz. butter

35 oz. flour

salt to taste

Bring veal bones in cold water to boil. Simmer for 2½ hours. Add carrots, onions, celery, and bouquet garni. Simmer for 2½ hours more and strain. Melt butter. Stir in flour (roux blanc), but do not brown. Add white stock, bring to boil, and simmer for ½ hour. Strain through cheesecloth. Salt to taste.

Sauce Poisson Blanc
White Fish Sauce

INGREDIENTS   YIELD: 1½ gallons

1½ gal. water

11 lb. fish bones

2¼ pt. white wine

juice of 1 lemon

2 onions, chopped

4 oz. carrots, chopped

4 oz. celery, chopped

1 bouquet garni (parsley, peppercorns,
  juniper berries, bay leaf)

14 oz. butter

14 oz. flour

dash of nutmeg

salt to taste

5 egg yolks

1 pt. heavy cream

Bring to boil cold water, fish bones, wine, lemon juice, onions, carrots, celery, and bouquet garni. Simmer for 45 minutes. Strain. Melt butter and add flour (roux blanc). Cool. Fill with fish stock. Simmer for one half hour. Strain through cheesecloth. Season with nutmeg and salt. Mix egg yolks with heavy cream. Whip into sauce. Strain. Salt to taste.

Sauce Poisson Rouge
Brown Fish Sauce

INGREDIENTS   YIELD: 1½ gallons

11 lb. fish bones

2 onions, chopped

4 oz. carrots, chopped

4 oz. celery, chopped

14 oz. butter

2¼ pt. red wine

juice of 1 lemon

1½ gal. water

Brown fish bones, onions, carrots, and celery in 2 oz. butter. Add red wine and lemon juice. Bring to boil. Add water and bouquet garni and simmer for 45 minutes. Strain. Melt remaining butter, add flour, brown, and cool. Add fish stock and simmer for 1 hour more. Strain through cheesecloth. Salt to taste.

(Cont.)

1 bouquet garni (parsley, peppercorns,
  juniper berries, bay leaf)

11 oz. butter

14 oz. flour

salt to taste

Sauce Gibier
Game Sauce

INGREDIENTS   YIELD: 1½ gallons

11 oz. bacon trimmings

11 lb. game bones and trimmings

2 onions, chopped

1 stalk celery, chopped

2 carrots, chopped

14 oz. butter

14 oz. flour

2¼ pt. red wine

1½ gal. water

1 bouquet garni (bay leaves, peppercorn,
  garlic cloves, juniper berries)

2 cups lingonberries

¼ cup sugar

juice of 2 lemons

salt to taste

Brown bacon trimmings, game bones, onions, celery, and carrots in butter. Stir in flour. Add red wine and bring to a boil. Add water and remaining ingredients. Simmer for 3 hours.

Sauce Bechamel
Creme Sauce

INGREDIENTS   YIELD: 2 gallons

2 onions, chopped

30 oz. butter

30 oz. flour

2 gal. milk

1 bouquet garni (bay leaf, peppercorns,
  whole cloves)

salt to taste

Saute onions in butter, stir in flour, and cool. Bring milk to a boil. Add roux blanc and bouquet garni. Simmer for ½ hour. Strain through cheesecloth. Salt to taste.

Sauce Tomate
Tomato Sauce

INGREDIENTS   YIELD: 24 servings

11 oz. bacon trimmings

2 lb. veal bones

3 onions, chopped

½ stalk celery, chopped

2 carrots, chopped

1 lb. fresh tomatoes, chopped

11 oz. butter

1 lb. flour

2 lb. tomato puree

5 stems parsley

2¼ pt. white wine

4 tbsp. sugar

juice of 2 lemons

1 bouquet garni (peppercorns, bay leaf,
  garlic cloves)

salt to taste

Saute bacon trimmings, veal bones, onions, celery, carrots, and tomatoes in butter till brown. Stir in flour, and add tomato puree and remaining ingredients. Bring to a boil and simmer for 1 hour. Strain. Salt to taste.

Sauce Supreme
Poultry Creme Sauce

INGREDIENTS

1 pt. heavy cream

4 oz. butter

juice of 1 lemon

dash nutmeg

Prepare as for Sauce Veloute using chicken bones in place of veal bones.

Add heavy cream and butter to strained Chicken Veloute. Finish with lemon juice. Add nutmeg.

Sauce Hollandaise
Whipped Butter Sauce

INGREDIENTS   YIELD: 6 to 8 servings

6 egg yolks

6 tbsp. water (or reduction)

1½ lb. clarified butter

juice of 1 lemon

cayenne to taste

salt to taste

Over double boiler, whip egg yolks with water (or strained reduction) till very creamy. Remove pot, whip, cool. Add clarified butter very slowly.

Reduction: Bring to boil 4 tbsp. vinegar, 5 tbsp. water, peppercorn, and 1 tsp. chopped onions. Reduce one third and cool.

NOTE   For vegetable dishes use water; for fish dishes use reduction.

Sauce Careme
Truffle Poultry Sauce

INGREDIENTS   YIELD: 4 servings

1 oz. brandy

1 tbsp. truffle, chopped

1 cup sauce supreme

Heat brandy, and ignite. Add truffle and sauce supreme. Bring to a boil.

Sauce Theresia
Cucumber Sauce

INGREDIENTS YIELD: 4 to 6 servings

1 onion, finely chopped

2 oz. butter

1 cucumber, peeled, cored, and diced

5 dill sprigs

1 bay leaf

1 cup sauce supreme

1 tsp. vinegar

dash sugar

Saute onion in butter. Add half the amount of cucumber and the dill sprig, bay leaf, and sauce supreme. Simmer for 20 minutes. Strain. Add vinegar, sugar, and remaining cucumber. Bring to a boil.

Sauce Vienna
Paprika Sauce

INGREDIENTS YIELD: 4 to 6 servings

2 onions, finely chopped

4 oz. butter

2 tbsp. paprika

3 oz. flour

1 cup chicken broth

1 tbsp. sour cream

salt to taste

white pepper, ground, to taste

Saute onions in butter. Stir in paprika. Add flour, and bring to a boil with chicken broth. Simmer for 20 minutes. Strain. Bring to a boil with sour cream. Season with salt and pepper.

Sauce Cumberland
Cranberry Sauce

INGREDIENTS YIELD: 6 to 8 servings

2 oranges

1 cup red wine

1 cup lingonberries

1 cup cranberries

1 cup madeira

juice of 1 lemon

1 tsp. dry mustard

1 tsp. Worcestershire sauce

10 whole cloves

Peel oranges and cut orange rinds thin in julienne. Bring ½ cup red wine and rind to a boil. Set aside. Bring remaining red wine, oranges, lingonberries, cranberries, madeira, and remaining ingredients to a boil and simmer for 1 hour. Strain and add julienne of orange. Cool.

Sauce Ambassadore

One cup sauce supreme with ½ cup finely diced chicken meat. Finish with 2 tbsp. heavy cream, dash nutmeg, and 1 tsp. butter.
  For fowl dishes.

Sauce Bearnaise

Five finely chopped shallots, 5 peppercorns, dash thyme, 1 bay leaf, 2 tbsp. vinegar, and ½ cup water, reduced and cooled. Strain and whip with 3 egg yolks, and 1 cup of clarified butter, as with hollandaise. Season with cayenne, chopped tarragon, and parsley.

For grilled meat and fish.

Sauce Bon Voyage

Five finely chopped shallots sauteed in 2 oz. butter. Add juice of 1 lemon, 2 tbsp. tomato sauce, and 2 tbsp. heavy cream. Strain. Mix with ½ cup white wine and julienne of 2 truffles.

For egg dishes, sauteed poultry, and vegetables.

Sauce Champagne Poulet

Five finely chopped shallots sauteed in 2 oz. butter. Add ½ cup white wine and 1 cup sauce supreme. Strain. Add ¼ cup champagne, 1 oz. cognac, 1 tsp. truffles, sliced, and 2 oz. butter.

For grilled poultry.

Sauce Barbecue

Saute 5 shallots in 2 oz. butter. Add ½ cup red wine, dash of rosemary, marjoram, 2 cloves crushed garlic, and 1 cup chili sauce. Finish with 1 cup of beef consomme, juice of 2 lemons, and 2 tbsp. mustard. Cool and brush meat or marinate.

For barbecued meat or chicken.

Sauce Bourguignonne

Five finely chopped shallots, 1 bay leaf, 3 juniper berries, 1 tbsp. parsley, 5 peppercorns, and 5 sliced mushrooms, sauteed in 2 oz. butter. Add 1 cup red wine, reduce, and mix with 1 cup demi glaze. Add pepper to taste.

For dark meat, chicken, and egg dishes.

Sauce Bordelaise

Five finely chopped shallots, 5 peppercorns, dash thyme, and 1 bay leaf simmered in 1 cup red wine. Mix with 1 cup demi glaze and strain. Add 2 tbsp. diced marrow.

For vegetables, and sauteed and roasted meat.

Sauce Bercy

Five finely chopped shallots sauteed in 2 oz. butter, cooked with ½ cup white wine mixed with ½ cup demi glaze. Season with pepper, finely chopped parsley, and diced marrow.

For roasts and grilled meat.

Sauce Berger

Five finely chopped shallots, sauteed with 2 cloves crushed garlic, ½ cup red wine, 1 cup demi glaze, 1 tsp. soy sauce, dash ginger, and 2 oz. sherry. Strain. Finish with 2 oz. butter.

For grilled meat, fowl, fish, or game.

COLOR PLATE 5. *Right:* Emince a la Fridolin (p. 25) and Rosti (p. 25). *Below:* Apple-Pecan Classic (p. 70).

COLOR PLATE 6. *Above:* Rock Cornish Hen Earl of Essex (p. 73). *Left:* Salmon Belvedere (p. 94).

COLOR PLATE 7. *Above:* Pot-Au-Feu Bonne Menagere (p. 24). *Left:* Big Apple Kebob Classic (p. 57). *Below, left:* Flaming Steak Zermatt (p. 100). *Below, right:* Somerset Salad (p. 10).

COLOR PLATE 8. *Above, left:* Classical Gourmet Punch (p. 23). *Above:* The World of Cheese. *Left:* Hawaiian Plantation Cake (pp. 155, 156).

Sauce Creole

Two medium onions, 2 tomatoes, and 3 green peppers, sliced, sauteed in 2 oz. butter with 5 sliced mushrooms, juice of 1 garlic clove, dash cayenne pepper and dash saffron with 1 cup of fish sauce.
For fish.

Sauce Champignons (Brown)

Fifteen mushroom stems sauteed in 2 oz. butter, with ½ cup red wine. Reduce to half. Add ½ cup demi glaze, simmer, and strain. Saute 15 sliced mushroom caps, and add to sauce.
For brown meat.

Sauce Champignons (White)

Fifteen sauteed sliced mushrooms, with 2 oz. sherry, and 1 cup sauce veloute. Strain. Finish with 15 sliced sauteed mushrooms, 2 oz. butter, and 1 oz. cognac.
For white meat or eggs.

Sauce Chevreuil

One cup sauce gibier reduced with ½ cup red wine and ½ cup demi glaze, juice of 1 lemon, dash cayenne pepper, and 2 oz. butter.
For sauteed game or roasts.

Sauce Bigarade

One cup brown duck sauce finished with 2 oz. white wine, and julienne of 1 orange rind.
For duckling.

Sauce Chasseur

Five finely chopped shallots sauteed in 2 oz. butter. Add 15 sliced mushrooms, ½ cup white wine, 1 cup demi glaze, and 3 diced, peeled tomatoes. Finish with 2 oz. butter and 1 tsp. chopped chives.
For sauteed or grilled meat.

Sauce Old Vienna

Saute 2 finely chopped onions. Add 1 cup beef consomme, 1 tbsp. finely chopped dill, juice of 1 lemon, dash of nutmeg, oregano, 1 cup sauce veloute, 1 oz. sugar, 2 tbsp. vinegar, pepper, salt to taste, and 2 tbsp. sour cream.
For boiled beef.

Sauce Glace de Viand

Five finely chopped shallots sauteed with 5 sliced mushrooms, 1 small bouquet garni, 1 cup meat glaze, and juice of 1 lemon. Finish with 2 oz. herb butter.
For grilled meat.

Sauce Mary

One tbsp. of chervil, tarragon, chives, 2 oz. white wine, and 1 cup poultry veloute. Finish with 2 oz. herb butter.
For poultry dishes.

Sauce Mousseline

One cup sauce hollandaise, finished just before serving time with ½ cup whipped cream.
For fish, vegetables.

Sauce Sirloin

One half cup soy sauce mixed with juice of 1 garlic clove, 1 tsp. mustard, dash chili powder, juice of 1 lemon, 2 oz. olive oil, and 1 cup demi glaze. Blend.

For barbecue.

Sauce Estragon

One half cup red wine, and 1 cup demi glaze, reduced to half with 2 tbsp. freshly chopped estragon leaves.

For meat and egg dishes.

Sauce Homard

One lb. lobster meat, sauteed with 1 cup diced vegetables. And 1 cup fish sauce, ½ cup white wine, and 2 oz. cognac. Strain. Add 1 cup diced lobster meat and finish with ½ cup heavy cream and 2 oz. butter.

For fish.

Sauce Newburg

Saute 1 cup fresh vegetables and one 1½ lb. lobster with shell. Simmer with 4 oz. cognac, ½ cup madeira, dash paprika, 2 cups fish sauce, and ½ cup heavy cream. Reduce and strain. Add 1 cup chopped lobster meat to finish.

For lobster or shrimp dishes, fish.

Sauce Hunter

Saute 5 finely chopped onions in 4 oz. butter till brown. Add ½ cup white wine, 2 tbsp. tomato paste, 1 cup demi glaze, 2 cloves garlic, and 1 small bouquet garni. Strain. Add 10 sauteed sliced mushrooms and 3 tbsp. julienne of ham. Finish with 1 tsp. sour cream. For grilled or sauteed meat.

Sauce Mornay

Three sauteed finely chopped onions. Add 1 cup sauce bechamel, and ¼ cup white wine. Strain. Add 2 tbsp. parmesan cheese.

For vegetables, egg dishes, fish, and white meat. Au gratin.

Sauce Venison

One cup sauce gibier mixed with 2 tbsp. lingonberries, and 2 tbsp. heavy cream, juice of 1 lemon, and 1 oz. vodka.

For sauteed or braised game.

Sauce Tashja

To 3 finely chopped sauteed onions add 2 shredded apples, 1 tsp. curry powder, 1 cup sauce bechamel, 1 tbsp. chutney, and ¼ cup heavy cream. Finish with 3 tbsp. coconut milk.

For fish, eggs, white meat.

Sauce Prague

To three finely chopped sauteed onions add dash paprika, 1 cup bechamel sauce, ½ cup consomme, 2 oz. heavy cream, juice of 1 clove garlic, 2 tbsp. tomato puree, and juice of 1 lemon.

For eggs, starch, white meat, or poultry.

Sauce Capitain

One cup sauce hollandaise, combined with 1 tbsp. blanched, chopped dill and 3 shrimp, finely chopped. Season with dash cayenne pepper, and juice of 1 lemon.

For fish.

Sauce London Classic

One cup butter sauce with 2 tbsp. freshly grated horseradish and ½ cup heavy cream. Strain. Mix with 3 egg yolks, 1 tsp. vinegar, and 2 tbsp. mustard.
 For boiled beef.

Sauce San Remo

One cup tomato sauce mixed with ½ cup demi glaze, 1 tsp. chopped parsley, dash cayenne pepper, and ¼ cup whipped cream.
 For meat, fowl, egg dishes.

Sauce Choron

One cup sauce bearnaise with 2 tbsp. tomato paste.
 For fish and grilled meat.

Sauce Nantua

One cup sauce bechamel simmered with ½ cup heavy cream, 4 diced shrimp, and 2 oz. white wine. Strain. Add 8 tiny shrimp and 2 oz. butter to finish.
 For fish.

Sauce Normandy

One cup fish sauce with ½ cup white wine, 10 sliced mushrooms, ¼ cup heavy cream, and 2 oz. butter.
 For fish dishes.

Sauce Au Porto

One cup hollandaise sauce with juice of 1 lemon and 2 tbsp. porto.
 For vegetables and fish.

Butter Mixtures

Butter mixtures are used for finishing sauces, or topping grilled or roasted meats, fish, fowl, or game. The various mixtures of shallots, garlic, or other basic ingredients belong to the mise-en-place in a classic kitchen. The mixtures are placed in waxed paper, rolled, and refrigerated. When hard, they are cut with a knife dipped in hot water. No more than 1 oz. per serving is used. To keep such mixtures on a station, they must be placed in ice water.

Almond Butter (Beurre d'Amandes—Mandel Butter)—one-half cup finely ground almonds mixed with 1 lb. butter and squeezed through a fine sieve.

Anchovy Butter (Beurre d'Anchois—Sardellen Butter)—4 oz. finely ground anchovies mixed with ½ lb. butter.

Caviar Butter (Beurre au Caviar—Kaviar Butter)—½ lb. butter spread on waxed paper, centered with 3 tbsp. caviar, and rolled.

Herb Butter (Beurre aux Fines Herbes—Krauter Butter)—4 shallots, 5 fresh tarragon leaves, 5 chervil leaves, 1 tsp. chives, and 5 sprigs parsley, all finely chopped and mixed with ½ lb. butter.

Meat Butter (Beurre Glace de Viande—Fleischglaze Butter)—½ lb. butter mixed with 5 chopped tarragon leaves, 3 peppercorns, 5 parsley sprigs, 3 shallots finely chopped, 1 tsp. soy sauce, and 1 tsp. demi glaze.

Shrimp Butter (Beurre aux Crevettes—Krevetten Butter)—½ lb. whipped butter with 5 finely ground shrimp, and dash paprika. Strained through a fine sieve.

Snail Butter (Beurre Escargots—Schnecken Butter)—5 finely chopped shallots with 5 sprigs of parsley, 3 cloves of garlic, and dash ground white pepper.

Tarragon Butter (Beurre d'Estragon—Estragon Butter)—10 finely chopped fresh tarragon leaves, mixed with ½ lb. butter, and squeezed through a sieve.

Captain's Butter (Beurre Maitre d'Hotel—Wurz Butter)—5 finely chopped shallots with 5 sprigs of parsley, juice of 1 lemon, 1 tbsp. mustard, and Worcestershire sauce. For various grilled items.

Side Dishes

Side dishes are vegetables, starches, potatoes, or fruit prepared to complement the entree. The various preparations of steaming, broiling, frying, braising, glazing, baking, and blanching have long been practiced by classical gourmets.

Artichoke Bottoms Morels

Fill 10 artichoke bottoms with 20 morels in 1 cup sour cream sauce with 5 tbsp. chopped dill. Place in a casserole and bake for 15 minutes at 400° F. Yields 10 servings.

Artichoke Hearts Roma

5 small young artichokes, cut and rubbed with lemon juice, and poached in 2 cups white wine. 2 cups finely diced carrots, celery, mushrooms, and shallots, sauteed in 4 oz. butter, and filled with 1 cup demi glaze and ½ cup red wine. Pour over hearts. Braise for 20 minutes. Yields 5 servings.

Cardons Espana

Only the heart of this giant artichoke plant is used, after removing all outside leaves. Boil in 1 cup lemon juice mixed with ½ cup flour, 1 gal. water, and ½ cup oil, up to 1½ hours. Cut into pieces. Saute in 4 oz. butter with ½ cup white wine, 5 diced tomatoes, 1 cup beef marrow, and 4 oz. cream. Finish with 2 tsp. chopped parsley and 2 oz. butter flakes. Yields 4–6 servings.

Eggplant Allumettes Old Vienna

Peel 2 medium eggplants, cut into long strips, and season with pepper and lemon juice. Roll in ½ cup chopped parsley. Dip in beer batter and fry till golden brown. Yields 4–6 servings.

Cucumber in Dill Sauce

Peel 3 cucumbers and remove seeds. Cut into 2-inch olive shapes. Saute in 4 oz. butter, and 1 cup cream sauce, 2 oz. chopped dill, 2 tbsp. white wine, and season with salt and pepper. Yields 4–6 servings.

Cauliflower Soufflet

One rose of cauliflower cooked, pureed, and mixed with 4 egg yolks and 6 whipped egg whites. Season with dash nutmeg. Place in buttered casserole, sprinkle with parmesan cheese, and bake at 350° F. for 20 minutes, or until light brown. Yields 4–6 servings.

Braised Cabbage Immigrant

Blanch 1 head green cabbage. Remove leaves and season with dash oregano, salt, and pepper. Roll into balls and cover with bacon strips. Saute 3 finely chopped carrots, celery, and onions. Fill up with ½ cup red wine and ½ cup demi glaze. Pour over cabbage rolls and braise for 20 minutes. Yields 4–6 servings.

White Cabbage Old World

Saute 1 cup diced bacon and 5 onions, sliced. Add 2 tsp. sugar and brown. Add ½ cup white wine, 1 head shredded cabbage, 2 juniper berries, 1 bay leaf, 2 tbsp. vinegar, and ½ tsp. caraway seeds. Cover and simmer for 45 minutes. Add salt and pepper. Yields 4–6 servings.

Red Cabbage Classic

Stick several cloves into an onion. Saute 1 cup of smoked bacon trimmings. Add 1 head of shredded red cabbage, 2 shredded apples, 2 onions, finely chopped, 1 cup red wine, salt, pepper, and a small bouquet garni. Braise for 45 minutes. Remove bouquet garni and onion with cloves. Yields 4–6 servings.

Brussels Sprouts Mornay

2 pints brussels sprouts cooked in salted water, drained, and seasoned. Cover with 1 cup sauce mornay, sprinkle with 2 tbsp. parmesan cheese and 4 oz. butter flakes, and bake at 375° F. for 25 minutes. Yields 4–6 servings.

French Beans Francaise

Cut 1 lb. blanched beans in 2-inch pieces. Saute in 4 oz. butter with 3 onions, sliced, 1 cup shredded lettuce, and 1 cup pearl onions. Add 1 tsp. flour, and ½ cup white wine and simmer for several minutes. Yields 4–6 servings.

French Beans Provencale

Saute 1 lb. beans with 3 sliced onions and 4 tomatoes, diced, in 2 oz. olive oil flavored with juice of 2 cloves of garlic. Add ½ cup white wine, 10 ripe olives, and 1 tsp. chervil. Yields 4–6 servings.

French Beans English Style

1 lb. French beans, ends snapped off. Boil in plenty of lightly salted water. Remove and serve with melted butter, au naturel. Yields 4–6 servings.

Carrots Champagne

Shape 5 carrots by cutting into olive forms. Saute in 4 oz. butter. Add ½ cup champagne and simmer till cooked. Season and sprinkle with freshly chopped parsley. Yields 4–6 servings.

Asparagus Spears Classic

Peel 20 stems, but do not touch the tips. Remove tough bottoms part. Bind together and boil in plenty of salted water for 20 minutes. Place on serving dish. Over double boiler, whip 3 egg yolks with 4 tbsp. orange juice and 2 oz. Grand Marnier. Remove. Add the zest from one orange and 1 cup of melted butter. Pour over asparagus spears. Yields 4–6 servings.

Endive Sorrel

Cook ½ lb. sorrel with dash of salt until soft. Braise 6 Belgian endive stalks in 4 oz. butter. In blender, combine 4 egg yolks with chopped sorrel. Add ½ cup melted butter as needed. Season and pour over endive. Yields 4–6 servings.

Zucchini Palermo

Slice 5 zucchini and saute in 2 oz. hot olive oil with 1 cup peeled, diced tomato, ½ cup sliced olives, and 3 onions, and juice of 2 cloves of garlic. Sprinkle with sea salt, freshly ground pepper, and 1 tsp. chopped fresh parsley. Yields 4–6 servings.

Turnips Puree

Boil 3 turnips, peeled, in salted water. Drain and puree. Mix with dash nutmeg and 4 oz. butter and season with salt and pepper. For proper consistency, add 2 tbsp. heavy cream. Yields 4–6 servings.

Stuffed Celeriac

Cut 5 celeriac in 2-inch by 1-inch pieces. Empty 5 celeriac in center and blanch in salted water. Puree 1 cup green peas with 2 oz. butter and salt and pepper. Fill centers with peas and celeriac pieces, cover with 1 tbsp. grated cheese each, and gratinee till golden brown. Yields 5 servings.

Gombos a La Creme

2 cups cut, blanched okra sauteed in 4 oz. butter. Combine with ½ cup white wine sauce and 2 tbsp. heavy cream. Yields 4 servings.

Maize Classic

Boil 2 cups of corn mixed with 1 cup heavy cream, 2 eggs, and ½ cup flour, till a heavy consistency. Season with nutmeg, salt, and pepper. Add a dash of baking soda. Fry one tablespoon at a time in hot oil till golden brown. Yields 4–6 servings.

Salsify au Beurre

Peel and cut 1 lb. salsify in 2-inch pieces. Boil in plenty of salted water. Saute in 4 oz. brown butter and sprinkle with 2 tbsp. chopped parsley. Yields 4–6 servings.

Pea Pods South Pacific

Stir 2 tbsp. curry powder into 4 oz. heated butter. Add 1 cup sliced onions and 1 lb. pea pods. Saute for 3 minutes. Add 1 tsp. sugar, 2 tbsp. soy sauce, 5 sliced water chestnuts, 1 cup diced pineapple, ½ diced mango, ½ lb. bean sprouts, and 5 sliced mushrooms. Mix 3 tbsp. pineapple juice with ½ tsp. cornstarch, and add to pea pods. Bring to a boil, and add salt and pepper. Do not overcook. Yields 6–8 servings.

Mushroom Grille

Remove caps from fresh mushrooms, brush with salted butter, and place under hot broiler. Sprinkle with 2 tbsp. chopped parsley and 2 tbsp. fresh sage. Yields 4–6 servings.

Spinach Timbales

Blanch 1 lb. spinach leaves. Grind finely. Mix with 4 oz. brown butter, ½ cup heavy cream, 3 whole eggs, dash nutmeg, and salt and pepper. Place in timbale forms and poach in water (covered) for 25 minutes. Turn spinach upside down. Yields 4–6 servings.

Spinach A La Creme

Blanch 1 lb. spinach leaves in boiling salted water. Remove and chop finely or grind. Mix with 1 cup cream sauce, and season with dash nutmeg, salt, and ground white pepper. Yields 4–6 servings.

Jerusalem Artichoke Palestine

Peel artichokes. Cut in sections, and boil in water with dash nutmeg, salt, and pepper. Strain and mix with 1 cup mashed potatoes, 4 oz. butter, and ¼ cup heavy cream. Yields 4–6 servings.

Flaming Onions

Blanch 1 lb. pearl onions in 1 cup white wine, with 3 cloves, for several minutes. Remove and saute at tableside. Melt 2 tbsp. sugar till golden brown and add onions. Pour in 2 oz. brandy, ignite, and add 2 tbsp. remaining stock. Yields 4–6 servings.

Bean Sprouts Oriental

Wash 2 pints bean sprouts. In large pan, heat 2 oz. olive oil until very hot. Add sprouts, 2 oz. butter, 2 tbsp. soy sauce, 1 tbsp. sesame seeds, salt, and pepper. Toss several times. Cook for 5 minutes until done. Yields 4–6 servings.

Haricots Blancs Mediterranean

Soak 1 lb. white beans in cold water for two hours. Remove tiny stones, and strain. Bring to boil with cold water, and simmer until beans are cooked. Saute 1 cup finely chopped onions in 2 oz. butter with ½ cup diced bacon. Add 4 diced fresh tomatoes, 2 cloves of garlic, crushed, salt, and freshly ground pepper. Add beans and ½ cup veal stock. Simmer. Sprinkle with chopped parsley. Yields 4–6 servings.

Lentils Tyrolienne

Soak 1 lb. lentils in cold water for several hours. Bring to a boil with 3 diced onions, 1 small bouquet garni, 2 cloves, 1 cup diced vegetables, 1 clove of garlic, and 3 strips of sauteed bacon. Fill with smoked ham stock, or add a piece of ham with water. Season with salt and pepper, and simmer till lentils are soft. Puree without bouquet garni. Finish with lemon juice and plenty of butter. Yields 4–6 servings.

Morilles Bordelaise Classic

Morels should be cleaned and washed; if dried, soak in red wine. Saute 5 finely chopped shallots in 2 oz. butter. Add 5 cups morels, lemon juice, 1 tsp. chopped parsley, a touch of garlic, ¼ cup red wine, and ¼ cup demi glaze. Bring to a boil and add 2 tbsp. heavy cream. Sprinkle with chopped parsley. Morels are from the expensive fungi family. Yields 4–6 servings.

Chanterelles Girolles Classic

These forest mushrooms have a brownish yellow color and a fine aroma. They can be prepared like any other mushrooms. The following method is my favorite:

Wash and remove the sandy part of the stems. Saute 5 shallots in 2 oz. butter, add 5 cups chanterelles, salt and pepper, and stir for 3 minutes. Add ¼ cup white wine and bring to boil. Add 2 tbsp. finely cut fresh dill and ½ cup heavy cream. Simmer for 5 minutes. Sprinkle with chopped dill. Yields 4–6 servings.

Les Truffles Diamond Classic

The most expensive of the fungi family is the truffle. Grown under the soil, it has a special aroma. Its color is black and it is used mostly for garnishing sauces or for decoration. Its origin is French. There are, however, white truffles from Italy that are imported commercially in cans. The classic preparation is to have fresh truffles (available in Europe) individually wrapped in pork fat, covered with parchment paper soaked in red wine, and placed under burning embers for ½ hour. They are then removed and placed in a silver tureen, sprinkled with champagne and aged cognac, and ignited.

English Style Potatoes

Potatoes are peeled, cut into olive forms, and boiled in lightly salted water. For various fish dishes.

Perigord Classic

Mash 6 potatoes and season with salt and pepper. Mix with 3 eggs, dash nutmeg, and 1 chopped truffle. Form into balls, and roll in 3 whipped eggs and ½ cup sliced almonds. Fry in hot oil till golden brown. Yields 4–6 servings.

Potato Classic

Boil 6 potatoes in jackets. Peel and slice. Place in casserole and cover with 1 cup of dill sauce (a light cream sauce with sour cream, chopped dill, and whisked egg yolk). Place in 350° F. oven and bake for 15 minutes. Yields 4–6 servings.

Anna Potatoes

Peel 6 potatoes, cut in round, even slices, and place in cold water. Remove to towel dry, and season with salt and pepper in 4 oz. hot clarified butter. Place in a round mold, in 5 or 6 layers, with additional butter between. Cover and bake for 45 minutes at 375° F. Turn to drain excess butter. Place on a platter and sprinkle with chopped parsley. Yields 4–6 servings.

Chateau Classic

Peel and cut 6 potatoes into large olive forms. Brush with butter and bake at 375° F. for 30 minutes till golden brown. Season with salt and pepper. Sprinkle with chopped parsley and serve with veal fond. Yields 4–6 servings.

Star Potatoes

Peel and cut 6 potatoes into 2-inch cubes. From each point, cut ¾ inch toward center all around. Place in water until needed. Fry at 400° F. for 5 minutes. Remove. Prior to serving time, place in 375° F. oil to finish. Season with salt and pepper, and brush with butter. Yields 4–6 servings.

Potato Noodle Classic

Boil, peel, and mash 4 potatoes with 4 oz. butter, 3 eggs, ¾ cup flour, salt, and ground white pepper. Form a dough. Make small, 2-inch long noodles. Place in salted boiling water. Boil for 12 minutes, covered. Remove to cold water. Place in toasted breadcrumbs mixed with butter and roll noodles till covered. Yields 2–4 servings.

Braised Cheese Potatoes

Peel 4 potatoes and cut into thin slices. Mix with ½ cup shredded Swiss cheese, salt, pepper, and nutmeg. Whisk 2 eggs mixed with ½ cup consomme. Rub buttered casserole with garlic. Put in potato slices, cover with egg mixture, and bake at 350° F. for 45 minutes. Sprinkle with chopped dill. Yields 2–4 servings.

Parisienne Classic

Cut out small, round potatoes from a large peeled one. Saute in 2 oz. butter till light brown. Roll in demi glaze and sprinkle with chopped parsley. Yields 1 serving.

Bird's Nest Classic

Peel 6 potatoes. Cut into thin, long julienne. Place in round ladle or nest form. Top with same and fry till golden brown. Remove carefully so as not to break nest. Fill with cooked carrots, turnips, peas, and mushrooms. Yields 4–6 servings.

Soufflet Classic

Mix 3 cups mashed potatoes with 4 tbsp. heavy cream and 3 egg yolks. Season with nutmeg. Fold in 3 whipped egg whites. Place in buttered earthenware dish and bake at 375° F. for 20 minutes. Yields 4–6 servings.

Sweet Potato Classic

Its basic preparation is like Pommes de Terre. The American Thanksgiving feast should never be without sweet potatoes. Boil them in their jackets till soft. Peel and cut in bite size portions. Fry in hot vegetable oil till golden brown. Place in maple syrup. Remove at serving time.

Yorkshire Classic

Mix 1 cup flour with ¼ cup milk, 3 egg yolks, salt, and nutmeg. Add 2 tbsp. roast beef drippings or kidney fat. Combine with 3 whipped egg whites. Fill greased tartlet cups half full and bake at 375° F. for 15 minutes. Serve with English style roasts. Yields 4–6 servings.

Roma Risotto Classic

Saute 3 finely chopped onions in 2 oz. butter. Add 1 cup rice, and a pinch of saffron. Fill with 2½ cups chicken or beef consomme, and season with salt and pepper. Bring to a boil, cover, and let simmer for 30 minutes. Add ½ cup diced ham, 1 chopped white truffle, and 2 tsp. parmesan cheese. Bake at 350° F. for 20 minutes. Yields 4–6 servings.

Italian Gnocchi Classic

Mix 1 cup milk, 2 oz. butter, salt, and nutmeg. Bring to a boil. Add 2 cups flour, stirring constantly, until mixture removes from pan. Remove. Beat in 2 whole eggs slowly and add ½ cup finely grated gruyere cheese. In boiling salted water, place teaspoonfuls of mixture. Do not put too many in the water at the same time. Cover and simmer for 15 minutes. Remove and place in buttered casserole. Cover with grated cheese and butter flakes. Bake at 350° F. till golden brown. Yields 4–6 servings.

Austrian Dumpling Classic

Saute 3 finely chopped onions in 2 oz. vegetable oil with 4 strips of diced bacon till golden brown. Dice 6 rolls in ¼-inch pieces and add. Whisk in 4 eggs mixed with 3 tbsp. milk just to soak. Season with salt and pepper. Add a pinch of chopped parsley and combine with 3 tbsp. flour. Form round balls 3 inches in diameter. Place in salted boiling water, bring to a boil, and simmer for 20 minutes, covered. Yields 4–6 servings.

Oriental Curry Rice Classic

Saute 3 finely chopped onions in 2 oz. butter. Add 1 tsp. curry powder, 2 cups rice, and ½ cup plum wine. Season with salt and pepper. Bring to a boil and simmer for 30 minutes. Add 2 tbsp. chopped almonds, 2 tbsp. seedless raisins, and ¼ cup dried fruit. Cover and complete cooking process for 15 minutes. Place rice in a ring form. Turn over on serving platter and surround with curry sauce. Garnish with fresh mint leaves. Yields 4–6 servings.

Fried Rice Classic

Set aside ½ cup ready cooked pork strips, ½ cup shrimp, 2 oz. crabmeat, 2 tbsp. diced bacon, 2 cups cooked rice, and ½ lb. bean sprouts. Saute in 2 oz. olive oil. Beat 2 eggs, add rice, and brown for 5 minutes, stirring lightly. Add 2 tbsp. soy sauce and simmer for several minutes. Add remaining ingredients, cover, and bake for 10 minutes. Sprinkle with freshly sliced scallions. Serve with sweet and sour sauce. Yields 4–6 servings.

Passion Fruit English Classic

Cut 10 fruits into pieces and soak in 4 oz. kirsch. Puree through fine strainer. Cut 4 pomegranates ½ inch from top. Empty apple and reserve seeds. Fill with passion fruit mousse, sprinkle with seeds, and heat in oven till warm. Accompaniment for game dishes. Yields 4 servings.

Glazed Red Bananas

Peel 6 red bananas and slice lengthwise. Cover with 4 oz. butter and brown sugar. Broil for several minutes. Yields 4–6 servings.

Island Coconut Classic

Cut coconut in half and remove milk. Fill with ham mousse, and decorate with sliced kumquats and mint leaf. Pour over honey with a touch of rum, ignite, and serve flaming. For Polynesian dishes. Yields 4 servings.

Pacific Guava Classic

Remove blossom from guava shells. Cut in half and remove seeds. Soak with allspice, cinnamon, whole cloves, sliced ginger root, sugar, and vinegar. Boil until guava is tender and juice has thickened. To store, seal in preservative jar while hot. For oriental dishes. Yields 4–6 servings.

Akee Paradise Classic

Simmer akee in a little red wine. Place in peeled avocado halves and bake for 5 minutes at 400° F. Serve with egg dishes. Yields 2 servings.

Hawaiian Pineapple Classic

Cut pineapple in half lengthwise. Remove core and cut meat into chunks. Mix with diced royale and apple. Decorate with slices of orange. Add lemon juice. Soak with kirsch and add rum for flaming. Yields 4 servings.

Malaysia Breadfruit Classic

This seedless fruit is cut in half, filled with diced mangoes and chestnuts, and covered with rum and sugar. Bake at 350° F. for 25 minutes. Yields 2 servings.

Pawpaw–Papaya Classic

Cut papaya in half, remove seeds, and sprinkle with lemon juice. Fill with raspberries and Grand Marnier. Bake for 15 minutes at 325° F. Yields 2 servings.

Tropical Mango Classic

Cut mango in half and remove seeds. Fill with puree of green bananas (mixed with lemon juice, boiled in water, and mashed). Decorate with red grapes and heat until hot. For meat dishes. Yields 2 servings.

Garnishes

Garnishes accompany the entree. In this section, we are going to present specialties that are different from the common side orders. A combination of various vegetables should always be served on a separate dish.

Asparagus Seville

INGREDIENTS	For 4	For 20
tomatoes	4	20
asparagus tips	16	80
butter, melted	1 tbsp.	¼ cup
breadcrumbs	1 tbsp.	1¼ cup
hard-boiled egg, chopped	1	5
parsley, chopped	1 tsp.	2 tbsp.
parmesan cheese	1 tbsp.	¼ cup
salt and pepper mixture	to taste	1 tsp.

Cut tops off tomatoes and empty centers. Fill with cooked asparagus tips mixed with butter, breadcrumbs, egg, parsley, parmesan, and seasoning. Bake in buttered dish for 15 minutes at 375° F.

Artichokes Calypso

INGREDIENTS	For 4	For 20
small artichokes	4	20
shallots, finely chopped	5	1 pt.
chanterelles	½ cup	2 cups
olive oil	⅛ cup	½ cup
chicken stock	½ cup	3 cups
salt	to taste	to taste
egg yolks	4	15
butter, clarified	½ cup	2 cups
cayenne	to taste	⅛ tsp.

Cut tops and stems off artichokes and trim leaves. In casserole, saute shallots and chanterelles in olive oil. Add artichokes, chicken stock, and salt. Cover and bake at 400° F. for 50 minutes. Whip egg yolks with one tablespoon of stock over double boiler until hot. Whip cold. Add clarified butter slowly by continuously whipping. Season with salt and cayenne. Serve artichokes in casserole with sauce on the side. Discard remaining stock.

Gourmet Potpourri Classic

INGREDIENTS	For 4 to 6	For 20 to 30
carrots	2	10
butter	½ cup	2 cups
morels, soaked	4	20
ham mousse	2 tbsp.	½ cup
demi glaze	½ cup	2 cups
cepes	½ cup	2 cups
salt and pepper mixture	to taste	to taste
salsify	2	5
white wine	½ cup	2 cups
marrons, peeled	8	40

Cut carrots in olive shapes, 2 inches long. Season and saute in butter. Stuff morels with mousse of ham. Bake with demi glaze. Saute cepes in butter, season, and add some demi glaze. Blanch salsify in salt water, saute in butter, and add white wine. Saute marrons in butter. Blanch artichokes in salt water, and finish in white wine. Dip truffles in beer batter and fry.

To arrange, place artichokes in center of silver platter with hollandaise sauce on the side. Place remaining vegetables around the artichokes. A culinary garnish.

(Cont.)

artichokes	1	5
truffles	4	20
beer batter	¼ cup	1 cup
hollandaise sauce	½ cup	2 cups

Endive Classic

INGREDIENTS	For 4	For 20
Belgian endive	4	20
butter	1 tbsp.	¼ cup
sugar	1 tsp.	2 tbsp.
juice of lemon	1	4
red burgundy sauce	4 oz.	3 cups

Cut endive lengthwise. Place in casserole with butter, sugar, and lemon juice. Bake at 375° F. for 40 minutes. Arrange on a serving platter and top with red burgundy sauce. Garnish with parsley sprigs.

Orloff Classic

INGREDIENTS	For 4	For 20
cucumbers	2	10
salt and pepper mixture	to taste	1 tsp.
butter	2 tbsp.	½ cup
heavy cream	¼ cup	2 cups
tarragon, freshly chopped	½ tsp.	2 tbsp.
3-inch tartlets	4	20
truffles, chopped	¼ tsp.	2 tsp.

Peel cucumbers, cut lengthwise, and remove seeds. Cut into 2-inch strips and form into olive shapes. Season and saute in butter for 2 minutes. Add heavy cream and tarragon, and bring to boil. Place in tartlets and sprinkle with truffles.

Gastronome Classic

INGREDIENTS	For 4	For 20
artichoke bottoms	4	20
small, olive-shaped potatoes	8	40
white wine	½ cup	2½ cups
truffles, chopped	¼ tsp.	1 tsp.
madeira sauce	4 oz.	3 cups
bernaise sauce	3 tbsp.	1 cup

Poach artichoke bottoms and potatoes in white wine. Remove. In center of artichoke bottoms, place potatoes and truffles. Cover with madeira sauce. In casserole, top each portion with bernaise sauce and place under salamander for several seconds.

Pommes Souffles Classic

INGREDIENTS	For 4	For 20
Idaho potatoes	4	20
salt	dash	to taste
vegetable oil, to fry		

Peel potatoes in oval shapes and place in water. Cut ⅜-inch slices on mandoline or slicer. Place in wet towel until frying.

To fry, use two casseroles with vegetable oil about 10 inches deep. Heat one to 325° F. and the other to 385° F. Drop slices into the 325° F. oil, a few at a time. Slide casserole back and forth to cook potatoes evenly for 4 minutes. Remove with skimmer. Place in 385° F. oil. As potatoes puff, remove and place on towel until serving time. At serving time, drop in 385° F. oil and they will puff again. Season with salt.

NOTE   Not all potatoes will puff. Use those that do not puff for boulangere potatoes.

Boulangere Classic

INGREDIENTS	For 4	For 20
medium potatoes	3	15
salt and pepper mixture	to taste	to taste
butter	4 tbsp.	1¼ cups
small onions, sliced	3	15
demi glaze	2 oz.	1 cup
parsley, chopped	1 tsp.	4 tbsp.

Peel potatoes, and slice into sections or form round balls. Season with salt and pepper, and saute in hot butter, with onions, till golden brown. Place on serving platter. Surround with demi glaze or juice from the accompanying meat. Garnish with parsley.

Bonne-Femme Classic

INGREDIENTS	For 4	For 20
large onions	2	10
butter	1 tsp.	2 tbsp.
mushrooms, sliced	2	10
parsley, chopped	1 tsp.	2 tbsp.
potato balls	8	40
salt and pepper mixture	to taste	to taste
white wine	½ cup	2½ cups
fennel, chopped	½ tsp.	2 tsp.

Peel onions. Cut in half and empty center of onion. Dice and saute in butter with mushrooms, parsley, and potato balls. Add seasoning, some wine, and fennel. Fill centers of onions and poach in white wine. If fish is poached, poach in the same liquid.

Aubergine Classic

INGREDIENTS	For 4	For 20
small eggplants	2	10
olive oil	2 tbsp.	¼ cup
tomatoes, peeled and diced	4	20
rice pilaf, cooked	¼ cup	1¼ cups
parmesan cheese	2 tbsp.	½ cup
sage	to taste	½ tsp.
salt and pepper mixture	to taste	to taste

Cut eggplants in half lengthwise. Empty centers and dice. Saute in olive oil with tomatoes. Mix with rice pilaf, some cheese, and season. Fill centers of eggplants with mixture. Sprinkle with remaining cheese and bake at 375° F. for 30 minutes.

Peasant Classic

INGREDIENTS	For 4	For 20
carrots, diced	1	5
peas	1 tbsp.	¼ cup
beans	4	20
parsnip, diced	1	5
brussels sprouts	4	20
medium onion, sliced	¼	1
butter	1 tbsp.	¼ cup
salt and pepper mixture	to taste	to taste
white wine	⅛ cup	½ cup
large potatoes, raw	4	20
hollandaise sauce	5 tbsp.	1½ cups

Clean all vegetables. Saute all but potatoes in butter and season. Add wine and simmer. Peel potatoes and cut in half lengthwise. Form in shape of boat and empty center. Bake in 350° F. oven for 45 minutes. Fill with sauteed vegetables. Cover with hollandaise sauce and brown under salamander for several minutes.

Sauerkraut Tartlets

INGREDIENTS	For 4	For 20
chicken liver pieces	4	20
butter	1 tsp.	2 tbsp.
bacon, diced	1 tbsp.	5 tbsp.
medium onion, sliced	1 tbsp.	2 onions
sauerkraut	4 tbsp.	1½ cups
white wine	2 oz.	1 cup
white pepper, ground	to taste	to taste
3-inch tartlets	4	20
Jarlsberg cheese slices	4	20

Saute chicken liver in butter. Remove liver and add diced bacon and onions. Do not brown. Add squeezed sauerkraut and wine, and season. Simmer for ½ hour, covered. Divide among tartlets. Top each with chicken liver and cheese. Place under salamander and melt cheese.

Rossini Classic

INGREDIENTS	For 4	For 20
shallots	1 tsp.	¼ cup
goose liver	4 slices	20 slices
butter, melted	1 tbsp.	¼ cup
large mushroom caps	4	20
truffle slices	4	20
madeira sauce	4 oz.	3 cups

Saute shallots and goose liver in butter. Place in each mushroom cap. Top with truffle slice and cover with madeira sauce. Bake for 15 minutes at 350° F.

11. Desserts, Cheeses, and Wines

Peach Benedictine

INGREDIENTS   YIELD: 1 serving

1 peach
2 oz. porto wine
2 oz. benedictine
½ cup crushed ice
whipped cream, for topping
2 fresh mint leaves

Boil peach with porto wine (covered). Cool. Mix remaining liquid with benedictine and crushed ice. Place in champagne glass and decorate with whipped cream and mint leaf.

Fondue Vienna Classic

INGREDIENTS   YIELD: 10 to 20 servings

3 oranges
3 pears
3 bananas
¼ cup shredded coconut
20 ladyfingers
1 tsp. cinnamon
¼ cup cocoa
2½ lb. chocolate
½ cup chocolate syrup

Peel and cut oranges, pears, and bananas into bite-size pieces. Place in a bowl. Place shredded coconut in a bowl with ladyfingers on the side. Mix cinnamon and cocoa and place in a bowl. Arrange bowls around fondue pot. Heat chocolate and syrup, and place in fondue pot. Dip each piece of fruit in melted chocolate mixture and accompaniments.

Classic French Croissants

INGREDIENTS   YIELD: 10 to 12 servings

1 tbsp. yeast
⅓ cup water
⅓ cup milk
salt to taste
4 tbsp. sugar
6 oz. butter flakes
2 cups flour
mixture of 1 egg yolk and 1 tsp. water

Dissolve yeast in 2 tbsp. warm water. Heat milk, remaining water, salt, sugar, and 2 oz. butter flakes till lukewarm. Place flour in bowl. Make a well in the center. Place milk and water mixture in center. Add yeast, form dough, and mix well. Let rise in warm place for about 45 minutes. Spread dough out on floured surface and let cool. Roll out dough into a rectangle. Cover with half the butter flakes. Fold in thirds. Roll out again, add remaining butter, and fold again. Chill in refrigerator for 1 hour. Remove and roll out a very thin, 4-inch wide strip. Cut into squares, and cut squares in half to make triangles. Roll each triangle from the point, and bend for half moon shape. Place on buttered baking sheet, and let rise in warm place for 1 hour. Brush with yolk mixture and bake at 425° F. for 15 minutes.

Charlotte Marquise Classic

INGREDIENTS   YIELD: 10 to 12 servings

30 ladyfingers

1½ cups whipped cream

2 oz. cognac

1 tbsp. gelatin

3 tbsp. water

5 tbsp. sugar

5 tbsp. candied fruit

whipped cream, for decoration

1 pt. fresh raspberries

Line bowl with waxed paper. Place ladyfingers on bottom and around bowl. Mix whipped cream with cognac and melted gelatin. Boil water and sugar for 5 minutes. Cool and add candied fruit. Chill. Mix with cream and half the raspberries. Pour cream in bowl and top with ladyfingers. Refrigerate for one hour. Turn upside down on serving platter. Decorate with whipped cream and place raspberries around.

Poppy Noodle Classic

INGREDIENTS   YIELD: 8 to 10 servings

12 oz. broad noodles

milk, for boiling

1 vanilla bean

salt to taste

6 oz. butter

8 oz. sugar

5 whole eggs, separated

5 tbsp. raisins

6 oz. poppy seeds, ground

cinnamon, to sprinkle

Boil noodles with milk, vanilla, salt, and 1 oz. butter. Chill well. Whip remaining butter with 4 oz. sugar and egg yolks, till creamy. Add raisins and poppy seeds. Mix half with half the noodles. Whip egg whites with 4 oz. sugar until firm. Mix with remaining noodles. Place noodles mixed with egg whites in a buttered casserole. Place remaining noodle and butter mixture on top and cover with remaining butter mixture. Bake at 350° F. for 35 minutes. Sprinkle with cinnamon and cut into portions. Serve hot.

Classic Apple Souffle, Old Vienna

INGREDIENTS   YIELD: 10 servings

10 old rolls or French bread

½ pt. milk

4 oz. rum

8 oz. butter

8 oz. sugar

rind of 1 lemon, finely grated

10 egg yolks

4 oz. flour

10 apples, cored and peeled

confectioner's sugar, to sprinkle

Peel rolls, cut into thin slices, and soak in milk and rum. Whip butter, sugar, and lemon rind. Add egg yolks slowly, beating till creamy. Add flour. In buttered casserole, place a layer of rolls, a layer of apples, and a layer of rolls. Cover with butter mixture. Bake at 350° F. for 25 minutes, or until golden brown. Cut into portions, and sprinkle with confectioner's sugar. Serve hot with Old Vienna Sauce.

For Old Vienna Sauce, whip 5 egg yolks with 2 tbsp. sugar and 2 cups white wine over double boiler, until hot. Serve separately or surrounding souffle on the serving dish.

Classic Gugelhupf

INGREDIENTS   YIELD: 8 to 10 servings

1 oz. yeast

½ pt. milk

1 lb., 2 oz. flour

4 oz. butter

4 oz. sugar

5 egg yolks

4 tbsp. raisins

rind of 1 lemon, finely grated

5 tbsp. cocoa powder

confectioner's sugar, to sprinkle

Mix yeast with 2 tbsp. lukewarm milk and dash of flour. Form dough, for testing. Let rise for 15 minutes. Mix remaining lukewarm milk, butter, sugar, egg yolks, raisins, lemon rind, and flour with yeast mixture. Form dough with wooden spoon. Add a little flour till dough separates from pot. Sprinkle with flour. Let rise ⅓ in warm place. Punch down and let rise again. Divide dough in half. Mix cocoa powder with one half of dough. Layer white and dark dough, alternately, several times in gugelhupf mold. Let rise again in warm place. Bake at 400° F. for 30 minutes, or until a long needle inserted in center comes out dry. Cool. Turn mold over on serving platter and sprinkle with confectioner's sugar.

Classical Gourmet Souffle

INGREDIENTS   YIELD: 4 servings

2½ tbsp. flour

1 cup milk

4 tbsp. sugar

dash of vanilla

2 tbsp. butter

2 tbsp. candied, diced fruit, soaked in coconut rum

5 whole eggs, separated

confectioner's sugar, to sprinkle

Mix flour with 3 tbsp. of milk. Bring remaining milk, 3 tbsp. sugar, and vanilla to a boil. Remove and mix flour into it. Bring to boiling point, stirring until smooth. Remove and add egg yolks, butter, and candied fruit. Beat egg whites and 1 tbsp. sugar until very stiff. Fold into the mixture. Heat the bottom of a buttered souffle dish, prior to filling. Fill and sprinkle with confectioner's sugar. Bake in preheated 350° F. oven for 18 minutes. The souffle must be served immediately—timing is very important.

Chocolate Mousse Classic

INGREDIENTS   YIELD: 5 to 8 servings

1 lb. semi-sweet chocolate

8 oz. sweet butter

6 whole eggs, separated

4 tbsp. sugar

champagne glasses

chocolate, for shavings

Melt chocolate in double boiler. Remove, add butter, and cool. Stir in egg yolks. Whip egg whites with sugar until stiff. Fold into mixture until consistency is creamy. Using a pastry bag, fill champagne glasses. Chill well. Sprinkle with chocolate shavings.

Baklava Hellene

INGREDIENTS   YIELD: 4 to 6 servings

1 cup walnuts, chopped

1 cup pistachios, chopped

1 cup almond pieces

½ cup sugar

¾ tsp. cinnamon powder

2 tsp. lemon rind, grated

1 lb. filo sheets

1 cup pancake syrup

1 cup honey

1 oz. brandy

1 cup sweet butter, melted

Mix together walnuts, pistachios, almonds, sugar, cinnamon, and grated lemon rind. Set aside. Place ⅓ of filo sheets, each brushed with butter, on top of each other in buttered baking pan. Spread half the nut filling over filo, and top with ⅓ more filo sheets, brushing each with butter. Spread remaining nut filling and place the remaining ⅓ filo sheets, each brushed with butter, on top. Press. Cut through sheets, making diamond shapes. Bake at 350° F. for 45 minutes, or until golden brown. Remove and cool. Bring pancake syrup with honey and brandy to boil. Pour over filo letting it soak thoroughly. Set aside for several hours until cold. Cut through previous cuttings. Remove from pan and place on serving dish.

South Pacific Wine Chateau

INGREDIENTS   YIELD: 4 servings

5 egg yolks

3 tsp. sugar

4 oz. plum wine

1 oz. pineapple liqueur

4 pineapple chunks

nutmeg, freshly grated

mint leaves, for garnish

Fill small pot with water, bring to boil. Use round bottom pan to whisk egg yolks, sugar, plum wine, and pineapple liqueur. Place over boiling water and whisk until eggs are thickened. Pour in champagne glasses. Place a pineapple chunk in each glass, sprinkle with nutmeg, and garnish with mint leaves.

Kaiser Classic

INGREDIENTS	For 4	For 40
egg whites	5	25
sugar	4 oz.	1 lb., 4 oz.
butter	4 oz.	1 lb., 4 oz.
almonds, chopped	4 oz.	1 lb., 4 oz.
semi-sweet chocolate, melted	4 oz.	1 lb., 4 oz.
white breadcrumbs	6 oz.	2 lb.
egg yolks	5	25
heavy cream, whipped	1 cup	5 cups

Beat egg whites with half the sugar. Whip butter with remaining sugar, almonds, and chocolate. Combine breadcrumbs with egg yolks. Fold in butter mixture. Place in ramequin. Place ramequin in boiling water that half covers it. Cover so the mixture can steam for 45 minutes. Serve hot or cold, decorated with whipped cream.

NOTE   Turn over to serve.

Mozart Classic

INGREDIENTS	For 6–8	For 32
almond paste	¼ cup	1 cup
confectioner's sugar	¼ cup	1 cup
egg whites	½	2
semi-sweet chocolate, melted	¼ cup	1 cup
semi-sweet chocolate	2 oz.	8 oz.

Combine almond paste, confectioner's sugar, and egg whites. Rub together. Form round balls. Roll in melted chocolate. Remove and roll in shredded chocolate. Arrange balls in champagne glass.

Cardinal Bread

INGREDIENTS   YIELD: 12 loaves

20 egg whites

1 lb. confectioner's sugar

45 egg yolks

1 oz. rum

8 oz. raisins

8 oz. granulated walnuts

1¼ lb. candied fruit

rind of 2 lemons, ground

1 tsp. vanilla

1¾ lb. flour

2 cups oil

Beat egg whites with half the sugar till very stiff. Whisk egg yolks with remaining sugar and rum. Add raisins, walnuts, candied fruit, lemon rind, and vanilla. Fold into egg whites. Fold in flour and slowly add oil. Divide among 12 loaf pans and bake at 350° F. for 45 minutes, until golden brown.

Anise Cookies

INGREDIENTS	1 Tray	18 Trays
eggs, separated	5	50
confectioner's sugar	5 oz.	6 lb.
flour	5 oz.	2½ lb.
milk	¼ cup	2½ pt.
anisette	½ oz.	2 oz.
anise	to sprinkle	to sprinkle

Beat the egg whites with half the sugar until very stiff. Blend egg yolks with remaining sugar, anisette, and milk. Add flour and fold in egg whites. Fill pastry bag and squeeze onto baking sheet lined with parchment paper. Sprinkle with anise. Bake at 375° F. for 20 minutes.

Grand Souffle Classic

INGREDIENTS	For 4	For 8
milk	1 cup	2 cups
sugar	5 oz.	10 oz.
butter	6 oz.	12 oz.
kirsch	3 tbsp.	6 tbsp.
flour	5 oz.	10 oz.
raspberries, fresh	1 pt.	2 pt.
egg whites	6	12
egg yolks	6	12
cocoa	to sprinkle	to sprinkle
confectioner's sugar	to sprinkle	to sprinkle

Bring milk, half the amount of sugar, butter, and kirsch to a boil. Add flour and stir until it easily separates from pan. Remove and add raspberries. Beat egg whites with remaining sugar until very stiff. Fold together with batter and egg yolks. In buttered, 6-inch souffle casseroles divide mixture and bake at 350° F. for 20 minutes. Remove and sprinkle with confectioner's sugar mixed with cocoa.

Flaming Sombrero Classic

INGREDIENTS   YIELD: 2 servings

2 oz. butter
2 oz. flour
½ cup milk
3 oz. sugar
2 tbsp. heavy cream
2 egg yolks
2 egg whites
1 oz. rum, warm
1 oz. Grand Marnier
3 tbsp. lingonberries, warm

Over heat, melt butter and flour mixed with milk and 1½ oz. sugar. Bring to a boil. Add heavy cream and stir in egg yolks. Beat egg whites with remaining sugar. Combine with batter. Using large, heated saute pan (14 inches), pour in mixture like a pancake, covering the sides also. Place in 375° F. oven and bake for 5 minutes, or until pancake is light brown and the sides stand up. Remove and place on platter. At tableside, pour warm lingonberries in center of "sombrero," fold over, and cover with Grand Marnier. Place rum in heated ladle, ignite, and ladle over folded sombrero, tossing gently.

Flaming South Sea Classic

INGREDIENTS   YIELD: 8 to 10 servings

Dough

½ oz. baker's yeast
1 tbsp. water
4 tbsp. milk
10 oz. flour
1½ tsp. sugar
3 oz. butter
3 eggs

Filling

3 papayas, peeled and sliced
4 bananas, peeled and sliced
juice of 1 lime

Place yeast, warm water, and 1 tbsp. milk in mixing bowl. Dissolve. Add flour and sugar. Blend with electric mixer at low speed for 3 minutes. Add eggs slowly until dough forms. Gradually add more milk and butter. Dough should stretch easily. Place in bowl and let rise in warm place for 20 minutes. Press down. Divide among savarin forms. Let rise again. Bake at 375° F. for 15 minutes until done. Cool. Turn onto serving platter decorated with palm leaves.

For filling, combine all fruit with lime juice, cinnamon, orange rind, and plum wine. Soak.

To flame, heat fruit mixture in sauce pan. Place in center of savarins. Flame heated Grand Marnier and rum. Ladle over fruit.

(Cont.)

dash of cinnamon, ground
rind of 2 oranges, shredded
1 Hawaiian pineapple, peeled and diced
½ cup plum wine

Flaming
Grand Marnier
dark rum

Apricot Classic

INGREDIENTS	For 4	For 24
apricots	8	48
sugar cubes	8	48
butter	6 oz.	2 lb., 4 oz.
flour	6 oz.	2 lb., 4 oz.
boiled potatoes	3	18
salt	pinch	dash
eggs	2	8
water	1 gal.	5 gal.
graham cracker crumbs	1 cup	6 cups
confectioner's sugar	to sprinkle	to sprinkle

Cut apricots on the side, remove pit, and replace with sugar cubes. Over the double boiler, mix butter with flour until dough separates from pan. Press cold potatoes through fine sieve. Combine with flour mixture, salt, and eggs, and form a dough. Knead and divide among apricots. Cover each apricot with dough. Place in boiling water and boil for 12 minutes. Remove, roll in graham cracker crumbs, and sprinkle with confectioner's sugar. Serve hot.

Parisienne Classic

INGREDIENTS	For 4	For 24
egg yolks	8	48
confectioner's sugar	2 tbsp.	¾ cup
zest of lemon	2 lemons	12 lemons
marsala	¼ cup	1½ cups
egg whites	8	48
granulated sugar	2 tbsp.	¾ cup
pistachios	1 tbsp.	⅓ cup
milk chocolate	2 oz.	12 oz.

Combine egg yolks, confectioner's sugar, lemon zest, and marsala. Whisk over double boiler till creamy. Beat egg whites with granulated sugar till very stiff. Fold in egg mixture and pistachios. Pour in champagne glasses and sprinkle with shaved milk chocolate.

California Grape Classic

INGREDIENTS	For 4–6	For 24–28
California white wine	2½ cups	1 gal.
sugar	4 oz.	1½ lb.
juice of lemon	1	6
whole eggs	6	36
cornstarch	2 tsp.	4 tbsp.
seedless grapes	20	180

Combine wine, sugar, lemon juice, eggs, and cornstarch. Whisk over double boiler until hot and creamy. Cut grapes in half. Place in champagne glasses and pour hot sauce over. Decorate with whole grapes rolled in sugar. Serve hot.

Cannoli Classic

INGREDIENTS   YIELD: 10 to 14 servings

Dough

1 cup flour
1 tbsp. butter
2 tbsp. sugar
2 oz. white wine

Filling

1 cup ricotta cheese
3 tbsp. sugar
1 tsp. vanilla
1 cup whipped cream
1 cup candied fruit
1 oz. brandy

To prepare dough, mix flour with butter and sugar. Add wine slowly, to absorb all flour. Roll out thin. Cut dough into squares, 4 × 4 inches. Roll out and place on cannoli stick or round pipe. Wet ends of dough and press together. Place pipe in 350° F. oil, and fry until golden brown.

To prepare filling, mix cheese with sugar, vanilla, and whipped cream. Soak finely chopped candied fruit in brandy, and fold into cheese mixture. Place mixture in pastry bag. Pipe through a large star tube to fill each cannoli. Sprinkle with confectioner's sugar, and arrange on silver platter.

Haagen Dazs Classic

INGREDIENTS   YIELD: 10 servings

1 qt. Haagen Dazs coffee ice cream
1 cup whipped heavy cream
2 oz. creme de menthe
1 pt. Haagen Dazs vanilla ice cream
½ cup candied fruit
1 qt. Haagen Dazs strawberry ice cream
½ cup whipped cream, for decorating
20 crystallized mint leaves
1 pt. fresh, ripe strawberries
4 oz. coconut rum

Spread coffee ice cream on bottom of 9-inch ring mold. Combine whipped cream with creme de menthe. Mix with vanilla ice cream and candied fruit. Spread on top of coffee ice cream. Top with strawberry ice cream. Place in freezer over night, or 8 hours. Remove, and dip in warm water for several seconds. Turn ring upside down on serving platter. Decorate with whipped cream and crystallized mint leaves. Return to freezer until serving time. Place fresh strawberries, soaked in coconut rum, in center of ring.

Crepes

Crepes are small, thin, round pancakes, with various fillings, rolled, sprinkled with confectioner's sugar, and burned with a hot needle in a diamond design. The basic, small crepe mixture consists of 2 cups of milk whisked with 1 cup of flour, 3 eggs, and a pinch of salt. Combine all ingredients and blend together. In a small frying pan, heat 1 oz. of butter and place a 2 oz. ladle of the crepe mixture, turning pan so the mixture can spread out. Brown on one side, turn it over and brown the other side. This will give you 14 pancakes, or yield 4–6 portions. Flavorings of kirsch, rosewater, or rum are optional. You need not put more than ½ oz. in the crepe mixture. When the crepes are completed, you may try to roll 4 crepes with a mixture of 4 oz. of cottage cheese, 1 tbsp. sugar, and ¼ cup of raisins. Place in flat, buttered, earthenware dish and cover with a mixture of 2 oz. of milk and 1 egg. Bake this at 375° F. for 20 minutes. This will give you an excellent dessert surprise.

Crepes Orange Classic—orange flavored, and filled with almonds, whipped cream, and rosewater. Sprinkled with orange zest and confectioner's sugar. Diamond design.

Crepes Irish Classic—flavored with kirsch, and filled with milk chocolate sauce. Flamed with cognac and covered with Irish cream.

Crepes Gastronome—flavored with Grand Marnier, and filled with strawberry puree and diced pineapples soaked in scotch whiskey. Sprinkled with confectioner's sugar. Diamond design.

Crepes Classical Gourmet—flavored with praline liqueur, and filled with vanilla cream mixed with whipped cream and gooseberries. Covered with gooseberry puree and sprinkled with pomegranate seeds.

Crepes Viennese—basic crepes filled with apricot jam, rolled, and sprinkled with confectioner's sugar. Diamond design.

Crepes San Remo—crepes flavored with galliano, and filled with lemon sherbet. Pour over more galliano, roll, and cover with chocolate sauce.

Crepes Olympic—filled with ladyfingers soaked in pear brandy, mixed with whipped cream and diced, candied fruit. Sprinkled with confectioner's sugar. Folded in diamond shapes with diamond design.

Crepes Sabra—filled with orange jam, flavored with cognac. Covered with sabra.

Crepes Laconia—flavored with orange blossom water, and filled with butter cream mixed with whipped cream, rosewater, rose petals, and confectioner's sugar. Diamond design, decorated with rose petals.

Crepes Casablanca—flavored with cognac, and filled with bing cherries and orange sherbet. Flamed with kirsch, and folded in diamond shape.

Crepes Flaming Pacific—flavored with pineapple rum, and filled with diced mangoes, pineapple, papayas, bananas, and Chinese gooseberries soaked in orange blossom water. Rolled, placed in large skillet with kahlua, and flamed with dark rum.

Crepes Big Apple—flavored with cointreau, and filled with sliced apples soaked in syrup. Flamed with kirsch.

Pancake Kaiser Franz Josef

INGREDIENTS   YIELD: 4 servings

4 eggs, well beaten

¾ cup milk

1¼ cups all-purpose flour

¼ cup sugar

salt to taste

1 tsp. oil

4 tbsp. raisins

¼ tsp. baking powder

3 oz. butter

confectioner's sugar, to sprinkle

ground cinnamon, to sprinkle

4 cups plums, boiled in red wine

Beat eggs and milk. Add flour, sugar, salt, oil, raisins, and baking powder. Let stand for 5 minutes. Melt butter in heavy frying pan. Add mixture and brown for 10 minutes on low heat. Turn and brown on other side for 10 minutes or till baked well through. Use 2 forks to score crosswise into 2-inch squares. Place pancakes on large platter, and sprinkle with confectioner's sugar and cinnamon. Serve plums with juice in side dish.

The World of Cheese

Cheese has a history of thousands of years—as long as milk has been known to man. Today, cheese is international. The Italians have their blue-veined gorgonzola and the hardest cheese of all, the parmesan. The Greeks have their feta made from goat's milk, salted, and preserved in a brine. Scandinavia offers the smooth jarlsberg, Holland the edam. The soft liederkranz comes from the United States. The white, velvet surfaced cheese, which ripens from the outside, is the fromage de brie from France.

Cheese can be served with drinks, with salads, with fruit, bread, sweet butter, wine, and as desserts, and Switzerland's gruyere cheese is used for fondues. Farmers around the world produce their own specialties. Perhaps the best of all is the classic pur chevre, made from goat's milk.

The Origin of Cheese

The cheesemaking process is basically unchanged from the centuries-old legend of its origin. It is said that a horseman poured milk into a container made from a young cow's stomach, and set out on a journey through the woods. He rode for hours over hills and valleys, and all the while the container bounced up and down. When he stopped to rest and to take a drink of the milk, the horseman discovered that it had become a sour, curd-like substance. This most primitive form of cheese was quickly adopted as part of the diet.

The ingredient in the young cow's stomach that separated the milk into white lumps and a watery liquid (curds and whey) is called rennet. In the natural cheesemaking process, the whey is stirred and a certain amount of hot water is added, causing the curd to shrink as it releases more whey. As the curdled substance yields more and more whey, stirring makes the curd firmer and drier. Steam is used instead of hot water to release whey near the end of this procedure. The firm curd is then placed in molds, where it begins to take on the familiar shape of cheese. The remaining whey is forced out as the cheese is wrapped in cloth and pressed, although various cheeses are developed by allowing some whey to remain. After several hours of pressing, the cloth is changed and the cheese is placed in a brine which causes the rind to form. Placed on a shelf to dry, the cheese is again covered in a cloth and transferred to a storage area where controlled humidity allows ripening to begin. If the temperature is altered, the cheese will not be the same. The qualities of the milk from cows grazing in one country will differ from the milk produced in another, so that the milk itself, as well as slight variations in the cheesemaking process, will make a certain type of cheese impossible to imitate.

It was the Greeks who gave cheese its name. The basket used to drain their cheeses was called *formos*, also known to the Romans as *caseus*. It became *cyse* to the Anglo-Saxons, and eventually evolved to the word "cheese." Today the Germans call it Käse, the Dutch call it Kaas, in Spain it is queso, the French know it as fromage, and the Italians call it fromaggio.

Among the beneficial nutrients contained in cheeses are:

Calcium—for bones and teeth, regulates activity of nerves and muscles, insures normal blood clotting.
Protein—builds and repairs body tissue, it is a major component of hemoglobin.
Vitamin A—for skeletal growth, skin and mucous membranes, normal eye functioning.
Vitamin B—regulates digestion, helps maintain functions of muscles, heart, nerves, and blood.

European Cheeses

Holland is known for two famous cheeses: edam and gouda. In making edam cheese, partially skimmed milk is combined with the usual whole milk. First, rennet is added to separate the curds from the whey. Then the curd is cut and churned in stainless steel vats before being placed in pressing molds with the correct edam shape. Whey is drained for several hours, then cheeses are placed in a salt water solution for five days.

About 800 years ago, farmers near the town of Edam discovered that treating the cheese with vermilion cloths gave it a reddish glow. The rind of Edam cheese, now world famous, is as renowned as its spherical shape and delicious flavor. Today a red wax coating is used instead of the vermilion cloths.

Gouda is made much the same way as edam, but uses only whole milk. Also, the curd is brought to a higher temperature before being poured into the molds. The result is a two-to-three month aging process, a softer-bodied cheese, and a sharper flavor.

Farmers near Gouda traditionally made cheese twice a day, after each milking, because only whole, fresh milk was used. Gouda cheese achieved a rich, buttery flavor and character all its own. Its distinctive shape, a large flat wheel with rounded edges, is still stocked at the market square in the town of Alkmaar.

Switzerland is famous for the Emmentaler Swiss. Aged four to eight months, it has a well-developed eye. Raclette cheese has a mild, unique flavor. Boiled in its natural rind and aged four to six months, the finished cheese weighs up to sixteen pounds. Sap Sago cheese is made from decreamed milk. Milled clover gives it a pungent flavor.

England's oldest cheeses are red, white, and blue variations of Cheshire English cheeses. Stilton, the "king" of English cheeses, has blue veins and a special, tangy flavor. Welshmen have their own favorite—Caerphilly, a creamy white cheese with a mild, delicate flavor.

France produces almost 400 varieties of cheese, each one as distinctive as a fingerprint. This selection includes cheeses made from cow's, ewe's, or goat's milk, or any combination. Each region of France has its specialty. Normandy is famous for unctuous Camembert and Pont l'Eveque; the Loire Valley and Poitou for tangy goat's milk cheeses; Alsace for robust Muenster; the Alpine region for firmer, subtly-flavored Reblochon and Beaumont; the Paris area for prestigious Brie; and the Pyrenees for Chiberta, firm and slightly nutty in flavor.

Types of Cheese

Double and Triple Creme Cheeses

What we Americans call cream cheese is a very distant relative to these rich, creamy, fresh cheeses from France. They vary in texture from thick, heavy sour or fresh cream, to semi firm cream. All are delicate with a refreshing tang. Many varieties are blended with a mixture of herbs and garlic or spices, such as pepper.

According to French law, these cheeses are classified double creme when they contain a minimum of 60 percent butterfat, and triple creme when they contain a minimum of 75 percent butterfat per gram.

These cremes are delightful at any time of the day, for any menu or snack. Simply spread them on crusty French bread and serve with fresh (non-citrus) fruits in season. Young, fruity wines are ideal to accompany these cheeses, particularly white and rose. Many Americans enjoy the herbed and peppered versions of these cheeses at cocktail hour. Among the cremes available are:

La Bouille—this rich triple creme has its own special tang.
Brillat-Savarin—from Normandy, this triple creme is a thick, plump white disk, with a buttery texture and elasticity.
Gervais—world renowned since 1850, Gervais is a tangy double creme from Normandy. Usually packaged in squares, its texture is similar to American cream cheese but its flavor is richer and slightly tangy. Pristine white in color, it is lightly salted and contains no preservatives.

Soft-Ripened Cheeses

These exquisite cheeses are the result of French cheesemaking genius. Soft-ripened or surface-ripened cheeses fall into two distinct categories: those with white powdery rinds, also called flowery or bloomy, and those with orange-colored washed rinds. Flowery rind cheeses are also referred to as soft paste cheeses. When fully ripened their crust is tinged reddish brown and the center is soft to the touch. A soft-ripened cheese with a washed rind is, as the name implies, washed in a brine solution and then brushed to keep the rind supple and moist.

In both instances the interior is golden yellow, creamy, buttery smooth, and slightly runny. The two types of rinds are edible, however, as the cheese matures the rind takes on a strong flavor and should be removed.

As with all French cheeses, this type must be served at room temperature.

Flowery Rind Types

Brie is the ultimate soft-ripened cheese. Its powdery, edible white crust is tinged light brown when fully ripened. The finest examples are named after their towns of origin: Brie de Meaux and Brie de Melun. Camembert, one of France's most popular cheeses of this variety, is known and admired throughout the world. Available in an 8 oz. round, it is a specialty of the province of Normandy. Coulommiers, like Brie, is produced in the Ile-de-France region outside of Paris. It is smaller and plumper than its cousin, but similar in flavor and texture.

Washed Rind Types

Muenster cheese has a strong aroma but is mild in taste. Plump, round, and rather orange in color, it is sometimes flavored with cumin or caraway. Vieux Pane is a large flat square produced in the south of France. It resembles Pont l'Eveque, but it is milder in taste.

Semi-Soft Cheeses

These cheeses are pressed, uncooked, and contain little water. Their slow maturing process allows them to be stored for longer periods of time than other highly perishable cheeses such as fresh cremes. They are mild in flavor with a clean, fresh tang which varies in strength depending on age. Most semi-soft cheeses have an inedible crust. Their interior is smooth, buttery, and slightly resilient to the touch. They slice easily and have good melting qualities making them ideal for cooking. They are also excellent for snacks.

Babybel is made from cow's milk. It is firm in texture and retains its freshness because the cheese is enveloped in a red paraffin wrapper. It has a slightly nutty flavor. Doux de Montagne comes in a 7 lb. round loaf with a brown rind. It has a pale yellow, creamy interior with small eyes. This Alpine cheese is mild in flavor. St. Nectaire is a cousin to Port Salut but its inedible crust is darkish brown.

Goat's Milk Cheeses | These cheeses are much prized by connoisseurs and almost every region of France has its own special goat's milk cheese. They are found in many sizes and shapes, including round patties, small logs, drums, pyramids, and loaves. Textures vary from soft but firm, somewhat like cream cheese, to extremely hard.

Chevres make excellent dessert cheeses, served with bread and fruit. Bucheron, a large 3½ lb. log from the Poitou region has a light edible rind, chalky center, creamy edges, and rich tangy flavor. Montrachet is made in the province of Burgundy, and always comes in the shape of a log. It is mild and creamy in flavor with a rind that may or may not be dusted with vine wood ash.

Roquefort | The "king" of cheeses, as it is known throughout the world, is made exclusively from ewe's milk in the south of France and aged and ripened in the limestone caves of the small village of Roquefort. It is unique, unlike any other cheese in flavor and texture. Authentic Roquefort can be easily identified by the red sheep emblem on the label.

Blue-Veined Cheeses | These cheeses have a blue vein marbling. Usually developed by natural fermentation processes, inoculation is sometimes used to start or hasten ripening and maturing. The term persille, which is often applied to these cheeses, has nothing to do with parsley. Rather it refers to the blue-green veining which looks like parsley. These cheeses have a tangy flavor, are usually semi soft, and are often crumbly, especially when cold. With few exceptions, such as Roquefort, almost all blue-veined cheeses are made with cow's milk. Natural blue cheeses are produced in many areas of France and are named after their region of origin.

Belle Bressane is shaped in a 4 lb. wheel with a center hole and comes from the region of Ain near the Alps. It is a buttery, blue-veined cheese made from cow's milk, with a soft-ripened rind. Bleu d'Auvergne is from the mountains of the rustic region of the Auvergne. This cheese is made from cow's milk in the form of a 5 lb. cylinder. It has a rich, sharp flavor. Fourme d'Ambert is produced in the mountainous area of Auvergne. This cheese is named Fourme after its shape, a tall cylinder. It is a particularly tangy cheese, sharper than most blue veined cheeses.

Semi-Hard and Hard Cheeses | These firm-textured cheeses are produced primarily in the mountains of France. They are cooked, then pressed, and come in the form of large wheels. In France, Gruyere is the generic name for all the big cheeses such as Beaufort, Comte, and Emmental. Usually they have many eyes, the size of which is helpful in identifying the various kinds. These popular cheeses are often used in gratine dishes, and in many other recipes.

Beaufort is produced in mountain chalets and dairies of the Jura and Savoie regions; a rich, strong example of Gruyere-type cheeses. It is pressed, uncooked cheese made in large wheels with an ivory interior and few small holes. Cantal, a native of the Auvergne region, is one of France's oldest and most famous cheeses. It has a piquant flavor but its hard crust is not edible. It is low in fat and high in protein, making it an excellent choice for dieters. Also, it is fine for cooking or as a simple table cheese with bread and red wine. A wheel may weigh as much as 100 pounds. Emmental Francais can be identified by its eyes which are relatively large. This cheese has a nutlike tang that adds zest to such dishes as quiches, fondues, and sauces.

Fondu or Processed Cheeses

Most of France's processed cheeses are a blend, with a creme de Gruyere as a base. They may be firm and heavy in texture or soft, smooth, and spreadable.

Gourmandise is a creamy spread made from Emmental blended with butter, milk, and cream. A party and dessert favorite, Gourmandise comes flavored with kirsch, walnut extract, crushed almonds, whole raisins, fresh herbs, port wine, and orange extract. La Vache Qui Rit pictures a laughing cow on the label. This has become an American favorite. It is available in cocktail size pieces or in packages of individual wedge shaped portions, plain or flavored with pimiento, caraway, or onion.

The Wine Cellar

Wines are divided into five categories:

appetizer wines
white table wines
red table wines
sweet dessert wines
sparkling wines.

Appetizer wines include dubbonet, vermouth, and sherry, and many brand names such as Cinzano, imported from France. In the continental manner, they are consumed "straight." Aperitif wines are made with the addition of herbs and other flavorings. The average alcohol content is 18 percent. Italian vermouth is much sweeter than the French. Vermouths are used for cocktails, for example, 1 part vermouth, and 2 parts of gin, vodka, or bourbon, with a twist of lemon.

White table wines vary in color from pale straw to deep gold to dark brown. The delicate flavor of a moselle from Germany, an alsatian from France, a gumpoldskirchner from Austria, or a California or eastern United States wine is best served with seafood, white meat, fowl, and soup. The average alcohol content is 12 percent.

Red table wines include the pink or rose wines. The average alcohol content is 12 percent. Burgundy (Bourgogne) wines from France are the most imitated in the world. The more outstanding Burgundy regions are Pomard and Chambertin. In Germany, it is the Blauer Spaetburgunder (Pinotnoir). Cultivated for over 500 years, these small, blue grapes, deep red inside, rank among Germany's best. Also noteworthy are the regions of Argentina, Austria, Italy, and the United States.

Sweet dessert wines generally average an alcohol content of 20 percent. The best known is port. Originating from Portugal, it is classified as tawny or ruby. Tawny is heavy bodied and ruby is the lightest bodied. Madeira comes from the coast of the small island of Madeira, which has a variety of grapes from its small vineyards. Sweet wines for the dessert table include sweet sauternes, marsala, tokay, sherry, and sparkling wines.

Sparkling wines, which go through a secondary fermentation, were discovered centuries ago. They are white, pink, or red and have a wide range of flavor, from dry to sweet. Their alcohol content averages 12 percent. The best known is Cuvee Dom Perignon, established in France in 1743, and known as champagne. Sparkling wines from other regions cannot be called champagne. Sparkling wines come from Italy, Germany, and the United States unknown to the western hemisphere is Cobetckoe Ntpnctoe from the U.S.S.R.

American Wines

Soil, climate, and type of vine are the factors that determine the character of all wines.

In America, California is the most widely known wine area. However, there are many states where wine is produced, including New York and Ohio. Both sweet and dry wines are produced in these areas. The southern areas of California produce sweeter grapes, because its climate is hot and dry. Northern regions in America produce drier wines due to their damp and colder weather.

United States Wineries

The nations's richest wine region is Santa Clara, producing more wine annually than the combined imports of Germany, France, Italy, and Spain. Here you can experience the refinements of a carefully maintained tradition, over 125 years old. Almaden Vineyards, Santa Clara's largest winery and one of the giant growers of premium varietals, holds the distinction of being California's first winery. It was founded in 1852 by a Frenchman named Charles Le Franc. The country's most famous premium wine labels offer a wide range of red, white, and sparkling wines, champagnes, and sherries. Surrounding wineries are:

San Martin Winery—Emerald Riesling, Cabernet Sauvignon.
Brookside Winery—Hausemarke Rhine, Hausemarke Rote.
Paul Masson Vineyards—Emerald Dry, Rubion.
Kirigin Cellars—on the southern slopes of the Santa Cruz Mountains in the Uvas Valley. Started in 1827 by an immigrant from Zagreb, Nikola Kirigin-Chargin. Now located in the historic Solis Rancho.
Live Oak Winery—started in 1912 by Eduardo Scagliotti. Suggested wine selections include Premium Burgundy, Chenin Blanc, Dry, Sweet, Medium.
Los Altos Rapazzini Brothers—Petite Sirah, Chenin Blanc.
Ridge Vineyards—its setting, high in the Santa Cruz Mountains, offers impressive views of the Santa Clara Valley. Selection, Zinfandels.
Pedrizzeti Winery—Barbera, Chenin Blanc.
Weibel Champagne Vineyards—as early as 1806, Mission San Jose yielded excellent wine. Established in 1869, it has a well-earned reputation for champagnes. Its grape variety originally imported from France.
Tureon and Lohr Winery—high quality to taste from the barrels. Established in 1972.
Mirassou Vineyards—Monterey Riesling, Gamay Beaujolais
La Purisima Winery—Begun in 1976, to offer fine quality California coastal wines.

America's oldest winery is located in New York's Hudson River Valley. Brotherhood is surrounded by countryside rich in history as well as scenery. Its historic underground cellars are the largest in the United States. In their shadowy coolness, wine ages and mellows according to the ancient art handed down through generations of master vintners. Champagne vaults and huge white oak casks line the native stone walls. Brotherhood, America's oldest winery, is in Washingtonville, New York.

Wine Tasting

Savor the experience and use sight, smell, and taste for the fullest enjoyment of fine wine.

1. Pour two ounces of wine into a glass. Holding the glass by the stem,

raise it to the light, and examine the color and clarity of the wine. It must be clear and brilliant, free of suspended material, never cloudy.

2. Swirl the wine around gently. This allows the wine to breathe and release its fragrance. Now sniff sharply to carry the aroma and bouquet to your nose.

3. Sip the wine without swallowing, and roll it around your tongue to expose every taste bud. Note the wine's body and richness. Swallow it, sense the warm flow, enjoy the finish of the wine.

Between tastings enjoy some cheese and bread. Why not begin the tasting and study of wines? And keep a record of your impressions.

III
The Versatile Chef

12. The Hawaiian Treasure Chest

It was springtime in New York when I came across the announcement of the biggest cook-off of professional chefs in the United States—to create something out of the ordinary with pineapple. It did not take me long to flambe some salads with pineapple, and to stuff some fish and birds with this exotic fruit. However, I put it aside for awhile. The summer and fall passed, but at Christmas I thought of a holiday cake. A pineapple cake. There wasn't much time before the closing of the competition. In a few days the creation had to be ready.

What about a burning torch in the evening—a flaming cake! This had never been done before. The result was the Hawaiian Plantation Cake, sitting on fresh pineapple and decorated with Hawaiian leis. This three-tiered cake, with macadamia nuts, ladyfingers, and marzipan, was ready for the closing date, and the beginning of the party. Honolulu, the dream of thousands of participants, came true.

Hawaiian Plantation Cake (3-Tiered)

INGREDIENTS YIELD: 48 to 60 servings

4 lb. almond paste

4 lb. confectioner's sugar

3 egg whites

24 egg yolks

9 oz. confectioner's sugar

1 qt. heavy cream

3 lb. sweet butter

6 oz. confectioner's sugar

150 ladyfingers

2 oz. Hawaiian pineapple rum

1 oz. milk

1 #10 can pineapple chunks in syrup, well-drained

30 macadamia nuts

4 tsp. cocoa powder

½ tsp. brown paste food color

½ cup confectioner's sugar

Rub almond paste, confectioner's sugar, and egg whites together thoroughly. Place in plastic bag until needed.

Combine egg yolks, 9 oz. sugar, and cream in a double boiler and whip over hot water until hot. Remove from heat and cool.

Whip butter with 6 oz. sugar. Mix in the chilled cream mixture.

Line 3 cake rings with waxed paper, one 12-inch, one 10-inch, and one 8-inch. Cover bottom of each with ladyfingers. Mix pineapple rum with milk, and use part to moisten ladyfingers.

Spread each with a layer of butter cream. Cover with pineapple chunks, pressing lightly into filling. Cover with more butter cream.

Repeat layers, cover top with remaining ladyfingers, and moisten each layer of ladyfingers lightly with rum/milk. Press ladyfingers on top together lightly. Chill thoroughly.

Turn cakes out upside down and remove rings and waxed paper. Roll marzipan in thin sheets large enough to cover tops and sides of cakes. Set 10-inch cake on top of 12-inch cake, and top with 8-inch cake.

Wrap macadamia nuts in marzipan and roll in cocoa. Arrange balls on each tier.

Color remaining marzipan with brown food color. Shape a miniature pineapple and set in center of top cake. Shape remaining marzipan into leaves, and arrange around the pineapple. Place 2 leaves beside each macadamia nut.

Sprinkle entire cake very lightly with confectioner's sugar to give frosted effect.

For display, stand entire cake on top of a Hawaiian pineapple. Cut another pineapple in half, empty shell, dice fruit, and flame with rum. Surround with fresh flowers for decoration. See Color Plate 8.

Hawaiian Plantation Cake

For the "richest taste," it serves 4 to 8,
for the "gourmet," it serves 8 to 12, and
for the "diet watcher," it serves 20 to 30.

INGREDIENTS   YIELD: INGREDIENTS

16 oz. marzipan

3 doz. ladyfingers

8 egg yolks

1 cup heavy cream

1 cup confectioner's sugar

1½ cups sweet butter

28 oz. pineapple chunks, drained

1 tbsp. rum

2 tbsp. milk

1 tbsp. cocoa

macadamia nuts

confectioner's sugar, to sprinkle

Mix egg yolks with cream and ½ cup confectioner's sugar. Beat over double boiler till creamy. Remove and chill. Whip butter with remaining confectioner's sugar, and combine with cold custard. Line 8-inch cake pan with waxed paper. Arrange a layer of ladyfingers on the waxed paper. Sprinkle lightly with rum and milk mixture. Spread half of the cream over ladyfingers. Arrange half of the pineapple chunks over cream, pressing them lightly into the cream. Cover with ladyfingers and moisten with rum/milk mixture. Repeat cream and pineapple layers, and top with more ladyfingers. Chill thoroughly. Unmold cake. Roll marzipan out thinly in a round circle and cover cake. Trim edges. Place back in refrigerator to keep cold. Wrap macadamia nuts in marzipan and roll in dry cocoa. Work 1 tbsp. cocoa into remaining marzipan. Roll out and cut leaves for decorations. Set macadamia nuts on cake, surrounded by marzipan leaves. Sprinkle entire cake very lightly with confectioner's sugar using a wire strainer. Refrigerate until serving time. See Color Plate 8.

Pineapple, The Glory of Hawaii

Waikiki Breakfast Special

INGREDIENTS   YIELD: 24 servings

24 English muffins, split

12 oz. butter

24 eggs

48 tomato slices

parsley, chopped, for garnish

24 slices Canadian bacon

3 lb. 12 oz. pineapple chunks, drained

1½ qt. cheese sauce, heated

24 parsley sprigs

For each serving, toast 1 muffin and spread with butter. Scramble 1 egg. Place 2 tomato slices on one muffin half, top with egg, and sprinkle lightly with parsley.

Fry Canadian bacon. Place 1 slice on second muffin half, and top with 2½ oz. pineapple chunks. Cover with 2 oz. cheese sauce. Garnish with parsley sprig.

Suggested garnish: Skewer of 1 tomato wedge and 1 orange wedge, with parsley sprig.

Golden Pineapple Royal Salad

INGREDIENTS   YIELD: 24 servings

1 #10 can pineapple chunks, in juice

1 cup sugar

1 tsp. salt

½ tsp. cinnamon

½ tsp. curry powder

½ cup lime juice

½ cup cornstarch

1 qt. mayonnaise

2½ qt. cooked chicken (or ham, lobster, or shrimp)

2 cups green pepper, diced

2 cups celery, diced

lettuce leaves, for garnish

24 pineapple slices

24 cherries

2 cups cashews or macadamia nuts

Drain juice from pineapple into saucepan. Add sugar, salt, cinnamon, curry powder, and lime juice. Heat to boiling.

Mix cornstarch with water. Stir into boiling juice. Simmer a few minutes. Remove from heat and chill.

Combine cold pineapple juice mixture with mayonnaise and blend well.

Mix drained pineapple chunks, chicken, green pepper, and celery. Add dressing and mix gently.

Serve on lettuce leaves, garnishing each serving with a pineapple slice, a cherry, and a sprinkling of nuts.

Pineapple Spinach Salad Oriental

INGREDIENTS   YIELD: 24 servings

2 lb., 8 oz. fresh spinach, washed and drained

1 lb. fresh mushrooms, sliced*

3 5-oz. cans water chestnuts, drained and sliced

1 qt. pineapple chunks, in juice, drained

4 large navel oranges, peeled and sectioned

¾ cup salad oil

6 tbsp. wine vinegar

6 tbsp. orange juice

3 tbsp. soy sauce

¾ tsp. Tabasco sauce

¾ tsp. salt

¾ tsp. dry mustard

Coarsely tear spinach into salad bowl. Add mushrooms, water chestnuts, pineapple chunks, and orange sections.

Mix oil, vinegar, orange juice, soy sauce, Tabasco sauce, salt, and mustard. Shake together well. Shake and add to salad just before serving. Toss lightly.

*Or use 1 8-oz. can sliced mushrooms, drained.

Pineapple Confetti Salad

INGREDIENTS   YIELD: 24 5-oz. servings

4 lb. dried beef, cut in strips

3⅔ qt. pineapple chunks in juice, drained

1 cup green pepper, coarsely chopped

½ cup pimiento, chopped

½ cup pineapple juice

3 cups mayonnaise

½ cup pineapple juice

2 tbsp. seasoned salt

2 tbsp. Worcestershire sauce

¼ tsp. Tabasco sauce

romaine lettuce, to line bowl

mixed salad greens, chopped (romaine, iceberg, red leaf lettuce)

Combine dried beef, pineapple chunks, green pepper, pimiento, and ½ cup pineapple juice. Mix together and chill at least 1 hour.

Mix mayonnaise with ½ cup pineapple juice, seasoned salt, Worcestershire sauce, and Tabasco. Chill.

Line serving bowl with romaine leaves and fill center with chopped salad greens. Top with meat-pineapple mixture.

Spoon dressing over salad just before serving. Toss lightly as salad is served.

Pineapple Spinach Salad With Mountain Brook Dressing

INGREDIENTS   YIELD: 25 portions

5 cups sour cream

2½ tsp. sugar

1¼ tsp. dry mustard

4 tsp. fresh lemon juice

2½ cups mayonnaise

3 tbsp. juice from canned pineapple

2½ tsp. capers

5 lb. spinach leaves

1 lb., 8 oz. fresh mushrooms (large)

lemon juice, for mushrooms

2 lb. California walnuts

1 #10 can pineapple chunks, in juice

Dressing

Mix together sour cream, sugar, and mustard. Gradually stir in lemon juice. Chill. Shortly before serving, blend in mayonnaise, pineapple juice, and capers.

Wash spinach thoroughly, at least 3 times, to remove sand. Drain well and remove stems. Tear leaves into bite size pieces.

Clean mushrooms, trim stems, and cut in medaillons. Dip in lemon juice to prevent darkening.

Toast walnuts in moderately slow oven (325° F.) about 8 minutes, until lightly toasted.

Divide spinach into 25 individual serving bowls. Top each with 4 or 5 mushrooms, 1 oz. walnuts, about 12 pineapple chunks, and 2 oz. dressing.

Annie's Flaming Spinach Salad

INGREDIENTS   YIELD: 24 servings

3 lb. fresh spinach leaves

1 cup bacon bits

¾ cup cider vinegar

juice of 3 lemons

½ cup sugar

2½ oz. Hawaiian teriyaki sauce

3 cups Hawaiian pineapple chunks

¾ cup brandy

Wash spinach, place in a large bowl, and refrigerate. Mix bacon bits with vinegar, lemon juice, sugar, teriyaki sauce, and pineapple chunks. Bring sauce to simmer. Pour sauce over spinach leaves, holding back bacon bits and pineapple chunks. Toss the salad and divide among 24 plates. Set aside. Continue simmering bacon and pineapple chunks. Add brandy and ignite. While flaming, ladle evenly over spinach mounds. Serve immediately.

Vegetable Salad Tropicana

INGREDIENTS   YIELD: 24 servings

3 qt. carrots, pared and thinly sliced

1½ qt. boiling water

1½ tbsp. salt

2½ qt. zucchini, cut in thin wedges

1 cup oil

½ cup white wine vinegar

½ cup lemon juice

4 tsp. salt

2 tsp. basil, finely crumbled

1½ tsp. mint, finely crumbled

2 tsp. dry mustard

leaf lettuce, for garnish

1¾ qt. pineapple tidbits, well drained

4 lb., 2 oz. cottage cheese

Place carrots in kettle with boiling water and 1½ tbsp. salt. Bring back to a boil, cover, and cook 5 minutes. Stir in zucchini, remove from heat, and cool. Mix oil, vinegar, lemon juice, salt, basil, mint, and mustard for dressing. Drain vegetables well, add dressing, and mix lightly. Chill several hours or overnight.

For each serving, place 2 oz. vegetable mixture in 8 oz. serving dish lined with small lettuce leaf. Top vegetables with 2 oz. pineapple tidbits. Add 2 oz. vegetables, 1 oz. pineapple, and top with 2¾ oz. (#16 scoop) cottage cheese.

Hawaiian Sundae Salad

INGREDIENTS   YIELD: 24 servings

1 #10 can pineapple chunks

leaf lettuce, for garnish

5 lb. cottage cheese

4 medium bananas

24 strawberries

24 parsley sprigs

salad dressing, as desired

Drain pineapple well. For each serving, line sundae dish with leaf lettuce. Add 3 oz. pineapple chunks, and 1 #12 scoop cottage cheese. Garnish with 2 thick unpeeled banana slices, 1 halved strawberry, and a small sprig of parsley.

Serve with sweet French or other desired dressing.

Pineapple Platter Salad

INGREDIENTS   YIELD: 24 servings

leaf lettuce, for garnish

3 lb. iceberg lettuce, shredded

48 (66 count) pineapple slices

3 lb. 8 oz. (¾ oz. slices) cold assorted meats

4 lb., 2 oz. cottage cheese

24 small pickles

24 cherry tomatoes

24 parsley sprigs

salad dressing, as desired

For each serving, line individual plates with leaf lettuce. Top with 1 cup shredded lettuce, 2 slices pineapple, 4 slices cold meat, and 1 #16 scoop cottage cheese. Garnish with pickle, cherry tomato, and parsley sprig.

Serve with desired salad dressing.

Hawaiian Garden Salad Bowl

INGREDIENTS YIELD: 24 servings

12 oz. mushrooms (small, sliced)
½ cup oil and vinegar dressing
leaf lettuce, for garnish
9 lb. iceberg lettuce, shredded
72 carrot slices, crinkle sliced
48 (66 count) canned pineapple slices
144 zucchini slices, thinly sliced
5 lb., 4 oz. cottage cheese
48 cherry tomatoes
24 thin cucumber slices
24 parsley sprigs
2½ qt. 1000 island dressing

Combine mushrooms with oil and vinegar dressing. Chill 1 hour or longer. Line individual serving bowls with leaf lettuce. Add 3 cups shredded lettuce. Arrange over lettuce 3 carrot slices, 2 well-drained pineapple slices, 6 zucchini slices, ½ oz. marinated mushrooms, and one #16 scoop cottage cheese.

On bamboo skewer, arrange 2 cherry tomatoes with cucumber slice between. Garnish bowl with skewer and parsley sprig. Serve 3 oz. dressing on the side.

1000 Island Dressing

INGREDIENTS YIELD: 2½ quarts

2 qt. mayonnaise
1 pt. chili sauce
2 tbsp. cider vinegar
1 tbsp. prepared horseradish

Mix all ingredients together well.

Flaming Veal Chops, South Pacific

INGREDIENTS YIELD: 24 servings

24 6-oz. veal chops with bone
salt and white pepper, ground, to taste
¼ lb. salted butter
72 avocado slices
1 lb. mushroom buttons
3 cups Hawaiian pineapple chunks
2 oz. brandy
1 cup sliced almonds, toasted
24 triangular croutons
watercress, for garnish

Sprinkle veal chops lightly with salt and pepper. Brown on both sides in butter. Transfer cutlets to serving casserole. Place 3 slices avocado on top of each chop. Keep hot. In same skillet, saute mushrooms and Hawaiian pineapple chunks. Pour brandy over and ignite. While flaming, ladle sauce over veal chops. Sprinkle with toasted almonds. Place one crouton to each chop. Garnish with watercress.

Chicken of Hawaii

INGREDIENTS   YIELD: 24 servings

36 8-oz. chicken legs, cut in half

salt and white pepper, ground, to taste

¼ lb. salted butter

¾ lb. carrots, cut in 1½ x ¼-inch strips

4 medium zucchini, cut in 1½ x ¼-inch strips

½ lb. celery stalks, cut in 1½ x ¼-inch strips

1 lb. fresh mushrooms, sliced

2 oz. brandy

10 tomatoes, peeled and quartered

juice of 10 garlic cloves

2 oz. Hawaiian teriyaki sauce

1 #10 can pineapple chunks, drained

4 cups white wine

1 cup sliced almonds, toasted

watercress, for garnish

Season chicken pieces with salt and pepper. Bake in 350° F. oven for 40 minutes. Place on serving dishes and keep hot. Melt butter and saute carrots, zucchini, celery, and mushrooms till tender. Add brandy and ignite. Add tomato wedges, garlic juice, teriyaki sauce, pineapple chunks, and white wine. Season with salt and pepper, and pour over chicken. Sprinkle with toasted almonds. Garnish with watercress.

Hawaiian Pineapple Dumplings

INGREDIENTS   YIELD: 4 to 6 servings

Dumplings

2 lb. potatoes

1 gal. water, to boil (lightly salted)

3 tbsp. sweet butter, melted

3 egg yolks

salt to taste

1 lemon rind, freshly grated

10 oz. all purpose flour

1 14-oz. can Hawaiian pineapple chunks, in heavy syrup, well drained

Dumpling Crust

6 oz. all-natural breadcrumbs

3 tbsp. sweet butter

Sauce

remaining pineapple syrup

2 oz. Grand Marnier

To prepare crust, melt butter in large pan, stir in all-natural breadcrumbs, and roast till golden brown.

To prepare dumplings, boil potatoes in lightly salted water. Remove, peel, and press through fine strainer. Mix in melted butter, egg yolks, salt, and lemon rind. Add flour and mix to a dough. Form 12 dumplings. Press each dumpling flat and fill with Hawaiian pineapple chunks. Form back into dumpling shape and place each in boiling water, stirring after 5 minutes very carefully to prevent dumplings from sticking to the bottom. Boil for 20 minutes. Roll each dumpling in prepared crust.

To prepare sauce, heat remaining pineapple syrup. Stir in Grand Marnier before serving.

To serve, arrange each hot dumpling, rolled in crust, on a serving platter. Sprinkle with powdered sugar and serve hot sauce on the side.

Polytalian Chicken Casserole

INGREDIENTS   YIELD: 24 servings

2 lb. broad noodles

1 cup onion, finely chopped

1 cup green pepper, finely chopped

2 garlic cloves, crushed finely

⅛ cup olive oil

salt and pepper to taste

2 bay leaves

1 tsp. thyme

½ tsp. oregano

3 lb. white chicken meat, diced

3 lb. fresh ripe, peeled tomatoes, diced in large pieces

1 #10 can pineapple chunks, drained

20 slices Swiss cheese

⅛ lb. parmesan cheese, grated

Cook 2 lb. broad noodles and drain. Set aside. Saute onion, green pepper, and garlic in olive oil. Add bay leaf, thyme, and oregano and continue sauteing until vegetables are transparent. Add chicken and tomatoes and bring to a boil. Slowly simmer 40 minutes. Place half of cooked noodles in bottom of deep casserole dish. Add chicken and tomato mixture on top. Top with remainder of noodles. Place a single layer of pineapple chunks on top of noodles. Top with cheese slices. Sprinkle with parmesan and place in 350°F. oven. Bake for 20 minutes.

Breast of Chicken Teriyaki

INGREDIENTS   YIELD: 12 servings

12 (7 to 8 oz. each) frozen chicken breasts, stuffed with brown and wild rice, thawed

3 tbsp. butter, melted

1½ cups syrup from canned pineapple

1½ cups unsweetened pineapple juice

6 tbsp. red wine vinegar

6 tbsp. soy sauce

2 tbsp. brown sugar

½ tsp. ginger, ground

¼ tsp. garlic, pressed

2 tbsp. cornstarch

½ cup sherry (dry)

12 pineapple slices, drained

Place thawed chicken breasts in baking pan and brush with melted butter. Bake at 400° F. for 20 minutes. While chicken bakes, combine pineapple syrup and juice with vinegar, soy sauce, sugar, ginger, and garlic. Heat to boiling. Mix cornstarch with sherry and stir into boiling liquid. Simmer 5 minutes. Pass sauce through strainer. Reserve 1½ cups. Pour remainder over chicken breasts. Bake 20 minutes longer, basting occasionally.

Place a pineapple slice on each chicken breast. Baste with sauce in pan. Bake 5 minutes longer, to heat pineapple.

Serve with 1 oz. reserved sauce over each portion.

Breast of Chicken Parmigiana

INGREDIENTS   YIELD: 24 servings

1½ cups onion, finely chopped

1½ cups celery, finely chopped

2 tbsp. oil

1½ qt. (½ #10 can) canned tomato sauce

1½ cups chicken broth

1½ cups white table wine

2 tsp. basil, finely crumbled

½ tsp. oregano, finely crumbled

1 tsp. salt

¼ tsp. white pepper

24 8-oz. half breasts of chicken

salt to taste

24 Swiss cheese slices

24 (66 count) canned pineapple slices

¾ cup parmesan cheese, grated

Saute onion and celery slowly in oil until soft but not brown.

Add tomato sauce, broth, wine, herbs, salt, and pepper. Heat to boiling, reduce heat, and simmer 20 minutes.

Sprinkle chicken lightly with salt. Arrange in oiled baking pan, skin side down. Bake in very hot oven (450° F.) 35 to 40 minutes, until cooked through.

Arrange a chicken breast in each individual baker. Ladle 3 oz. sauce over. Top with Swiss cheese slice and pineapple slice. Sprinkle with 2 tsp. parmesan cheese.

Heat in microwave oven. Brown lightly under salamander.

The Hawaiian Pineapple Classic

INGREDIENTS   YIELD: 4 servings

4 8-oz. boneless breasts of chicken

1 tsp. salt

black pepper, freshly ground to taste

4 tbsp. butter

12 shrimp, peeled and deveined

1 large carrot, cut in 1½ × ¼ inch strips

1 zucchini, cut in 1½ × ¼-inch strips

¼ lb. fresh mushrooms, sliced

½ oz. brandy

1 14-oz. can Hawaiian pineapple chunks, in own juice, drained

1 oz. teriyaki sauce

½ oz. Hawaiian pineapple liqueur

2 tomatoes, peeled and cut in wedges

2 oz. remaining pineapple juice

½ cup white wine

Season chicken breasts with dash of salt and pepper. Bake in 350° F. oven with 2 tbsp. butter for 35 minutes. Baste several times with butter from pan. Saute, in remaining butter, the shrimp, carrots, zucchini, and mushrooms, until tender. Season with salt and pepper to taste. Add brandy and ignite. Then add remaining ingredients, except shredded coconut, and bring to a boil. Pour over chicken breasts and bake for 10 minutes more. Remove and place on serving platter. Sprinkle with coconut.

Special arrangement: Arrange two napkin horns on the serving platter. Decorate horns with exotic flowers. Place fresh Hawaiian pineapple on dining table. A side order of rice is an accompaniment.

Pineapple Chicken Salad

INGREDIENTS   YIELD: 24 servings

12 oz. white agar-agar strips, cut in 3-inch lengths

3 cups eggs, beaten

1½ qt. cucumber, cored

3 cups cooked chicken, shredded

1½ qt. crushed pineapple in syrup, well drained

1 qt. carrots, shredded

¼ cup sesame seeds, lightly toasted

2 tbsp. dry mustard

¼ cup water

1 cup soy sauce

1 cup vinegar

½ cup sugar

1 cup sesame oil

3 tbsp. peanut butter, smooth

Soak agar-agar strips in warm water ½ hour. Drain and squeeze out excess water. Pan fry eggs in thin sheets. Cut in ⅛-inch shreds.

Cut cucumber in 2-inch lengths and slice medium thin.

On large platter layer, in this order, agar-agar strips, shredded egg, cucumber, chicken, and drained pineapple. Sprinkle evenly with carrot. Chill. At serving time, sprinkle sesame seeds over center of salad. Serve with dressing.

To prepare dressing, mix mustard to a smooth paste with water. Combine all remaining ingredients, and mix until smooth.

Variation: Shredded deep-fried wonton noodles may be substituted for agar-agar strips, if desired. Use 1½ lb. wonton noodles for 24 servings.

Stuffed Pineapple Chicken Breast Waikiki

INGREDIENTS   YIELD: 24 servings

6 cups (approximately) juice drained from crushed pineapple

2 cups (approximately) juice drained from ½ #10 can mushrooms

3 cups lemon juice

1½ cups soy sauce

3 tbsp. ginger, ground

24 (6 oz. each) boned, half breasts of chicken

1 lb. (approximately) bacon slices, diced

1 qt. onions, diced

1 qt. (approximately ½ #10 can) canned mushrooms, coarsely diced

½ #10 can crushed pineapple in juice, drained

½ cup parsley, chopped

1 qt. sour cream

salt and pepper, to taste

2 cups flour

1 tbsp. salt

1 tbsp. garlic powder

1 tbsp. sage

2 tsp. curry powder

Combine pineapple juice, juice from mushrooms, lemon juice, soy sauce, and ginger in stainless steel pan. Make an incision in chicken breasts for stuffing. Place breasts in marinade and let stand about 1 hour.

Saute bacon until crisp. Drain, reserving bacon drippings. Add onions, mushrooms, crushed pineapple, and parsley to bacon, and saute 3 or 4 minutes. Add sour cream, and cook, stirring constantly, until most of the liquid is reduced. Season to taste with salt and pepper. Spread in large pan to cool. Portion stuffing with #12 scoop, making 24 portions.

Mix flour, salt, garlic powder, sage, curry powder, pepper, thyme, and ginger together thoroughly.

Reserve 2 to 3 cups marinade for gravy. Turn remainder into sautoire.

Place stuffing in incision in chicken breasts, and pack meat around it, using skin to pack tightly. Dredge breasts in flour mixture, and place close together, closed side down, in sautoire. Bake at 375° F. for 30 to 40 minutes, basting chicken every 10 minutes with reserved bacon drippings. Remove baked chicken from sautoire and keep warm.

Mix cornstarch with reserved 2 to 3 cups marinade.

Reheat marinade from sautoire to boiling. Stir in cornstarch mixture and cook, stirring constantly, until thick and glossy. Add remaining ½ can pineapple, and salt and pepper as needed. Arrange chicken breasts on serving plate, and cover with gravy. Garnish each with pineapple slice and parsley.

(Cont.)

2 tsp. white pepper

1 tsp. thyme

1 tsp. ginger, ground

½ to ¾ cup cornstarch

2 to 3 cups marinade

½ #10 can crushed pineapple, drained

24 pineapple slices

24 parsley sprigs

Sweet and Sour Alaskan King Crab

INGREDIENTS   YIELD: 24 servings

½ cup butter

2 cups onions, diced in 1-inch pieces

4 medium green peppers, diced in 1-inch pieces

1½ cups pineapple juice

¼ cup malt vinegar

2 tbsp. fresh lemon juice

4 tbsp. soy sauce

1 cup chili sauce

½ cup sherry wine jelly

2 (13½ oz.) cans pineapple tidbits (or chunks), in juice

2 lb. Alaskan king crab meat

2 tbsp. sugar

2 tsp. salt

1½ tsp. fresh ginger root, crushed

¼ cornstarch

¼ cup water

Melt butter in saucepan. Add onions and green peppers. Saute over medium heat 5 minutes, until tender-crisp. Add pineapple juice, vinegar, lemon juice, soy sauce, chili sauce, and wine jelly. Simmer 3 to 5 minutes. Add pineapple, crab meat, sugar, salt, and ginger. Simmer 5 minutes.

Mix cornstarch with water. Stir slowly into the mixture. Bring to a quick boil, and remove from heat. Serve with rice pilaf.

NOTE   Cornstarch quantity may be increased for thicker consistency, if desired.

Pork Loin Chops Hawaiian

INGREDIENTS   YIELD: 24 servings

48 chops (4 oz. each) boneless, center cut pork loin

salt to taste

white pepper to taste

1 cup flour

2 #10 cans pineapple chunks in heavy syrup

1 cup sugar

2 lb. butter

2 #303 cans bing cherries, drained

24 fresh mint sprigs

Trim all fat from pork chops. Season with salt and pepper. Dust lightly with flour. Drain pineapple chunks, reserving syrup. Mix sugar with reserved syrup.

Melt butter in large frying pans and brown pork over medium high heat. When chops are golden, drain most of the butter from pans, and add syrup/sugar mixture. Braise pork until cooked through and glazed. Remove pork to hot platter and keep warm.

Add pineapple chunks and cherries to glaze remaining in pan, and heat thoroughly. Remove fruit with slotted spoon and arrange over pork, allowing about 8 pineapple chunks and 4 cherries per serving of 2 chops. Garnish each serving with fresh mint sprig.

Chaudeau Aloha

INGREDIENTS   YIELD: 24 servings

1 #10 can Hawaiian pineapple chunks

2 oz. Grand Marnier

32 egg yolks

½ cup sugar

1 cup pineapple juice

2 cups Hawaiian pineapple wine

2 orange rinds, freshly grated

1 whole nutmeg, grated

24 stem mint leaves, for garnish

Drain pineapple, reserving juice. To prepare bolla long stem glasses, mix some sugar and drop of egg shade. Dip wet ring of glass into mixture for frosting. Divide the pineapple chunks into 24 glasses.

Set round bottom pan into bottom of double boiler and bring water to boil. In round bottom pan whisk Grand Marnier, egg yolks, sugar, pineapple juice, and Hawaiian wine until sugar is dissolved. Place over hot water jacket. Whisk gently until eggs thicken or mixture loosens from side of pan. Pour mixture evenly over pineapple chunks. Sprinkle with orange rind and nutmeg. Garnish with stem mint leaves.

Pineapple Cheesecake Tortoni

INGREDIENTS   YIELD: 30 4-oz. servings

1½ qt. canned, coarse, crushed pineapple in juice, drained

1¾ cups sugar

½ cup juice from pineapple

½ cup candied cherries, coarsely cut

8 oz. cream cheese

3 oz. light rum

1 qt. heavy cream

1½ cups powdered sugar, sifted

1 tbsp. vanilla

¼ tsp. salt

2½ cups macaroon crumbs

Combine pineapple, sugar, and pineapple juice. Boil together until thick, stirring occasionally. Cool and stir in cherries. Soften cream cheese. Beat in rum, mixing until smooth.

Beat cream with powdered sugar, vanilla, and salt, to soft peaks. Fold in cheese mixture.

In individual serving glasses, place a #40 scoop pineapple mixture. Top with #24 scoop of cheese/cream. Sprinkle with 1 tbsp. macaroon crumbs. Repeat pineapple and cheese layers as before. Top with 1 tsp. pineapple and light sprinkling of crumbs. Freeze until firm.

Pineapple Crepes Tropicana

INGREDIENTS   YIELD: 1 serving

1 tbsp. butter

3 tbsp. brown sugar

½ oz. syrup from pineapple

3 oz. canned pineapple chunks, drained

½ oz. rum

½ oz. banana liqueur

2 crepes, rolled or folded

Melt butter in chafing dish or small skillet. Add sugar and pineapple syrup. Simmer until thickened. Add pineapple chunks and cook until well glazed, spooning syrup over pineapple as it cooks. Add rum and liqueur, ignite, and spoon over pineapple until flames die out. Serve over crepes.

Pineapple Dessert Sauce

INGREDIENTS   YIELD: 2 quarts

1 cup juice from crushed pineapple

12 oz. brown sugar

2 cups light corn syrup

2 qt. canned, coarse, crushed pineapple, in juice, well drained

6 oz. white creme de cacao

Combine pineapple juice, sugar, and corn syrup. Heat to simmering to dissolve sugar. Add drained pineapple. Simmer 10 minutes. Cool. Stir in creme de cacao. Serve over ice cream or other desserts.

Grasshopper Parfait

INGREDIENTS   YIELD: 75 servings

1 #10 can crushed pineapple

3¾ cups sugar

5 oz. white creme de cacao

2½ gal. vanilla ice cream

2 qt. creme de menthe

whipped cream (optional), for topping

Combine undrained pineapple and sugar. Cook until thick, stirring frequently, about 20 minutes. Cool. Stir creme de cacao into pineapple sauce. Chill.

To assemble parfaits, layer 1½ oz. pineapple sauce, 4 oz. ice cream, and ¾ oz. creme de menthe in 7 oz. parfait glasses. Store in freezer. If desired, top with rosette of whipped cream at serving time.

Hawaiian Luau Flambe

INGREDIENTS   YIELD: 6 servings

3 Hawaiian pineapples, split in half lengthwise

1 papaya

1 bunch green grapes (tropical)

2 bananas

2 tangerines

2 figs

1 persimmon (sweet tropical fruit)

½ melon, in season

1 cup granulated sugar

1 cup Hawaiian rum

1 oz. Southern Comfort

Empty meat from pineapple, and set pineapple aside. Clean all tropical fruits, dice, and mix. Add rum and granulated sugar and marinate for a few hours. Saute in a pan. Add Southern Comfort and ignite. Pour fruit into pineapple shells.

Make a meringue by whipping 6 egg whites till very firm, and adding 1 lb. confectioner's sugar.

Use pastry bag to decorate and cover pineapples, and place ½ eggshell into meringue, next to pineapple leaves. Brown in oven at 350° F. for 2 minutes. Remove. Fill eggshell with Southern Comfort and ignite. Serve flaming.

Garnish with fresh strawberries and mint leaves.

Pineapple Crisps with Ginger Sauce

INGREDIENTS   YIELD: 50 servings

1 #10 can pineapple slices, 52 count

8 oz. butter

¼ cup sugar

8 large eggs

pinch of salt

2 lb. flour

3¼ cups raspberry jam

4 large eggs, beaten

oil for deep frying, as needed

⅞ cup sugar

4½ cups (approximate) syrup from pineapple

7 tbsp. cornstarch

1 cup water

2 tsp. ginger, ground

Drain pineapple in strainer over bowl, while preparing pastry, saving syrup for sauce.

Cream butter with ¼ cup sugar. Beat in 8 eggs, one at a time. Sieve salt with flour, and knead into creamed mixture. Allow pastry to rest for ½ hour. Cut pastry into 6 pieces. Roll one at a time about 1/16-inch thick, and cut in rounds with a 3¾-to-4-inch cutter.

Lay a pineapple slice on each of 50 pastry rounds. Fill center of pineapple with a teaspoon raspberry jam. Brush edges of rounds with beaten egg. Cover with remaining pastry rounds, and press edges together firmly. Deep fry pastries at 360° F. until golden brown. Drain on absorbent paper. Sprinkle generously with sugar.

Strain reserved pineapple syrup into saucepan and heat. Mix cornstarch with water and ginger. Stir slowly into simmering pineapple syrup using wire whip. Cook, stirring, until thickened. Serve sauce over pineapple crisps. (Makes about 7 cups sauce.)

Pineapple Mousse Torte

INGREDIENTS   YIELD: Two 10-inch tortes, 12 to 16 servings each

32 pineapple chunks in syrup, drained

4 oz. cointreau

2 10-inch sponge cakes* 1-inch high

½ cup red currant jelly

8 oz. instant vanilla mousse mix

3 cups crushed pineapple in juice, drained

½ cup sliced almonds, toasted

1½ qt. whipping cream

32 strawberries, halved

currant jelly, for dipping strawberries

2 to 4 oz. bitter chocolate, shaved

Marinate pineapple chunks in cointreau several hours. Drain, saving marinade.

Cut sponge cakes into 2 equal layers, ½-inch high. Spread bottom half with warmed currant jelly. Set top layer in place, and soak with cointreau drained from pineapple.

Prepare vanilla mousse as can directs, beating 3 to 5 minutes in mixer. Fold in well-drained crushed pineapple. Spread a 1-inch layer on top of each torte. Cover sides of torte lightly with remaining mousse, dipping spatula in hot water while icing sides.

Cover sides of tortes with toasted almonds. Refrigerate 1 hour or longer.

Mark tops of tortes into 12 to 16 wedges. Whip cream, turn into a pastry bag, and pipe design on tops of tortes. Decorate each wedge with marinated pineapple chunk, a half strawberry dipped in melted currant jelly, and chocolate shavings.

*Recipe follows.

American Sponge Cake

INGREDIENTS YIELD: 2 to 3 10-inch
sponge cakes, 1-inch high

2⅓ cups granulated sugar

1¼ cups whole eggs

¼ cup egg yolks

½ tsp. vanilla

¼ tsp. salt

grated orange peel from ½ orange

¾ cup milk

2 tbsp. butter

3 cups cake flour

¼ tsp. baking powder

Heat sugar in mixer bowl over water bath. Remove from heat. Add eggs and yolks, vanilla, salt, and orange peel. Beat at high speed, until thick and lemon colored, about 10 minutes. Meanwhile, heat milk and add butter to melt.

Sift flour with baking powder. At low speed, fold flour mixture into egg mixture alternating with milk and butter. Fill greased and floured (or parchment lined) torte molds half full with batter. Bake at 300° F. approximately 30 to 40 minutes. Cool cakes before removing from pans.

Pineapple Sunset

INGREDIENTS YIELD: 24 individual pies

3 cans (10 oz. each) condensed milk

3 cups graham cracker crumbs

24 pineapple slices (from 20 oz. cans)

½ pint whipping cream

1 can (11 oz.) mandarin orange sections

sweet chocolate curls, for decoration

Cover cans of milk with boiling water. Boil 3 to 4 hours, replacing water as needed. Chill 24 hours or longer.

Sprinkle graham cracker crumbs in bottoms of 24 individual pie plates, 5 to 6 inches in diameter. Open cans of milk on both ends, slide out milk, and slice each into 8 rounds. Place on top of crumbs. Top each with a pineapple slice. Whip cream. Turn into a pastry bag fitted with star tube. Pipe onto pies in decorative swirls. Decorate tops of pies with orange sections and chocolate curls.

13. Management Techniques

Management Techniques of an Executive Chef

How to Manage a Kitchen

To manage a kitchen effectively, the chef must be in complete control of supervision, preparation, storage, and standards of service. Only then can you assure proper service. Whether you have a large or small kitchen, the basics remain the same—the menu, ordering of merchandise, receiving of goods, preparation of food, and the final presentation. No one can say it is easy for the chef. The chef will always be blamed if food costs are too high, if sales are too low, or if the food is inedible. Poor service and sanitation are also usually blamed on the chef.

A Day in a Hotel Kitchen

Any day in the kitchen actually began three days earlier, when the price quotation was taken to purchase the quality food needed. If the delivery is late, don't hesitate to tell the dealer that if it happens again it will be the last delivery. The dealer needs the business and you need the merchandise. You can get the merchandise somewhere else, but a dealer has to search for business.

The basic preparation has to be done the day before. This includes getting the supply ready for the different stations, preparing basic stocks, butchering meat, cleaning fish, and preparing vegetables and basic desserts. Also set up your galantines. This setting-up is called "mise en place."

Let us view an actual day, starting with breakfast. Basically, the cooks arrive at 5 or 6 am and the doors open at 7 am. Eggs are placed at room temperature, and those to be scrambled are whipped with milk and strained. The bacon, preset yesterday, is ready to be cooked, and the ham is sliced for grilling. The cereal is set up for mixing. The fruit is cut in the pantry. The baker gets the danish in the oven ready for the opening. The dining room tables are set, and the room service captain has the time order ready to be picked up. The banquet maitre d' checks a thousand details for the breakfast buffet. Not one sick call from an employee—this is a good start for the day.

Later in the day comes the potage, the garde-manger, and the entremete preparations. The steward's department is functioning properly. The chef checks his production guideline. The requisition has been made to the food storeroom and the supply is being delivered. Sauces and roasts are in the oven, the soup is cooking, the meat is cut, salads are being prepared, vegetables are being peeled, the cake is being sliced in half for final decoration, the creams are whipped, and the stations are preset for the lunch service. The leftovers are utilized for the employees' lunches. By 9:45 am, the chef is getting a nervous stomach, having his first cup of coffee, and settling the dispute over the increase in guarantee. The solution to a sudden increase in the number guaranteed at a banquet is to increase the productivity of preparation. At 10 am, there is a meeting on new menu development. Also charts are designed to control food costs (roasting meats at correct temperatures, item counting on production, and production scheduling). Employee work schedules and progress reports are reviewed. Meat inspection and grading, purchase orders, price quotations, handling of requisitions, food cost analysis, daily sales for cost, butcher tests, menu counts, payroll costs, sanitation inspection, energy conservation, and inventory turnover are discussed. Participants at the meeting are the chef, the assistant chef, the steward, and the banquet chef.

At 11 am, the production line is being checked, tasting the items to be served for the midday meal, to assure quality and preparation completion. Lunch is served and all food items are properly garnished for the service personnel.

Inventory is taken for ordering for the next day. Setting up of all the different items used for dinner preparation goes on. Mise en place for the following day. At 3:30 pm, lunch for the crew; at 4 pm, a meeting with personnel to ensure proper communication, followed by various department meetings. Did the guests complain about slow service? Is this the result of improper supervision and training of service staff, inadequate equipment in the dining room or kitchen, friction among employees, or the travel distance from the kitchen to the guest?

The banquet is set up. Guarantee changes in the last minute—a large group arrives without notification to the chef. All these problems must be solved at the various meetings. At 5 pm, the setup is almost complete for the evening. A round of checkup and tasting. Three cooks are absent. The chef is preparing special dishes for the guests. Classic touches must be given to these dishes. Productivity must be increased to compensate for the no-shows.

All this can be arranged simply by being organized. Develop a routine of proper preparation, whatever the size of your operation. Set guidelines. The chef must be the motivating factor.

Menu Planning for the Restaurant

Menu planning is an art that requires knowledge of food preparation and presentation. It depends on the season of the year, the kind of customers of the establishment, and the personnel who must achieve the standards set by the establishment. High standards do not always guarantee qualified personnel. Training in this area is needed and the menu should be planned to achieve high standards. The budget should be set according to the items featured on the menu.

The Menu Cover

The design must complement the establishment. A seafood specialty house might feature a perfect drawing of a lobster or king crab. A continental restaurant might have its name hand-written or use a classic piece of art, such as, a landscape painting, a Roman statue, or a picture related to the land of origin (a winery with food, a map with different cities, or a region with its specialty). An oriental restaurant's menu might use a jade plate with food drawings, or an oriental tree with a statue from this culture. A middle eastern restaurant might show a dried fruit arrangement, or hand-designed plates.

The Written Menu

After the cover is designed and the size of the menu established, the written menu should be arranged. This can be done in several ways.

I. A La Carte Headlines

Le Service Exclusivement a la Carte

Recommandons	Appetizer and Salad
Potages	Soup
Poissons	Fish
Entrees	Main Course
Legumes	Vegetable
Entremets	Desserts
Cafe	Coffee

II. Complete Dinner

Les Specialites de la Maison

Pate de Campagne a la Gelee

Billi-Bi Aux Paillettes

Steak au Poivre Royale

Poulet en Cocotte Grand Mere

L'Agneau au Curry Orientale

Sole Belle Meuniere

La Cote de Veau Normande

Laitue de Saison

Peches Flambees

Crepes Suzette

Fraises Romanoff

Cafe

III. Oriental Gourmet Dinner

Dim Sum

China's Special Meat Pastry

Yen Wor Tong

Bird's Nest Soup

Hung Shu Gai Kew

Chicken meat blended with snow pea pods, water chestnuts, and fresh vegetables of the Orient.

See Gyp Ha

Shrimp with bamboo shoots, mushrooms, and scallions, blended with oriental spices.

Yang Chow Rice

Oolong Keemun Tea

IV. More Extensive A La Carte
Headlines

Les Hors-d'Oeuvre Froids

Les Hors-d'Oeuvre Chauds

Potages

Poissons et Crustaces

Les Viandes

Grillades

Legumes

Les Salades

Desserts et Fromages

Cafe

These samples, whether written in French or another language, must have an attractive layout. This is the first impression the customer gets of your establishment. Moreover it must be easy to read. The dishes (particularly when prepared for connoisseurs) must be selected with imagination. No dish should be repeated on the menu.

Once the mise en place takes place, both in the dining room and the kitchen the eye appeal of the food and the service must be attended to as carefully as the preparation of the menu. Service and food must be of the highest order when presenting a classic gourmet meal. Classic is the highest quality or grade produced and served. It also stands for simplicity and perfection of cuisine.

Creating a Menu

To create a menu, it is very important to follow a few simple steps:

1. Determine the nature of your establishment. Is it classic, elegant, continental, or ethnic?

2. Tailor your menu to your establishment.
   The classic menu is written in French with an explanation in the country's native language underneath. For example:
   Quennelles de Homard Mari Lois
   Mousseline of Lobster—Truffle Sauce
   The elegant menu is written in the language of origin. For example:
   Icelandic Cod Calypso
   Cod fillet poached in white wine, with shrimp and sauce hollandaise
   The continental menu might read:
   Tournedos Sauce Choron
   The ethnic menu is written in the original language with translations. For example:
   Gefullte Lachsforelle
   Stuffed Salmon Trout
   After completing these steps, it is necessary to outline the menu, which then can be described in different words.

Example I

Appetizer
Soups
Fish
Entree
Vegetables
Dessert

Your Way of Living
Tureens
Treasures of the Sea
Selection for the Gourmet
Vegetable Kingdom
From the Patisserie

Example II

Hors d'Oeuvre	Appetizer	Antipasti
Potages	Soups	Minestre
Poissons	Fish	Pesce
Entrees	Entree	Carne
Legumes	Vegetables	Legumi
Dessert	Dessert	Dolci

Example III

Exotic Appetizers and Soups
Gourmet Specialties
Dessert or Flaming Dishes

Creativity is a must in your menu. Your headlines must reflect the style of your creations. Whether handwritten or in classical print, it must be simple and readable. Whatever kind of paper, wood, cloth, or blackboard is used must be of good quality. This assures your guest of the quality of your establishment. The menu is the first impression of the food you serve. Never make a spelling mistake or list an item under the wrong classification. Always explain your dishes in a simple way. Never let the printer make a decision on appearance. He takes the easy way out. Don't have too many items on your menu. Have selections in each category that the kitchen can handle. Always consider your kitchen space. Production, if not properly handled, can ruin the appeal of the menu.

Once you have double-checked your menu selection, the type setting, the quality of the paper, and the cover, you are ready for a proof from the printer. Make sure you approve the menu proof before it goes into production. This eliminates delays and misunderstandings.

Your Menu—The Key To Success

I have observed in many food establishments that nine out of ten waiters cannot explain to guests the makeup of particular items on the menu. This brings us back to where we started. If your menu explains what the dish consists of, you save time and embarrassment for your service personnel. However, service personnel should be able to explain each dish. This is a selling tool. If the kitchen runs low on an item, you can compensate by explaining to guests the dishes you prefer to sell. And it eliminates time running to the kitchen and back.

Now your guest has the explanation on the menu of the food to be served, and the service personnel can explain anything that puzzles the guest. How wonderful! But suppose the food does not taste the way the menu describes it. What can be done? Invite the chef to dinner. Let him sit down and criticize his own menu. Let him tell you what is wrong and you will have the best critic there is in any establishment.

Practical Food Preparation

Soups This category includes clear soups, consomme garni, thick soups and cream soups, puree soups, special soups, soups with fish or crustaceans, and cold soups. Four to five hours is sufficient time for setting the basic stock. Soup should be started as early as possible in the morning, and finished as close as possible to serving time.

Appetizers Prepare for galantines, pates, terrines, mousse, and marinades a day in advance. The appetizer whets the guest's appetite and allows time for the entree to be prepared in the kitchen. It should be pleasantly seasoned, not too spicy, and not too filling. Hot appetizers should be light in consistency. Appetizers can be presented in the dining room on a rolling cart.

Breakfast Eggs Egg dishes, whether poached, fried, scrambled, or omelettes, with garniture or without, must be made to order.

Fish Boiled, fried, grilled, poached, braised, or gratinated—fish should be prepared as close as possible to serving time. Season lightly to preserve the flavor.

Sauces Basic stocks for sauces should be prepared the day before. This assures a stronger flavor for each dish made to order. Sauces should be finished prior to serving time.

Poultry Poultry, including duck, chicken, birds, goose, and turkey, can be braised, boiled, roasted, stuffed, sauteed, or souffled.

Game Rabbits, venison, wild boar, deer, and game birds should hang several days prior to preparation. The classic way of roasting brings out the wild flavor.

Meat Meat should always be served after fish. It can be prepared in casseroles or in cocotte; grilled or sauteed; roasted on a spit or boiled; stewed or raw.

Side Dishes Vegetables, potatoes, pasta, salads, or fruit should be served in small portions to complement the main dish.

Desserts Sweets can be served hot or cold, made to order or frozen, whichever is preferred. There are souffles, dumplings, pancakes, puddings, strudels, fruit, chaudeau, cakes, or tarts. Roman punch can be included too.

Quality Control of Purchasing

To control food quality, one must learn the standards of grade marks and inspection stamps. Grade marks reflect quality. Inspection stamps mean the inspector has checked the grade, the plant operation, and the processing, packing, and sanitary requirements. Quality products do not always command higher prices; demand and supply set the product price. The more supply available, the lower the price. You must set specifications for weight and grade in order to determine the best price quotations. Grading factors for all products are: color, character of tenderness, texture, maturity, and uniformity of size and shape. For example:

quality of beef—bright red in color, the flesh is firm, fine grained, and well-marbled

quality of lamb—finely grained and pinkish red in color

quality of veal—milk fed, the flesh pinkish in hue

quality of pork—soft gray pink color, white fat.

Beef

Gooseneck Round boneless—the part remaining after removal of the inside round, knuckle, shank meat, and all bones. Weight 18 to 20 pounds.

Beef Tenderloin (defatted)—removed from the full loin, cut starting at the round end of the loin, follow the seam over the hip bone, and loosen the butt end of the tenderloin. Trimmed so that the fat is removed from the top to the blue tissue. Weight 5 to 6 pounds.

180 Strip Loin (boneless)— all bones and cartilage removed. No more than 1 inch of fat on top and 3 inches from the cut to the meat at the large eye. Weight 18 to 20 pounds.

Top Sirloin Butt (boneless)—the top sirloin butt is the thicker upper portion, separated from the bottom sirloin by cutting the natural muscle seam. Weight 7 to 8 pounds.

107 Rib—this oven-prepared rib is a portion of a 7-rib bone, the exposed meat removed. The rib is tied to hold it in place. It measures one inch top fat, and 3 inches from the cut to the large eye. Weight 24 to 26 pounds.

Specifications for buying beef are:

U.S. Prime	U.S. Commercial
U.S. Choice	U.S. Utility
U.S. Good	U.S. Cutter
U.S. Standard	U.S. Canner

Lamb

Rack of Lamb—portion of the bracelet. Double rack has 8 ribs on each side. Not to exceed 4 inches from the center flesh to the cut. Weight 7 pounds.

Lamb Shoulder—these are the remaining foresaddles after removal of foreshanks, briskets, bracelet, and neck. Cut between the 4th and 5th ribs. Weight 10 to 12 pounds.

Lamb Legs (double)—after removal of the loin, the remaining hindsaddle. Top fat not to exceed ½ inch. Weight 16 to 18 pounds.

Specifications for lamb are: Prime, Choice, Good, Utility, Cull. A-Lamb, B-Yearling Mutton, C-Mutton.

Veal

Rack of Veal—veal racks are cut starting at the 12th rib, 4 inches from the rib eye muscle, in a straight cut to the 6th rib, again 4 inches measured in a straight line. Weight 14 pounds.

Veal Legs (double)— remainder of the hindsaddle, after removal of the loin. The tail bones and the fat must be removed. Weight of single, 40 to 45 pounds.

Specifications for veal are: Prime, Choice, Good, Standard, Utility, Cull.

Pork

Ham—fat remaining on the skinned surface must be smooth, not exceeding ½ inch. Weight 16 to 18 pounds.

Loin—the regular loin has the blade in. The line of separation must be straight and parallel. The fat thickness over the loin is not to exceed ¼ inch. Loins with damaged ribs or split back bone to be excluded. Weight 10 to 12 pounds.

Spareribs—the belly portion of the pork carcass.
Specifications for pork are: U.S. No. I, II, III.

Poultry

U.S. standard Grade AA is for young, fine-grained birds with full breast and no feathers. No discoloration permitted. Other U.S. Grades are A, B, and C. B is for birds setting poorly, with fleshed breast, some discoloration or bruises. C is evidence of poor bleeding, feathers, bad bruises, and partly inedible carcass.

Eggs

U.S. Grades AA, A, B, and C. Grades are determined by size, and exterior and interior appearance. Priced according to size. Size classes are: Jumbo, Extra Large, Large, Medium, and Small.

Butter

Graded in terms of Score 93 and above, the best available. Grades AA, A, B, and C. U.S. inspection stamp for verification.

Cheeses

Type of Cheese	Per Case
Split Midget, 90 days	2, 5½ lb. each
Sharp cheddar	2, 10 lb. each
Cream cheese	10, 3 lb. each or 1 30 lb. or 36, 3 oz. each
Cottage cheese	4, 5 lb. each
Muenster	6, 5 lb. each
Mozzarella	8, 5 lb. each
Neufchatel	10, 3 lb. each
Blue wheel	3, 6 lb. each
Abbey port salut	4, 6 lb. each
Brie	6, 2.2 lb. or 2, 4.5 lb. each
Camembert	12, 8 oz. each
Gouda	4, 9 lb. each
Bel paese	2, 4 lb. each
Parmesan	2, 12 lb. each
Jarlsberg	2, 20 lb. each

Fish

Fish can be purchased in many forms, such as, fresh, frozen, pickled, salted, smoked, and canned. Today, quick freezing and refrigeration assure freshness throughout the country, not just for those living next to the seashore. The fish is flown to assure proper freshness, and even quick frozen at sea. There are fat and lean fish. Fat fish include blue fish, herring, eels, and salmon; lean fish include cod, flounder, and haddock.

To assure good fish, check for bright skin, tight scales, firm flesh, and clear eyes. When cut, the meat must stick firmly to the bones. Fresh fish, at delivery, should always be packed with ice. This assures proper handling.

Dry Goods

Dry goods are canned and boxed. Read the label of each product to determine the ingredients, pieces, liquid, and weight. Storage temperature is the primary factor in storage life, along with humidity, type of container, vacuum, and nature of the product. The chemical reaction on canned goods doubles for each 180° F. The perfect storage temperature is 65° F. All commercially canned foods are safe providing the container is not leaking or bulging. Should this occur, do not taste or eat. Return to the supplier for proper credit.

Fresh Vegetables and Fruits

Grading is not as applicable due to the fast changes in quality and handling. It is practical to order by brand name to assure proper quality. Some gradings call for U.S. Fancy, No. I, or II.

Fresh items arrive packed per pound, count, and weight. For example:

Artichokes	Per piece
Beans	Per pound
Cabbage	Per crate pounds
Carrots	Per pound 50
Leeks	Per bunch each
Lettuce	Per box count 24
Potatoes	Per box count 90
Parsley	Per bushel 50 pieces
Shallots	Per pound
Tomatoes	Per box 25 pounds
Turnips	Per bag 50 pounds
Watercress	Per bunch 25 box

Control Guides

The following are sample control guides to facilitate management of your establishment:

Daily Employee Schedule
Daily Menu Count
Sales Analysis, Daily—Annually
Meat Roasting Chart
Daily Guideline of Production
Potential Food Cost
Operational Food Cost.

Table 14.1 Daily Employee Schedule

WEEK NAMES	TOTAL HOURS	MON.	TUES.	WED.	THURS.	FRI.	SAT.	SUN.
AM Cook	40							
PM Cook	40							
Butcher	40							
Pantry	40							
Garde- Manger	40							
Total	200							

Table 14.2 Daily Menu Count

ITEM	PORTIONS PREPARED	LEFT OVER	SOLD	MENU COUNT	VARIOUS + −
Appetizer					
Lachs	25	4	21	21	0
Foie Gras	25	—	25	24	−1
Entree					
Chicken Breast	30	2	28	28	0
Sirloin Steak	30	1	29	30	+1
Vegetable					
Spinach Timbale	30	5	25	25	0
Asparagus	30	2	28	28	0
Dessert					
Sacher Torte	24	4	20	20	0
Raspberry Mold	25	—	25	25	0

At the end of the day, this control will show any discrepancies due perhaps to cashier errors, or other circumstances.

Table 14.3 Sales Analysis

CATEGORY I DAILY BUDGET	ACTUAL	PROJECTED	LAST YEAR	PREVIOUS YEAR
$2,315	$2,500	$2,415	$2,261	$2,000

CATEGORY II ANNUALLY RESTAURANT	TOTAL	JAN.	FEB.	MAR.	APR.	MAY	JUNE
Budget	389,000	50,000	45,000	60,000	74,500	80,000	79,500
Last Year Actual	380,000	48,000	44,000	58,000	75,000	79,000	76,000

If properly planned, this analysis can give you an overall look at the operation.

Table 14.4 Roasting Chart

DESCRIPTION OF ITEM	TIME IN	TIME OUT	TRIMMED RAW WEIGHT	COOKED WEIGHT	LOST WEIGHT	%	ROASTING
Lamb	11 am	12:45 am	7 lb.	6 lb., 13 oz.	3 oz.	2.7%	200°F.
Roast Fillet of Beef	11 am	12:30 am	5 lb.	4 lb., 12 oz.	4 oz.	5%	200°F.
Roast Beef	11 am	4:30 pm	19 lb.	18 lb., 5 oz.	11 oz.	3.7%	225° F.

Example:
The roasting time for the roast beef was 5½ hours for a 19 lb., trimmed rib. Convert the weight into ounces—19 ×16 = 304 oz. raw and 293 oz. cooked (11 oz. lost). The weight loss in percentage—293:304 = .963. Now bring the weight back to 100%. Subtract 963 from 1000 which equals 3.7% of your original loss. If you cut a 13 oz. portion, your yield would be 22½ cuts of meat.

In these examples, the meat is very rare. If the roasting temperature is higher, the meat shrinkage is greater and more weight is lost.

Table 14.5 Daily Guideline of Production

ITEMS	MONDAY PREP.	LEFT	TUESDAY PREP.	LEFT.	WEDNESDAY PREP.	LEFT	THURSDAY PREP.	LEFT	FRIDAY PREP.	LEFT.	SATURDAY PREP.	LEFT	SUNDAY PREP.	LEFT
Salad														
Portion Meat														

Use this form for daily production and inventory. List as many items as prepared.

Table 14.6 Potential Food Cost

Take a sample of a roast fillet of beef with truffle sauce, a roast potato, and a side order of a whole grilled tomato.
Ingredients Yield: 12 6-oz. portions

		Cost Price
roast fillet of beef	5 lbs. raw—4½ lbs. cooked = 72 oz.	$5 per lb. = $25.00
salt, pepper	dash	12¢
oil	4 oz.	8¢
truffle sauce	24 oz.—12 2-oz. portions	25¢ per lb. = $3.00
roast potatoes	3 lb.	$1.30 per lb. = $3.90
butter	4 oz.	$1.50 per lb. = 38¢
grilled tomato	12	12¢ each = $1.44
butter	4 oz.	$1.50 per lb. = 38¢
watercress	2 bunches	40¢ per lb. = 80¢
		TOTAL = $35.10

The total of $35.10, divided by 12 portions, yields a cost per person $2.93, rounded out. With a selling price of $10.95, the food cost percentage is 26.7%.

Table 14.7 Operational Food Cost (Monthly)

Last Day Inventory	$13,000.00
Plus Purchases	$20,300.00
Total	$33,300.00
Minus Previous Inventory	$12,000.00
Total	$21,000.00
Minus Credit	$ 800.00
Total	$20,000.00
Divided by Total Sales	$70,000.00

Accurate Food Cost—29.2%.

Appendices

Appendix 1.
Metric Conversions:
The Formula for
Cooking

Ounces	Grams	Pounds	Kilograms	Pints	Litres	Gallons	Litres
1	28	1	0.5	½	.236	1	3.8
2	56	2	0.9	1.0	.473	2	7.6
3	85	3	1.4	1½	.709	3	11.4
4	113	4	1.8	2.0	.946	4	15.1
5	141	5	2.3	2½	1.183	5	18.9
6	170	6	2.7	3.0	1.419	6	22.7
7	198	7	3.2	3½	1.656	7	26.5
8	226	8	3.6	4.0	1.893	8	30.3
9	255	9	4.1	4½	2.129	9	34.1
10	283	10	4.5	5.0	2.366	10	37.9
11	311	11	5.0	5½	2.602	11	41.6
12	340	12	5.4	6.0	2.839	12	45.4
13	368	13	5.9	6½	3.075	13	49.2
14	396	14	6.4	7.0	3.312	14	53.
15	425	15	6.8	7½	3.549	15	56.8
16	453	16	7.3	8.0	3.786	16	60.6
		17	7.7			17	64.3
		18	8.2			18	68.1
		19	8.6			19	71.9
		20	9.1			20	75.7
		25	11.34			30	113.6
		30	13.61			40	151.4
		40	18.14			50	189.3
		50	22.68			60	227.1
		60	27.22			70	264.9
		70	31.75			80	302.8
		80	36.29			90	340.7
		90	40.82			100	378.5
		100	45.36				

Liquid

1 litre = 4 cups = 32 oz. = 2 pints = 1 quart (4 quarts = 1 gallon)
¾ litre = 3 cups = 24 oz.
½ litre = 2 cups = 16 oz. = 1 pint
¼ litre = 1 cup = 8 oz. = ½ pint
⅛ litre = ½ cup = 4 oz.
          ¼ cup = 2 oz. = 1 portion

Other Measurements

dash   = ⅛ teaspoon
 3 tsp. = 1 tbsp.
 4 tbsp. = ¼ cup
 8 tbsp. = ½ cup
12 tbsp. = ¾ cup
16 tbsp. = 1 cup

Appendix 2. Special Occasions in Other Languages

Blessings on Your Baptism *(English)*
  Zur Taufe *(German)*
  Heureux bapteme *(French)*
  Per il Battesimo *(Italian)*
Bon Voyage *(English)*
  Gute Reise *(German)*
  Bon voyage *(French)*
  Bon viaggio *(Italian)*
Best Wishes on Your Anniversary
  Zum Jubilaum *(German)*
  Heureux jubile *French)*
  Per il giubileo *(Italian)*
Best Wishes on Your Engagement *(English)*
  Zur Verlobung *(German)*
  Heureuses fiancailles *(French)*
  Per il fidanzamento *(Italian)*
Best Wishes on Your Confirmation *(English)*
  Zur Konfirmation *(German)*
  Confirmation *(French)*
  Per la confirmazione *(Italian)*
Congratulations on Your Wedding *(English)*
  Zur Vermahlung *(German)*
  Heureux mariage *(French)*
  Per il sposalizio *(Italian)*
Congratulations *(English)*
  Wir gratulieren *(German)*
  Nos felicitations *(French)*
  Congratulazioni *(Italian)*
Golden Anniversary *(English)*
  Zur goldenen Hochzeit *(German)*
  Pour les noces d'or *(French)*
  Per le nozze d'oro *(Italian)*
Good luck *(English)*
  Viel Gluck *(German)*
  Bonne chance *(French)*
  Buona fortuna (auguri) *(Italian)*
Good Luck in the New Year *(English)*
  Viel Glück im neuen Jahr *(German)*
  Nos meilleurs voeux pour l'an nouveau *(French)*
Happy Mother's Day *(English)*
  Zum Muttertag *(German)*

Pour la fete des meres *(French)*
per la giornata della mamma *(Italian)*
Happy Easter *(English)*
  Frohe Ostern *(German)*
  Joyeuses Paques *(French)*
  Buona Pasqua *(Italian)*
Happy Birthday *(English)*
  Zum Geburstag *(German)*
  Heureux anniversaire *(French)*
  Per il compleanno *(Italian)*
Happy Holiday *(English)*
  Frohe Festtage *(German)*
  Joyeuses fetes *(French)*
  Buone Feste *(Italian)*
Happy New Year *(English)*
  Prosit Neujahr *(German)*
  Bonne annee *(French)*
  Buon Anno *(Italian)*
First Holy Communion *(English)*
  Zur Heiligen Kommunion *(German)*
  Pour la sainte communione *(French)*
  Per la prima comunione *(Italian)*
Merry Christmas *(English)*
  Frohe Weihnachten *(German)*
  Joyeux Noel *(French)*
  Buon Natale *(Italian)*
To My Dear Mother *(English)*
  Der lieben Mutter *(German)*
  A ma chere maman *(French)*
  Alla cara mamma *(Italian)*
Welcome *(English)*
  Willkommen *(German)*
  Soyez les bienvenus *(French)*
  Benvenuti *(Italian)*
Best Wishes on Your Silver Anniversary *(English)*
  Zur silbernen Hochzeit *(German)*
  Pour les noces d'argent *(French)*
  Per le nozze d'argento *(Italian)*
Best Wishes
  Herzlichen Gluckwunsch *(German)*
  Nos voeux sinceres *(French)*
  Felicitazione *(Italian)*

Appendix 3. Spices and Herbs

Spices and herbs were once coveted like gold. Traders grew wealthy as they discovered new lands and brought back the new and unusual. Indian spices were among the greatest discoveries traders ever made. New discoveries were cultivated in vegetable gardens. Several herbs were mixed together to flavor soups, stews, and stocks. A new mixture, called a bouquet garni, brought the flavor of cooking to perfection; a touch of spices finished the taste. The spice shelf is a meeting place for the very ancient and the very new. Many of its products have not changed since the history of spices and herbs was first recorded.

Allspice—Spice
Pea-sized fruit of a West Indian tree. Native to India. Flavors of cloves, nutmeg, and cinnamon.
Gourmet uses—whole or ground.
Relishes, preserves, cakes, stews, meats, soups, sauces.

Angelica—Herb
Licorice flavored plant, related to celery. Stalks are crystallized with sugar.
Gourmet uses—stalks.
Cakes, desserts, confectionary.

Anise—Seed
Licorice flavored fruit of small plant.
China, Mexico, Mediterranean origins.
Similar to caraway but grown in hotter climates.
Gourmet uses—seed.
Cookies, rolls, candies, cakes, breads, soups, fruits.

Basil—Herb
Plant leaves of the mint family. Native to India and Persia.
Gourmet uses—leaves or sweet basil.
Soups, stews, meats, sauces, fish, eggs, cheeses.

Bay Leaves—Herb
Green leaf of evergreen laurel tree. Mediterranean origin.
Gourmet uses—bay leaves.
Stews, fish, meats, soups, sauces, vegetables.

Borage—Herb
Cucumber flavored plant. Spanish origin.
Gourmet uses—leaves.
Salads and sauces.

Caraway—Seed
Dried fruit of parsley family. Northern Europe and Asia.
Gourmet uses—seeds.
Pork, meats, bread, vegetables, stuffings, cakes, cheeses.

Cardamon—Seed
Tiny seeds, browned in the sun. Guatemalan and Indian origin.
Gourmet uses—whole or ground.
Curry sauces, cakes, bread, pastries.

Cayenne—Spice
Ground from the hottest pepper pots. Louisiana and African origin.
Gourmet uses—whole or crushed red pepper.
Poultry, sauces, relishes, meats, cheese dishes.

Celery Seeds—Seed
Brown fruit of the parsley family. Indian and French origin.
Gourmet uses—seeds or ground.
Pickling, salads, sauces, stuffings, vegetables, bread.

Chervil—Herb
Sweeter, more aromatic leaf; resembles parsley. Peasant origin.
Gourmet uses—leaves.
Soups, sauces, salads, fish, egg dishes, butter.

Chili Powder—Blend
Mixture of other spices; oregano, cumin seeds, sometimes garlic.
Mexican origin.
Gourmet uses—chili powder.
Fish, sauces, relishes, stews, soups.

Chives—Herb
Slender leaves, onion flavored. Peasant origin.
Gourmet uses—chive stalk.
Soups, egg dishes, salads, butter, cheeses.

Cinnamon—Spice
Bark of the laurel tree family, Ceylon origin.
Gourmet uses—stick or ground.
Pies, puddings, rolls, breads, fruits, beverages.

Cloves—Spice
Flower buds of evergreen clove tree. West Indies and Indonesian origin.
Gourmet uses—whole or ground.
Baked hams, stews, cakes, fruit, meats, soups, marinades.

Coriander—Seed
Dried fruit of parsley family. Flavor resembles that of lemon peel and sage.
   North African and Argentinian origin.
Gourmet uses—seeds or ground.
Salads, meats, pastries, soups, vegetables, stuffings.

Cumin—Seed
Caraway type herb seed. Mediterranean, Mexican, and Far Eastern origin.
Gourmet uses—seed or ground.
Breads, cheese, stews, soups, meats, curry dishes.

Curry Powder—Blend
Blend of different spices including cumin, ginger, turmeric, and several
   red pepper varieties. Indian origin.
Gourmet uses—curry powder.
Soups, sauces, fish, meats, dressing, eggs, poultry, rice.

Dill—Herb
Parsley family herb. Leaves and seeds. European and Indian origin.
Gourmet uses—leaves or seeds.
Sauces, soups, vegetables, dressing, meats, fish, salads.

Fennel—Herb
Licorice flavored, parsley family herb. Italian origin.
Gourmet uses—leaves or seeds.
Soups, stews, rolls, pies, vegetables, cakes.

Fenugreek—Spice
Aromatic bittersweet spice. Moroccan and Indian origin.
Gourmet uses—ground.
Curry dishes, pickling.

Garlic—Herb
Strong, pungent section of bulb. Peasant origin.
Gourmet uses—bulb.
Whole, chopped, crushed, or juices for meats, poultry, vegetables, salads, dressings.
Ginger—Spice
Fragrant, pungent root grown in Jamaica, China, and Japan.
Gourmet uses—whole or ground.
Sauces, Pies, Bread, Meats, Vegetables, Curry Dishes
Horseradish—Herb
Strong, hot root of peasant origin.
Gourmet uses—root.
Meat, sauces, soups, pickling.
Juniper—Spice
From evergreen tree grown in Africa.
Gourmet uses—berries.
Game, marinades, pork, sauces.
Mace—Spice
Orange red skin covering nutmeg. Fruit of evergreen tree. Fragrant of nutmeg and cinnamon. East Indian origin.
Gourmet uses—ground.
Fish sauces, rarebits, cake, cream, fish stew, meats.
Mahaleb—Spice
Small flowering tree seeds of Persian origin.
Gourmet uses—seeds.
Cakes, breads.
Marjoram—Herb
Dried green herb of mint and oregano family. Hungarian and South American origin.
Gourmet uses—leaves or ground.
Stews, meats, fish, poultry, vegetables, soups, salads.
Mint—Herb
Dried leaves of sweet peppermint. Peasant origin.
Gourmet uses—flakes or leaves.
Soups, stews, meats, sauces, stuffings, fruit.
Mustard—Seed
Small seed of different colors, dark brown and yellow. Asiatic origin.
Gourmet uses—ground, powder, dry, seed.
Soups, sauces, vegetables, dressings, salad, meats, fish.
Nutmeg—Spice
Seed inside the kernel of fruit of nutmeg tree. East Indian origin.
Gourmet uses—whole or ground.
Stews, custards, pies, vegetables, desserts.
Oregano—Herb
Dried leaf of mint family. Mexican and Italian origin.
Gourmet uses—ground or leaves.
Soups, salads, sauces, fish, meat, vegetables.
Paprika—Spice
Powder made from dried pits of capsicum. Hawaiian origin.
Gourmet uses—ground.
Fish, stews, meats, sauces, poultry, vegetables, salads.

Parsley—Herb
A classic for centuries in European cooking. Peasant origin.
Gourmet uses—leaves.
Garnishes, stews, sauces, soups, meats, stocks.
Pepper—Spice
White or black peppercorns. Dried berry. East Indies origin.
Gourmet uses—whole, cracked, ground, coarse ground, whole green
    peppercorns in brine or wine vinegar.
For all foods except sweets.
Poppy—Seed
Opium poppy is a European cooking classic. Far Eastern origin.
Gourmet uses—seeds.
Bread, desserts.
Rosemary—Herb
Grayish leaf, strong and pungent. Peasant origin.
Gourmet uses—leaves.
Meats, poultry, fish, soups.
Saffron—Spice
Dried stigma of a variety of crocus. Whole or powdered. Mediterranean
    and Asian origin.
Gourmet uses—ground or whole.
Soups, sauces, curries, rice, cakes.
Sage—Herb
Dried leaf of the mint family. Mediterranean origin.
Gourmet uses—rubbed, ground, leaves.
Poultry, meats, stuffings, breads, fish, salads.
Savory—Herb
Dried leaf of a widely grown herb of the mint family. Peasant origin.
Gourmet uses—rubbed, ground, leaves.
Poultry, sauces, salads, vegetables, stuffings.
Sesame—Seed
Small honey colored seed of Asian origin.
Gourmet uses—seed.
Rolls, dessert, candy.
Shallots—Herb
Onion family, very delicate bulbs. Peasant origin.
Gourmet uses—bulb.
Meats, poultry, sauces, fish.
Sorrel—Herb
Aromatic herb. Peasant origin.
Gourmet uses—leaves.
Poultry, pork.
Star Anise
Blend of different spices including cloves, fennel seeds, anise, pepper.
    Chinese origin.
Gourmet uses—powder.
Soups, sauces, meats, vegetables, poultry.
Tarragon—Herb
Dried leaf of anise type flavor. Peasant origin.
Gourmet uses—ground or leaves.
Marinades, salads, sauces, meats, soups, fish.

Thyme—Herb

Leaves of widely grown mint family plant. Southern European origin.

Gourmet uses—ground or leaves.

Fish, stews, game, marinades, stuffings, meats, soups.

Turmeric—Spice

Powder made from dried root of ginger family. Chinese origin.

Gourmet uses—ground.

Salads, dressings, sauces, rice dishes, meats, fish.

Fine Herbs

A mixture of chopped parsley, chervil, tarragon, watercress, shallots, and sweet marjoram.

Bouquet Garni

For flavoring stocks, soups, and meat dishes. It is composed of bay leaves, peppercorns, tarragon, savory, chervil, celery, chives or dried orange peel, and garlic. Various uses in food preparation.

Spice Blends

Apple pie spice, barbecue spice, cinnamon sugar, gumbo blend, herb seasoning, hickory smoked salt, Italian seasoning, lemon pepper, mixed pickling spice, poultry seasoning, pumpkin pie spice, seafood seasoning, seasoned or flavored salt, seasoned pepper or shrimp spice.

Products associated with the spice shelf include: orange or lemon peel, cream of tartar, beef, chicken, and fish stock base, sour salt, meat tenderizer, and MSG (monosodium glutamate).

Glossary

Abalone Shellfish native to California.

Accent Monosodium glutamate, seasoning for cooking.

Agar-agar Tasteless gelatine made from seaweed; also called Chinese gelatine.

Aging Term for meat tenderness.

Agneau Lamb.

A la Carte To choose from menu selection dish by dish.

A la Mode Prepared a certain style.

Albatross Sea bird; only young birds should be prepared, like wild duck.

Alcohol Liquid distilled from fermented grains or fruits.

Al Dente Cooked to the point of being finished, as with pasta.

Alfalfa Seed, leaves, of Asian origin.

Allemande Basic white veloute with egg yolk.

Allumette Small strip of puff pastry or cake, cut in matchlike strips.

Amandine Garnished with almonds.

Ambrosia Marinated fruit with sugar and liquor.

Americaine Prepared as native to America.

Ananas Pineapple.

Anchovy Small salt-water fish fillet, packed in brine or marinated in oil.

Andalouse Province of southern Spain.

Anglaise Style of English cooking.

Anjou Pear Firm, juicy winter pear, originally from France.

Anna Potatoes Thinly sliced potatoes baked in buttered casserole.

Annatto Seeds, used for food coloring.

Antipasto Hot or cold hors d'oeuvre.

Aperitif Cocktail (drink) served before the meal.

Appetizer Food served before the meal.

Aquavit Scandinavian liquor served ice cold.

Argenteuil City near Versailles, France, known for asparagus.

Aromatic Herb flavored.

Arrowroot Starch made from American or West Indian tropical plant, which is used to thicken stocks.

Artichoke Garden plant with flowery head and leafy bottom. The heart and bottom are edible when cooked.

Artichoke Jerusalem Vegetable that is usually boiled.

Aspic Reduction of liquid from meat, fish, poultry, bones, or vegetables, with gelatine added.

Assam Black tea of Indian origin.

Assistant Cook Person assigned to assist at various preparation stations.

Aubergine Eggplant.

Au Bleu Fresh fish poached in salted water with carrots, celery, onion, bay leaves, lemon, and vinegar.

Au Gratin Sprinkled with cheese, baked or put under salamander until brown.

Au Jus Served with its own natural juice.

Au Lait Beverage served with milk.

Auslese White wines made of ripened grapes.

Avocado Tropical fruit with dark green to purplish skin whose meat has an oily, nutty flavor.

Bain-Marie Hold in steam table or double boiler.

Baklava   Very rich, sweet dessert in which dough is filled with a butter and nut mixture, and soaked in syrup.

Ballottine   Boned chicken leg, or any kind of meat, game, or fish, stuffed with forcemeat and rolled.

Bamboo Shoots   Young shoots are eaten raw, marinated, or canned.

Banquet Chef   Person in charge of all banquet functions.

Barquettes   Tartlets formed like boats which are baked and filled with mousses of meat, fish, or poultry and decorated.

Baste   Pour stock over food when roasting.

Batter   Mixture of flour, liquid, and eggs.

Bay Leaf   Sweet and spicy leaf; of Mediterranean origin.

Bearn   French province where Sauce Bearnaise originated.

Bechamel   Sauce named for Louis De Bechameil.

Beef Stroganoff   Fillet of beef, cut in strips and sauteed with mushrooms, demi glaze, and sour cream.

Beer Batter   Mixture of flour, eggs, and beer.

Beeswax   Wax used for tallow figures.

Belgian Endive   Spears, yellow in color, with slightly bittersweet taste.

Bercy   Sauce named for town near Paris. Shallots and white wine reduced; pepper and demi glaze added; finished with marrow.

Bergamost Wild   Minty leaves of North American origin which are used for tea.

Beurre   Butter.

Beurre Noir   Brown butter.

Bibb Lettuce   Small and very tender lettuce.

Birch   Bark, leaves, used for tea.

Biscuit   Floury confection.

Blackberry   Brewed leaves and roots make a mild flavored tea.

Blanc   White.

Blanquette   Veal, lamb, or chicken stew with white sauce; ragout.

Bombay Duck   Dried fish used for curry dishes.

Bombe   Ice cream shaped in a mold.

Bonbon   Candies usually dipped in chocolate fondant.

Boneset   Brewed leaves make a bitter flavored tea.

Bonito   Fish of the mackerel family.

Borage   Stems, flowers and leaves have a cucumber flavor.

Bordelaise   French region where Sauce Bordelaise originated. The sauce is made with demi glaze, red wine, and marrow.

Borsch   Hot or cold beet soup originating from Russia.

Boston Lettuce   Round, loose head, excellent for basic coverings of salad plates, or with oil and vinegar.

Bouchees   Small puff pastry made with various fillings.

Bouillabaise   Seafood stew with twelve Mediterranean fish and crustaceans, and flavored with saffron.

Bouillon   Broth of beef, veal, mutton, fish, or poultry with vegetables and aromates.

Boulangere   With onions and sorrel.

Bouquet Garni   Fresh herbs, placed in a cheesecloth bag, and used for soups, stews, and sauces.

Bourgeoise   Style of baking in earthenware dish with shallots, vegetables, and red wine.

Bourguignonne   Seasoned with red wine, small onions, and glazed.

Braise   Cook slowly in small amount of liquid.

Breading   Coated well with flour; placed in milk and egg wash; dipped in breadcrumbs. For meats, vegetables, fish, croquettes.

Brine   Solution of salt, vinegar, or any added preservative.

Brochette   Beef, lamb, fish, etc., served on a skewer with mushrooms, tomatoes, onions, peppers, etc.

Broiler Cook   Person in charge of all grilled items.

Brown Roux   Melted butter, combined with flour, and heated until golden brown.

Brunoise   Diced vegetable combination of carrots, celery, leeks, and turnips.

Butcher   Preparation of all meat.

Butter Cream   Filling for cake.

Butternockerl   Dumpling consisting of butter, egg yolk, flour and egg whites.

Cacao   Seeds are used to make cocoa and chocolate.

Cacciatore   Aromatic seasoning with tomato and wine of Italian origin.

Caesar Salad   Salad with romaine, egg, lemon juice, anchovies, olive oil, parmesan cheese, garlic, seasoning, and croutons.

Calenula   Flowers, petal forms with mild flavor; of Southern European origin.

Calvados   Brandy made from apple cider.

Camembert   French cheese.

Camomile   Plant whose flowers are dried and used for tea and medicine.

Canape   Appetizer made of small pieces.

Canard   Duck.

Cannoli   Fried pastry shell filled with whipped cream and sweetened ricotta cheese.

Capon   Male chicken, castrated before ten months old, and averaging six lbs; provides juicy and tender meat.

Cappucino   Espresso coffee with cinnamon and hot milk.

Caramel   Melted sugar heated until golden brown.

Carob   Fruits and seeds, cut and powdered (raw or roasted) which have a chocolate-like flavor; of Mediterranean origin.

Carp   Fresh-water fish.

Carre D'Agneau   Loin of lamb.

Cassata   Mixture of four layers of ice cream, filled with whipped cream, liquor, dried fruit, and nuts.

Casserole   Earthenware dish for baking and serving food.

Castor Sugar   Finely granulated sugar.

Caviar   Salted roe of various sturgeon or fish; best served on ice in its original container.

Cayenne Pepper   Hot, red powder, used for seasoning.

Celeriac   Root, also called celery knob.

Celery   Herb whose stalks are sometimes blanched.

Celery Seed   Seed from wild celery, used as a spice.

Celestine   Sliced pancakes.

Cepe   European gourmet mushroom with dark brown cap.

Cervelle   Brains, soaked and blanched.

Challah   Yeast raised bread, made with eggs.

Champignon   White field mushroom.

Chanterelle   Yellow wild mushroom of European origin.

Charlotte   Molded dessert, with ladyfingers and a custard or whipped cream filling.

Chasseur   French term for hunter's style; A dish made with mushrooms, tomatoes, shallots, and wine.

Chateaubriand   Cut from the center of beef tenderloin.

Chaud   Hot.

Chef   The titles of executive chef, head chef, chef steward, or working chef include the same duties in the kitchen, knowledge of administrative, production, gourmet cooking, dining room service, and all stations of preparation in any form in the kitchen.

Chef de Partie   Person in charge of a preparation station for various categories (saucier, broiler, garde-manger).

Cherry Jubilee   Often written cherries jubilee, pitted black cherries, flamed with brandy and poured over ice cream.

Chicory   Curly plant, which is dark green outside and yellow inside.

Chief Steward   Supervisor of the stewards, porters, cleaners, and dish washers.

Chinese Anise   Star anise.

Chinese Cabbage   Plant with green leaves and white center, used for Chinese cooking and salads.

Chinese Five Spices   Mixture of ground star, fennel, anise, cinnamon, cloves, and szechuan pepper.

Chrysanthemum   Use whole flower or petals as a Mediterranean garnish.

Chutney   Dish made of mangoes, tamarinds, raisins, garlic, sugar, vinegar, lemon, and cayenne; of Indian origin.

Cochon De Lait   Suckling pig.

Cockie-Leekie   English soup with leeks and fowl in chicken consomme.

Cocktails   Drinks or food served before the meal.

Compote   Fresh fruit, cooked in syrup and served cold.

Compound Butter   Butter mixture of various herbs or flavorings.

Concasser   Chopped tomatoes.

Conch   Southern shellfish used for chowder or stews.

Consomme   Clear stock from any kind of meat.

Coq Au Vin   Chicken sauteed in caramelized sugar with burgundy wine, demi glaze, pearl onions, and mushroom bottoms.

Cornstarch   Thickening agent, mixed with water for glossy finished products, sauces, etc.

Coupes   Ice cream served in a champagne glass with fruit or sauces and topped with whipped cream and liquor.

Court Bouillon   Stock prepared for fish cooking.

Couscous   Made from semolina or other wheat or starch; of Middle Eastern origin.

Cream Chantilly   Whipped cream sweetened and finished with vanilla and flavoring.

Crepe   Pancake.

Croquette   Minced food (potato, meat, etc.) formed and rolled in flour, egg, and breadcrumbs and deep fat fried.

Crouton   Diced bread fried in butter.

Crown Roast   Rack of lamb, veal, or pork formed to a crown, tied together, and roasted.

Crystallize   Coating of any kind with sugar formed into crystals.

Cuisine   Various styles of cooking.

Cumberland Sauce   Sauce made from currant jelly, lingonberries, orange, lemon, port wine, and seasoning.

Dampfgulyas Natural beef gulyas with raw potatoes and red paprika slices.

Darjeeling Area in India where the famous Darjeeling tea is grown.

Date Fruit from the date palm tree; originally from the Middle East.

Deglaze Stirring in liquid to loosen drippings from pan.

Degrease Removal of fat from any kind of stock or juice.

Demi Glaze Reduction of Sauce Espagnole.

Demi Tasse Half cup; after dinner coffee.

Dijon Mustard Mustard seasoned with wine, vinegar, and spices; originated in Dijon, France.

Dill Sauce Butter, flour, chicken stock, and chopped dill, finished with sour cream and seasoning.

Dobos Torte Thin layers of sponge cake, filled with chocolate butter cream, and covered with caramel glaze.

Dough Mixture of flour and liquid.

Drawn Butter Melted butter.

Dredging Coating with flour.

Duchess Potatoes Mashed potatoes mixed with eggs, butter, nutmeg, and seasoning, formed through pastry bag, and baked in oven.

Dusting Sprinkling with confectioner's sugar or flour.

Duxelles Chopped onions and shallots sauteed in butter, and finished with chopped mushrooms, chopped parsley, and seasoning.

Eclair Oblong pastry shell filled with custard or whipped cream.

Ecrevisse Fresh-water crayfish.

Egg Fruit Very sweet orange or yellow fruit, which is used for preserves.

Eggplant Purple skinned fruit, also called aubergine.

Eggs Benedict Poached eggs on Canadian bacon and toasted English muffin topped with Sauce Hollandaise.

Egg Wash Egg yolk mixed with water or milk, used for glazing pastry.

Emince Finely cut.

Enriched Flour Bleached flour with vitamins and minerals added.

Entrecote Sirloin steak cut from shell between two ribs.

Escargot Snail.

Escarole Broad, loose-leafed, dark green lettuce which is bitter in taste.

Escoffier Auguste, 1846–1935. Author of *Le Guide Culinaire*, which became the bible of cooking.

Espagnole A basic brown sauce originally from Spain.

Estragon Tarragon.

Executive Chef Person responsible for food standards, purchasing, coordinating the banquet, restaurant, and room service departments, and all food related preparation areas.

Extract Concentrated liquid of stock.

Faisan Pheasant.

Farce Finely ground stuffing made from meat or fish with egg whites, seasoning, and cream.

Feta Greek cheese made from sheep's milk or goat's milk and preserved in a salt brine.

Fillet Mignon Cut from beef tenderloin.

Fine Herb Dressing Chopped basil, parsley, oregano, and garlic, mixed with mayonnaise, vinegar, mustard, salt, and pepper.

Finnan Haddie Smoked haddock, cooked in cream.

Flageolet Small green bean originating in France.

Flambe   Flaming with liquor.

Fleuron   Puff paste, half moon garniture.

Florentine   Italian style, food served with spinach.

Flounder   Flat fish of good quality.

Fondant   A soft, creamy confection used for covering or icing of cakes, nuts, canned fruit or petits-fours.

Fondue   Gruyere cheese melted with other cheeses and mixed with vodka or brandy; or simple meats, vegetables, or fish, cooked in hot oil, and dipped in condiments.

Fontina   Delicate, creamy Italian cheese.

Food Cost   Determined basic cost, divided by selling price.

Food Poisoning   A term for a bacterial condition that produces toxins causing gastrointestinal disorders.

Foo Young   Egg souffle with various vegetables, meats, or fish.

Forcemeat   Finely minced meat.

Framboise   Raspberry.

Fricandeau   Loin of veal that has been larded.

Fried   Cooked in oil.

Fromage de Chevre   Goat cheese.

Frying Liquid   Rendered beef or pork fat, vegetable shortening, oils.

Fumet   Stock made of bones and trimmings, reduced for stronger flavor.

Galantine   Poultry, meat, or fish, boned and stuffed with forcemeat, poached and chilled.

Garde-Manger   Cold preparation and decoration of appetizers, meat, fish, canapes, salad dressings, and sandwiches.

Garniture   Garnish.

Gastronome   A gourmet with refined taste.

Gaufrette   Small, thin, fan-shaped wafer imported from France.

Gazpacho   Cold soup, of Spanish origin, with fresh tomato, garlic, peppers, olive oil, lemon juice, vinegar, cucumber, and seasoning.

Gherkin   Small pickled cucumber.

Giblets   Heart, gizzard, and liver of fowl.

Ginseng   Bitter flavored roots and leaves, used for teas.

Glace   Ice cream.

Gnocchi   Italian dumplings made from potatoes or pasta, with cheese and poached.

Gorgonzola   Italian blue-veined, creamy cheese.

Gouda   Mild, yellow Dutch cheese.

Gourmet   Connoisseur of food and wine.

Granite   Ice made with syrup.

Green Tea   Tea made from nonfermented leaves.

Grouper   Fish of the sea bass family.

Gruyere   Mild cheese with high butterfat content.

Guacamole   Highly seasoned avocado spread.

Gugelhupf   Viennese cake made from yeast raised dough, with raisins.

Guinea Fowl   Small bird of African origin.

Haggis   Scottish sausage, consisting of liver, heart, lung, and seasoning. boiled in sheep's stomach.

Halvah   Middle Eastern confection made with honey and sesame seeds.

Haricot Vert   Green string bean.

Hasenpfeffer   Hare marinated in wine, onions, vinegar, spices, and herbs, braised, and finished with sour cream.

Herb Butter   Butter mixed with herbs.

Hibiscus   Flowers of Asian origin used for tea.

Hoisin Sauce   Soy bean and spice sauce.

Hors d'Oeuvre   Canape or appetizer.

Huitre   Oysters.

Hummus   Chickpeas pureed in different ways; of Middle Eastern origin.

Iceberg Lettuce   Firm, round head of lettuce with light green leaves.

Icing   Sugar, butter, egg white, and cream mixture used for decorating cakes.

Irish Soda Bread   Round bread made with baking soda, raisins, and molasses.

Italian Bread   Bread made with yeast which is similar to French bread, but shorter and thicker.

Jam   Cooked, sweetened puree of fresh fruit.

Jambalaya   Creole cookery usually consisting of rice, tomato, red pepper, shellfish, ham, or poultry, and onions.

Jambonneau   Pork leg.

Japanese Tea   Green tea.

Jardiniere   Diced, mixed vegetables, used for a la jardiniere (garnish).

Jarlsberg   Beer or cheese from Norway.

Jerusalem Artichoke   Sweet tuber of a tall sunflower which looks like a potato; can be cooked or eaten raw.

Julienne   Any vegetable cut into long strips.

Kaiserschmarren   Omelet made with flour, raisins, and baking powder, sprinkled with powdered sugar, and served with plum compote; originated in Vienna.

Kale   Cabbage family greens.

Kaltschale   Cold fruit soup with liquor.

Kebob   Meat on a skewer; of Arabic origin.

Kelp   Seaweed, with a mild to bitter flavor.

Kiev   Stuffed with herb butter, breaded, and fried, as with Chicken Kiev.

King Crab   Delicately flavored, large red crab from the north Pacific.

Kipper   Popular fish in Britain which is usually served smoked.

Klosse   Meat dumplings.

Knead   Pressing or mixing of dough.

Knodel   Dumpling.

Kohlrabi   Vegetable similar to a turnip and related to cabbage family.

Kosher   Food that is ritually fit and prepared according to Jewish law.

Kreplach   Small noodle dough square filled with chicken or meat.

Kromeskies   Meat croquette, dipped in batter and fried; also, in French, cromesquis.

Kuchen   Yeast raised coffee cake made with plums or fruit.

Lachs   Salmon.

Ladyfingers   Sponge cake mixture which is piped through pastry tube.

Lamb   A sheep fewer than twelve months old.

Langouste   Lobster-like crayfish.

Lard   Rendered fat or pork strips cut to julienne for inserting in meat.

Latkes   Pancakes made from raw potatoes.

Leek   Vegetable similar in appearance to a large scallion, which is related to the onion family.

Legumes   Vegetables.

Lemon Grass   Leaves and stems which provide a lemon like flavor used for tea; of West Indian origin.

Lentils   Dried seeds from the pea family.

Liederkranz   Soft ripened cheese with a piquant flavor.

Lily Buds   Buds of Chinese lilies.

Lingonberry   Red berry, smaller than a cranberry.

Linguini   Long, flat, thin noodles.

Linzer Torte   Rich dough with nuts and spices; torte is lattice covered and filled with raspberry jam.

Live Breadcrumbs   Trimmed white bread, finely chopped.

Lotus   Water lily used in Oriental cooking.

Lovage   Leaves, seeds and stalks which have a celery-like flavor.

Lox   Smoked salmon.

Lyonaise   Made with sauteed onions.

Macadamia Nut   Nut grown in Hawaii.

Macaroon   Cookie made of almond paste, egg white, and sugar.

Macedoine   Fresh fruit marinated with liquor or a vegetable mixture served hot or cold with butter or cream; also called Madedoine.

Madeira Sauce   Demi glaze flavored with madeira.

Madrilene   Hot or cold tomato flavored consomme.

Maison   Cooked according to the house recipe.

Maitre d'Hotel   **1)** A mixture of butter, lemon juice, mustard, Worcestershire, salt, and pepper; **2)** The person in charge of the dining room, also called the headwaiter.

Maize   Corn.

Manhattan Clam Chowder   Soup made with diced vegetables, tomatoes, clams, clam stock, and seasoning.

Marinara   Spicy tomato sauce with garlic, onions, and oregano.

Marmite   Stock pot. Petite marmite is a small casserole with consomme, vegetables, meat, and chicken.

Marron   Chestnut.

Marrow   Substance in the center of bones; which is used in soups, stews, or sauces.

Marzipan   Confection consisting of equal amounts of almond paste and confectioner's sugar, with a little egg white.

Mayonnaise   Mixture of egg yolk, oil, seasoning, vinegar, lemon juice, Worcestershire sauce, and mustard.

Medaillon   Small, round piece of meat.

Melba Sauce   Raspberry sauce.

Meringue   Egg whites beaten with sugar until extremely firm.

Meuniere   Food sauteed in butter with lemon juice and chopped parsley.

Minestrone   Italian vegetable soup, with pasta.

Mire-poix   Mixture of cut vegetables (onions, carrots, celery, leeks), sauteed with peppercorns, bay leaf, thyme, garlic, and bacon.

Mise-En-Place   Preparation, or station set up.

Mixed grill   Lamb chops, kidneys, liver, bacon, and sausage broiled and served with grilled tomato.

Mock Turtle Soup   Browned calves head soup.

Molasses   Dark, rich syrup.

Montmorency   With sour cherries.

Morel   Oval-capped, brown, wild mushroom.

Mornay Sauce   White cream sauce with grated cheese.

Moussaka Middle Eastern dish consisting of baked eggplant, ground lamb, onions, and spices.

Mousse Finely textured dish, made from various meats, fish, or sweets, combined with egg whites and cream.

Mousseline Sauce Hollandaise sauce with whipped cream.

Mulligatawny Indian soup made with stock of vegetables and chicken, flavored with curry.

Nantua Sauce Bechamel sauce with crayfish, shrimp, or lobster added.

Napoleon Puff paste layers filled with custard mixed with whipped cream and sprinkled with confectioner's sugar.

Nesselrode Pie Pie crust filled with whipped cream mixed with candied fruits and rum and topped with shaved chocolate.

Newburg White roux with paprika, milk, fish stock, and shallots, strained and seasoned.

New England Clam Chowder Creamy soup made with clams, clam stock, potatoes, onions, and seasoning.

Night Chef Person in charge of the kitchen, after chef or sous-chef have left, until closing time.

Nockerl A light dumpling, made with flour, oil, eggs, milk, salt, and pepper, mixed and squeezed through a pan with large holes into boiling, salted water and sauteed in butter.

Noisette Small, round cut of lamb or fillet.

Oat Straw Mild flavored stems used for tea; of Mediterranean origin.

Okra Green seed pod of large herb used in Creole cooking.

Orange Water Made from distilled orange blossoms; used for baking and flavoring.

Ossobuco Braised veal shank in olive oil with tomatoes, diced vegetables, and wine; an Italian specialty.

Oxtail Used for soups or stew; braised with diced vegetables and wine.

Oysters Rockefeller Oysters in half shell, topped with chopped spinach, butter, seasoning, and crumbs, placed on rock salt and baked.

Paella Rice dish with saffron, shellfish, clams, chicken, sausage, lobster, and seasoning.

Papillote Buttered heavy paper in which food is wrapped for cooking.

Parsnip Edible root, with a somewhat sweet taste.

Passion Flower Mild flavored leaves, and flowers used for tea, of United States origin.

Pasta Types of noodles made from semolina and water, or with eggs.

Pasteurize Heat to a temperature of 150° F.

Pastry Chef Supervisor of the pastry department and its related preparations.

Pastry Flour Very fine, low gluten flour.

Pate Ground veal, pork, fowl, or game mixed with pork fat, brandy, and truffles, seasoned, and baked.

Patty Shell Puff paste shell filled with various meats or fruit.

Paupiette Stuffed with various mixtures and rolled.

Pecan Nut grown in southern part of the United States.

Peking Duck Specially prepared duck, coated with honey and roasted; of Chinese origin.

Perigourdine A la perigord, with truffles and goose liver.

Persimmon Sweet, orange skinned fruit larger than apricot; of South Sea origin.

Petit   Small.

Petit Four   Individually arranged cookies or small cakes, covered with icing and decorated.

Petits Pois   Young, tender peas.

Phylo   Very thin, flaky pastry, also spelled filo.

Pie Dough   Consists of flour, butter, egg, salt, and water.

Pike   Fresh-water fish with firm flesh.

Piquant   Seasoned for the appetite.

Poach   To cover with liquid and simmer.

Poisson   Fish.

Pomegranate   Deep red colored fruit, larger than an apple, with edible seeds and pulp.

Poppy Seed   Black seeds of the poppy plant.

Port Du Salut   Creamy, soft cheese with yellow, edible crust.

Porterhouse Steak   Thick cut of choice beef from largest portion of the tenderloin muscle.

Potage   Cream or veloute soups.

Potatoes Delmonico   Diced potatoes, finished with diced green pepper, cream sauce, and diced red pimiento.

Potpourri   Several meats and various vegetable arrangements.

Praline   Pecan candy, cooked in brown syrup, with praline liqueur and vanilla added.

Prime   Best grade of meat.

Prosciutto   Dry cured Italian ham.

Provencale   Provence cooking with tomato, garlic, and olive oil.

Puff Paste   Flour, salt, and water, rolled out, with butter folded in.

Puree   Any food put in a blender or pressed through a sieve.

Quail   Tender bird of the partridge family.

Quenelles   Small dumplings made of meat, fish, or poultry seasoned with nutmeg, egg whites, and cream.

Quiche   Pastry shell filled with eggs and cream mixture, seasoning and various meats or vegetables added.

Ragout   Stew.

Ramequin   Small baking dish.

Ratatouille   Vegetable dish consisting of eggplant, tomato, zucchini, garlic, and seasoning.

Ravigote Sauce   Mixture of capers, pickles, parsley, chopped hard-boiled eggs with yolks, lemon, tarragon, oil, and mustard.

Reduce   Decreasing the volume of liquid by simmering.

Remoulade   Spicy cold sauce made with mayonnaise with chopped gherkins, herbs, capers, and mustard.

Rhubarb   Vegetable with a pinkish stalk.

Ricotta   White, creamy, Italian cheese.

Rijstafel   Dutch/Indonesian rice dish.

Risi-Bisi   Risotto mixed with peas.

Risotto   Italian rice dish with parmesan cheese.

Rissole   Ground meat mixtures, wrapped in pastry shaped like turnovers and fried.

Rock Cornish Hen   Cross breed of Cornish and Plymouth Rock fowls.

Roe   Fish eggs.

Rollatine   Veal stuffed with prosciutto and cheese, rolled and sauteed.

Romaine   Lettuce with long, narrow, coarse leaves.

Roquefort   Marbled, blue green, semi-soft cheese.

Roquefort Dressing   Mixture of mayonnaise, dry mustard, vinegar, onion juice, water, crumbled roquefort cheese, salt, pepper, and cayenne.

Rose Water   Distilled rose petals.

Rote Grutze   Pudding with raspberries cooked in wine; dessert of German origin.

Rotisserie   Oven with spit for rotating food.

Roulade   Meat slice with various fillings of bacon, pickle, hard-boiled eggs, and onions, rolled, seasoned, braised with wine, and finished with cream.

Roux   Mixture of fat or butter and flour to thicken sauces; white, gold, and brown are three types of roux.

Royale   Mixture of eggs and cream; this custard is cut in various shapes for garnishing.

Rye Flour   Dark flour made from rye grains.

Sabayon   Mixture of egg yolks, sugar, and wine whipped over double boiler; used in fruits or cakes.

Sacher Torte   Chocolate cake glazed with apricot jam and covered with chocolate fondant, which originated in the House of Sacher, a hotel in Vienna.

Salad Russe   Mixture of chopped pickles, potatoes, celery, carrots, tongue, ham, capers, anchovy fillets, and lemon juice mixed with mayonnaise.

Salpicon   Various ingredients cut into small pieces and bound with sauce.

Salsify   Carrot-shaped root vegetable whose flavor resembles that of an oyster.

Saltimbocca   Veal sauteed with prosciutto.

Sarsaparilla   Roots of American origin.

Saute   Cooking food rapidly in a pan with small amount of heated fat or butter.

Scaloppine   Thin, sauteed slice of meat; of Italian origin.

Schnitzel   Veal cutlet pounded, breaded in flour, eggs, and breadcrumbs, and sauteed in butter or fried in deep fat.

Seasoning   Ingredients added to bring out the flavor.

Seviche   Raw fish, scallops, marinated in lemon juice and seasoned.

Shad Roe   Eggs of shad fish baked in butter.

Shchi   Russian sauerkraut soup.

Shirred Eggs   Eggs broken into individual buttered ramequins and cooked in an oven until whites are firm.

Simmering   Brought to boiling point, but not boiled.

Sorbet   Sherbet.

Soubise   Veloute base sauce made with chopped shallots.

Souffle   An entree or dessert, consisting of stiffly beaten egg whites and a combination of milk, flour, and egg yolks.

Sous-Chef   Person responsible for total kitchen operation, including preparation of food and personnel supervision.

Stock   Reduced liquid of meat, fish, etc. slowly simmered with vegetables.

Stroganoff   Fillet of beef, sliced in strips and sauteed in butter with wine and sour cream.

Stuffing, Chestnut   Dressing made of diced rolls with chestnuts, thyme, poultry seasoning, eggs, and fine herbs.

Sukiyaki   Beef, pork, or chicken with vegetables, such as mushrooms, or bamboo shoots, sauteed briskly in oil, with soy sauce added; of Japanese origin.

Su-Shi   Combination of raw fish and rice; of Japanese origin.

Tagliatelle   Italian noodles, cooked in salt water, and served with butter and parmesan cheese.

Tamale   Spicy Mexican dish of minced meat and corn meal, wrapped in corn husks, dipped in oil and steamed.

Tamarind   Tree fruit from India which is used for preservatives.

Tapioca   Starchy substance, prepared from the root of the cassava plant.

Tarragon   Herb used for flavoring food.

Tartlet   Small tart used for appetizer and dessert fillings.

Tempura   Japanese style of cooking; food is dipped in batter and fried.

Terrapin   Fresh-water turtle found on the eastern and Gulf coasts of the United States.

Terrine   Earthenware dish used for pates.

Timbale   Small, round-shaped mold.

Toffee   Candy made of sugar solution.

Torte   Cake made of flour, eggs, and sugar; butter-filled and glazed.

Tortue   Turtle.

Tournant   Relief cook for all stations of various preparation areas.

Tournedos   Fillet cut from the beef tenderloin.

Trifle   English dessert made of sponge cake soaked with brandy, custard, and strawberry jam, and topped with whipped cream.

Truffle   Black or white fungi found underground and used for garnishes and sauces.

Tureen   Deep fish for serving soups or sauces.

Vanilla   Long bean used for aromatic flavoring in desserts.

Vanille Steak   Viennese culinary steak, rubbed with garlic and marinated in oil, sauteed au natural.

Veau   Veal.

Veloute Sauce   White sauce made from chicken, veal, or fish stock.

Venison   Term for wild deer, game.

Vinaigrette   French dressing with chopped chives, pickles, chopped hard-boiled eggs, and seasoning.

Vol-Au-Vent   Large puff pastry or patty shell, filled with creamed meat, fish or poultry.

Wasabi   Roots of Asian origin; the powder is also called Japanese horseradish.

Water Chestnut   Nut-like fruit of Asian water plant; used in Oriental cooking.

Watercress   Green leaves with stem used for garnishes and salads.

Westphalian Ham   Smoked ham; originated in Germany.

White Roux   Melted butter mixed with all-purpose flour.

Wild Rice   The seeds of tall water grass, brownish-white color, also called Indian rice; grown in United States.

Wok   Round bottomed cooking pan used for stir frying in Chinese cooking.

Worcestershire Sauce   Dark brown, piquant sauce, containing soy sauce; of English origin.

Yeast   Microscopic living plant, producing fermentation.

Yerba-De-Mate   Cut leaves of South American origin. Tea used in Paraguay.

Yogurt   Creamy fermented milk with specific bacterium.

Yorkshire Pudding   Popover made with roast beef drippings; of English origin.

Zabaglione   Sabayon made with marsala; of Italian origin.

Zest   Extremely thin peels of lemon or orange, finely cut, used for flavoring.

Zucchini   Green summer squash.

Zwiebel Roastbraten   Shell cutlet, seasoned and sauteed with sliced onions, sprinkled with crisp, deep fat fried sliced onions.

Index